EMOTIONAL
DIFFICULTIES
IN READING

Emotional Difficulties in Reading

by BEULAH KANTER EPHRON, ED. D.

[*A Psychological Approach to Study Problems*]

GREENWOOD PRESS, PUBLISHERS
WESTPORT, CONNECTICUT

154996

372.4
E 63

The Library of Congress has catalogued this publication as follows:

Library of Congress Cataloging in Publication Data

Ephron, Beulah (Kanter)
    Emotional difficulties in reading.

    1. Reading, Psychology of. I. Title.
[BF456.R2E65 1972]   428.4'2'07   79-138226
ISBN 0-8371-5583-5

DEDICATED

to the memory of my mother and father

DORA AND JOSEPH KANTER

———————

CONTENTS

PREFACE

THE PURPOSE of this book is to clarify the role of psychotherapy in adolescent and adult remedial reading. The application of psychoanalytic thinking to a school situation is not a new idea; Freud recommended that education make use of the findings of psychoanalysis (20).[1] Nor is it a new idea that emotional difficulties and reading disabilities are linked together. In 1936, Phyllis Blanchard stated:

". . . the reading disability often arises from the same source of difficulty in emotional development, and in the same manner as the accompanying personality or behavior problems or neurotic symptoms, such as fears, illness without physical basis, infantile regressions, and the like. . . .

"While sex conflicts are evident in many reading disability cases, even more pronounced, in the material produced in treatment interviews, are difficulties in establishing masculine identifications and in handling aggressive impulses, together with excessive anxiety and guilt over destructive, hostile and sadistic feelings (8)."

Undoubtedly a great deal of pertinent material about emotional difficulties in reading resides in the literature of psychoanalysis and non-directive counseling, since it is likely that a large proportion of psychoanalytic and counseling cases might also be classified as cases of reading and study disability. Except when the particular symptom of reading disability is specified, this material is lost to the literature of remedial-reading research.

[1] All numbers in parentheses, when not preceded by any letters, refer to the numbered Bibliography on p. 285.

The reader who wishes to obtain a background in the area of reading disability and emotional difficulties is referred to the contributions of the many investigators who have endeavored to understand the role of emotional factors both as cause and result of reading disability.[2]

The case-study method of research seems to have been recognized as an especially appropriate method for exploring reading disability. The literature in the field of adolescent and adult remedial reading (ages twelve and above) contains at least forty published case studies.[3] However, the spirit and the purpose of the case-study method are lost when insufficient attention is paid to the "why" and "how" of information obtained. The following story about a recent case presentation in the Adolescent and Adult Reading Center at Teachers College may serve to illustrate this point.

A student reported that her client's mother had read to the boy all his life, and that now she was not going to do it any more. It did seem odd that the boy at age sixteen still wanted his mother to read to him. Until the student read aloud her verbatim notes of her interview with the mother, it was not apparent that the mother had always resented reading to the boy, and thus she had not given him the affection implied by the factual story of a mother reading to her child.

The student was advised to read to the boy, but to introduce this activity with the words—and, most important, *with the warm feeling*—"Let me read this story to you; I would *so enjoy doing it.*" It was true that she enjoyed reading to him, for this student is a soft, maternal woman with real concern for her adolescent students, and with a lively joy in their success. The results were almost immediate and quite astounding, so much so that one of his teachers asked what had suddenly produced such an improvement in the boy's attitude and work.

If this case, written up and published as a case study, were simply to state the fact, "The mother read to the boy all his life," the truth

2 Among these are the following: Axline (2), Bills (5), Blanchard (6, 7, 8, 9, 10), Dickinson (14), Edelston (16), Gann (22), Gates (23, 24), Gray (25, 26, 27), Jackson (35), Klein (37), Kunst and Sylvester (38), Missildine (45), Monroe (46, 47), Redmount (49), Robinson (54), Russell (57), Sherman (58), Soles (60), Stewart (63), Strang, (64, 65, 66, 67), Tulchin (68), Vorhaus (69, 70, 71), Wiksell (73).

3 Refer to: Blanchard (6, 7, 8, 9, 10), Cooper (12), Davis (13), Eberl (15), Ehrlich (17), Font (18), Gates (23), Gray (25, 26), Gunzberg (28), Hansburg (29), Harris (30), Hrastnik (32), Hutchinson (33), Robinson and Savery (55), Russell (57), Simpson (59), Stauffer (62), Stewart (63), Vorhaus (69), Watts (72), Witty (74), Witty and Kopel (75), Young (76).

would be distorted, since the implication of givingness would not be a fact. Thus, the oversimplified, oversummarized, starkly "factual" accounts of cases may distort reality and make the cases difficult to understand.

This writer would like, therefore, to see the literature of case studies expand in the presentation of verbatim material. Then, students reading a case study would feel almost as though they were participating in a case conference in which verbatim interview material was the focus of attention. This book tries to provide that kind of experience.

One of the major challenges of this book has been the interpreting of the case material. Trying to account for the way a person feels and behaves, or even just to adequately describe his overt behavior, leads one into inevitable oversimplification. One cannot speak of an individual's appearance, thoughts, words or deeds without observing, "But there is so much more to it." The use of projective techniques provides a pattern for describing personality configurations, but this still leaves the picture incomplete.

Perhaps the only way of finding courage to go on with a clinical study is to warn the reader that here no story is the whole story, that the hypotheses presented are not considered absolute and that other investigators might suggest different explanations or modifications of these. Having uttered these warnings, the writer perhaps can rest in the hope that the reader, at all times, will be alert, creative, aware—taking nothing as final, but eagerly moving from each discovery to further ones; never resting too long on any conclusions, but working constantly toward increased understanding.

Who will be the reader of this book? Though the framework of this study places it in the field of adolescent and adult remedial reading, many principles of guidance, counseling, teaching and learning emerge from the material and promise to make it of interest to school psychologists and guidance personnel not engaged specifically in reading work. It should be useful to all teachers who have the courage, vision and inner freedom to see what is to be seen and feel what is to be felt, without being overwhelmed by the challenge.

This book is most particularly addressed to students of remedial reading, who, it is suggested, will get the greatest good out of it by using it as a work-book, as material for group discussion, and as a supplement to their own experience with actual cases. It should be understood that the cases presented in this book are not considered samples of perfect interviews, or models for students to follow. It is hoped that the process of evaluating the strengths and weaknesses of these interviews will stimulate students to develop their own philosophy of interview technique. Similarly, the paragraphs entitled "Discussion," which follow each interview, are not offered as comprehensive evaluations. They are intended to supply descriptively some of the non-verbal material—such as voice, manner, appearance—and to stimulate and supplement the student's own thinking about the interview.

EMOTIONAL
DIFFICULTIES
IN READING

The Surface Threads

I AM A POOR READER

Almost everyone who comes for reading help has the self-concept that he is a poor reader. The qualifying word "almost" is used because of those adolescents who reluctantly come to the reading clinic at the behest of parents and/or teachers, though they themselves see no need for it.

At Teachers College, the course called "The Improvement of Reading for College Students and Adults" is composed mostly of graduate students, people who have read well enough to attain the graduate-school level of academic achievement. There are also in the group some college students, a few high school students, and occasionally one or two foreign students having a language problem.

The range of reading ability as objectively measured by a standardized test runs from zero to the ninety-ninth percentile, yet all of the sixty or more students consider themselves poor readers, else they would not have enrolled in this course. Because of their eagerness for help, their low self-evaluation as students, and their anxiety about their work, this group has been described as being "highly motivated and full of despair." Despite great differences in actual skill, they show this universality in self-concept: "I am a poor reader."

I WANT TO LEARN TO READ FASTER

In five years of work in remedial reading, this writer has never heard anyone ask for help in obtaining more pleasure from reading. The idea of enjoying oneself with a book does not appear among the requests for help. The most frequent, perhaps universal, request is for increased speed. These are familiar questions: "What is considered normal reading speed . . . ?" "How fast should I be able to read . . . ?" "Will I be able to read more words per minute, more pages per hour if I take the course . . . ?"

I NEED HELP WITH RETENTION

"I read and read and then can't remember what I've read. . . ." "I realize as I get to the bottom of the page that I have not really *seen* a word that I've 'read.'" This surface thread is tied in with a lack of interest, for many possible reasons, in the reading material. The individual is not paying real attention, for many possible reasons, to the printed page. He cannot follow this surface thread to its inter-connections in order to see why this is happening to him. Without help, he does not realize the existence of the interconnections. He keeps trying to force himself to pay attention, and he feels more and more defeated and hopeless as he fails to remember because he is not really seeing.

I Cannot Concentrate

When this thread is followed all the way, it usually leads to the sources of all the other reading troubles. One who cannot concentrate will soon add, "My mind wanders away from what I'm reading." Now, one of the most interesting bits of data in the whole collection of material is this fact: In over two hundred instances, the writer asked the question, "Where does your mind go when it wanders?" In every case, without exception, the individual seemed surprised by this question; he had never thought to follow the wanderings of his mind to see what was distracting him. His energies were expended in a strenuous effort to force his attention upon the task at hand, away from whatever preoccupations were clamoring for attention, away from problems calling for solution. Since forcing is unsuccessful, the result is a losing battle, accompanied by feelings of helplessness and bewilderment.[1]

I Have the Bad Habit of Reading Word-by-Word

The reader who reads "word-by-word" gives equal stress, time and value to every word. He cannot omit a single word without a nagging feeling that something important has been missed, and he retraces his steps to pick up the missing word. It is chiefly because of the word-by-word reading that the Harvard Films [2] are used in the Improvement-of-Reading course. There is no magic in a mechanical stimulus, but the films do lead the students to make an important observation about themselves. Phrases flash by, never to return. The students groan. They have not had time to look long and thoroughly at every word, to go back and make sure they have missed nothing, and they are certain they will not be able to recall much of the material. However, when

[1] Reik states: "We often hear that a patient cannot concentrate his attention, without thinking that it is already concentrated upon a subject, unknown or unconscious to him." Reik, Theodor (50, p. 169).

[2] A tachistoscopic device by which phrases are flashed in sequence on a movie screen.

they are tested on their retention of the article, they are pleasantly surprised to discover that most of it has been absorbed. They learn, therefore, that they are capable of observing a great deal without conscious awareness of the act of observation. They learn that a quick exposure to the material is sufficient, that lingering and re-reading is unnecessary. The next step is to transfer this learning from the films to the printed page. Unfortunately, making this transition is not easy. Too many unconscious forces get in the way.

There Must Be One Best Way to Read

The conception of being "a better reader" is usually expressed in terms of reading faster and remembering more. To achieve this goal, all other reading goals are abandoned, and the student applies to every reading challenge his chief objective: "Faster!"

Professor Strang tries to meet this demand by suggesting that good reading consists of developing a repertory of reading skills and applying these skills appropriately in terms of the kind of material being read and the purpose for which it is being read. One would not sensibly read Keats, Dickens and Dostoievsky the same way one would skim the headlines of the *New York Times,* study a chemistry experiment, think through an engineering problem or peruse a lease on an apartment. Each reading situation calls for an appropriate response.

Students do not reject this approach to reading, since its validity is self-evident. However, they tend to veer back irresistibly to the expression of a wish for *faster reading*—no matter what the material may be. "Look at our bibliographies for all our courses," they say. "We have to read fast or we can't get through the semester." Yet, "We have to read slowly and carefully, else we won't remember." It is as if, to meet this dilemma, there must be *one best way to read.*

I Have the Bad Habit of Procrastination

Recently, a young man who had come to the Reading Center to speed up his reading confessed that he had carried an "incomplete" at a graduate school for five years. All he had to do to fulfill his obligations to the course was to write a brief essay. He had the intelligence, the experience and the knowledge, but he could not get the paper written. It is unusual for an incomplete to stand for five years, but it is not unusual for students to procrastinate.

The "bad habit" of procrastination is so prevalent, in fact, that the colloquialism, "cramming," came into existence to name the feverish activity which is the inevitable sequel to procrastination. A graduate student said, "Cramming became·so ingrained in me that now, even when I am thoroughly well prepared for an examination, it is hard for me to resist staying up all night to study, though I know it would do me more good to get eight hours' sleep."

Procrastination and cramming: twin socio-psychological phenomena that haunt every campus. What are the underlying causes?

READING MAKES ME NERVOUS

Restlessness, irritability, drowsiness, unaccountable fatigue, a desire to close the book and do almost anything except read—these complaints are frequent. "I haven't the patience to sit still. . . ." "I keep getting up and going out for coffee or a cigarette—anything for an excuse. . . ." "Gosh, I keep thinking how I'd rather be outdoors. . . ." "I get so fed up, I feel as though I'll shriek if I have to sit there and read one more minute . . . !" "I get so nervous sitting in the library. I always think I'll do better at home. But at home it's worse, because I start wandering around. . . ." "I've always loved reading novels, but as soon as I have to read something for school, I get jittery. . . ." "It's hopeless. It's too much. What's the use. . . ."

The Underlying Threads

All the underlying threads emerge as various expressions of fear. The list is long and intertwined. Enumeration of the most important threads will involve unavoidable repetition and overlapping. But fear is basic: [3] I am afraid to take chances; I am afraid to make a mistake; I am afraid of freedom; I am afraid of responsibility; I am afraid to succeed; I am afraid to fail; I am afraid of my own feelings; I am afraid of criticism; I am afraid I'll appear ridiculous; I am afraid people will find out; I am afraid of being imperfect; I am afraid to have fun. . . . Each unconscious attitude, or underlying thread, involves many of these and other fears, all interrelated. The individual does not sense them as specific fears; he is aware only of vague anxiety, emotional and sometimes physical malaise, feelings of helplessness, hopelessness, bewilderment, "lack of self-confidence," "nervousness" and other signals of deep distress.

[3] According to Theodor Reik, the goal of psychotherapy was formulated by Ernest Jones as "the achievement of relative fearlessness."

I Do Not Know What to Feel

When the Spaniards conquered Peru, they found in this strange land a belief in one virginal goddess, which reminded the Spanish Jesuits of the Holy Virgin and provided a connecting link between an alien culture and their own. This bit of history comes to mind in connection with a story about a Philippine girl who was a student in an American college. Because the external circumstances of her case were so strikingly different from those of the other students, the connecting links made by similar unconscious attitudes were dramatically highlighted. Let us refer to her as "Jasmine." She was so much like a flower, delicate, fine-featured, with creamy skin and soft ways. She came into the Reading Center one day for an interview, which proceeded as follows:

"I say I have a reading problem. I take your course because I cannot read; I cannot get my work done. But this is silly, because I can read, but I cannot concentrate!"

"You mean your mind wanders away from what you are reading?"

"Yes! It wanders and wanders."

"Do you ever follow it to see where it wants to go?"

"Well . . . no. I try to make it stay where it should!"

"Perhaps the problems it is trying to solve are more urgent than the reading."

"Oh. . . ." She gazed out the window.

"Tell me about it."

"Shall I start from the beginning?"

"Start wherever you like."

"Well. . . . I was living happily at home, in the Philippines. I was content. I was engaged to be married, and I was content. One day I got a letter from my uncle and aunt who live here in New York. They said, 'Jasmine, why are you content to go on that way? Don't you want to be an educated, cultured person? Come to New York. Go to a graduate school. Get a higher degree. Make something of yourself. You could live with us. Come!' " Jasmine began to weep.

"My boy-friend did not want me to go. It meant postponing our marriage for a year. He said he would break our engagement if I left. I did not believe he would. He has not, but I miss him.

"My aunt and uncle have four little children. The youngest is less than a year, the oldest is eight. The same week I got here, my aunt and uncle left for a trip to California. They are still gone. I sit in the library and I try to concentrate, but how can I concentrate if I am wondering what to buy for supper that all the children will be sure to eat. I cook for them and take care of them, and it is a very big responsibility. I do not know what to feel."

"You do not know what to feel?"

"Well, you see, I know I should be grateful to them for this big opportunity which they have given me, but I do not feel grateful! I feel I would like to move out. I would so much like to live in the International House. I think if I could live in the International House and no longer have to take care of the four little children, I could study and I could concentrate."

She paused, sighed, and looked at the interviewer apprehensively.

"Do you think I am very wicked and ungrateful?" she asked.

"No, I do not."

"Do you think I would be very bad if I moved out and lived in the International House?"

"It sounds sensible."

"Oh, thank you! That is what I have done, but I was afraid I was being very ungrateful. I did not know what I should feel."

Jasmine had already summoned her relatives home and had arranged for a room in International House, but she became frightened that she had done something wrong. During the rest of this interview she talked of other experiences in which she had been similarly afraid. As she left, she said, "Now I shall have no reading problem." And this proved to be correct.

Jasmine's story is not presented here to show how much can be achieved in one interview. It is rare that this much is accomplished so quickly. One wonders whether she has, since then, had any further trouble with trusting her own feelings and taking a chance on them. One would guess that she has had more of the same self-doubt, as such basic fears are not fully routed quite so easily.

What were Jasmine's fears in this particular instance? She was afraid of feeling what she did feel, anger. She was afraid no one could like her if she felt angry when she was expected to feel grateful. She was afraid she could not like herself if she did not live up to her own standards of feeling only what one *ought* to feel. Her fears carried her away from a belief in her own feelings and their validity; she became confused and ended up with, "I do not know what to feel."

This fear of feeling what one really does feel—especially if the feeling is rage—is so prevalent that one must watch for it in every case. Almost everyone feels it is dangerous to be angry. An angry person is not a lovable person. An angry person will be punished for his anger. Someone will get back at him. No one possibly can like him. No one will want to be with him. He will be all alone. These are the frightening exaggerations that cause the true emotion to be forced out of awareness. It requires energy to keep it out of the way, to hold it back. Sometimes this effort is so fatiguing that little energy remains for work (1). Also, holding back one strong feeling may involve holding back all strong feeling; if a little bit is let out, more may come bursting forth. Thus, when one tries to encourage a very slow reader to develop "a positive attack on the printed page," one may be urging him to do something he is not able to do, because he is afraid of letting out any aggression whatsoever; to actively "go after" the words and concepts on a page would mean a freeing of energies which he has all tightly dammed up, for safety's sake.

"I am afraid to feel what I feel" may refer to any number of emotions which, because of some conditioning in the person's life, it seems dangerous to sense. Love, affection, passion, ambition, hope, joy—any of these, all of these, and many more than these may be freighted with feelings which the individual is afraid to face, afraid to feel, afraid to know.

It is oversimplification merely to state that the fear of one's own feelings interferes with reading enjoyment and reading efficiency. Seeing this important fear as it manifests itself in actual case material is the best, perhaps the only, way to obtain a clear understanding of its many ramifications. The reader will recognize its powerful role in a human being's life when reading about a young man named Ralph later in this study (cf. 4). It is a thread that runs through and around all the other threads of unconscious attitudes about to be enumerated.

I Am Afraid to Take Responsibility for a Choice

A young man having trouble with his law books was asked, "Is this the study of your choice?" He replied, "What do you mean?" The question was rephrased, "Have you always wanted to study law?" He replied, "Of *course* I want to be a lawyer." He thought a moment, then, "I don't know what else I could be."

Trouble with concentration is often a clue to poor vocational choice, or, rather, no vocational *choice*. The individual has made no active selection of career; he simply finds himself preparing for one. He is sitting in the library, struggling to learn history, or psychology, or chemistry, or engineering, or business administration, or transportation, or textiles, or pharmacy—and he has never given time or real thought to what he most wants to do with his life.

Perhaps he is reading law books because it has never occurred to him to actively question his father's expectation that he join the firm. His attention, therefore, is not on the material in the books, since he has no vital interest in *learning law,* but only the goal of *becoming a lawyer.* To have a goal instead of a purpose and direction means that attention is not flowing into the learning process itself, where it belongs, but is caught in a vision of a final position in life.

Perhaps the channels of communication are so inadequate between him and his parents that he cannot express to them any doubts he may have about their choice for him. Self-assertion then may make its way through distorted channels. Instead of realizing and saying directly, "I am not so sure, Mother and Dad, that I am interested in law; I'd like time and opportunity to explore some other studies"—instead of speaking these words, he may express them indirectly and unconsciously through self-sabotage, failing the courses, not being able to concentrate on his books, not being able to remember the lectures. For further discussion of this thread, see the paragraphs about "Inner Resistance."

To change one's vocational plan seems to mean admitting a mistake. This puts an additional burden on the individual when he tries something new, for to change *again* would be unbearably humiliating. Changes of direction that often quite naturally result from growth are not regarded as evidence of expansion and learning, but as signs of weakness, vacillation, defeat, undependability.

Teachers and parents create and continually reinforce this fear of change. A high school lad of sixteen was chided by his guidance teacher for wanting to drop a certain subject and change to another closer to his heart's desire. The teacher said, "Don't be a quitter." This was outrageously inappropriate to the circumstances, since this particular boy had always had the problem of erring on the side of excessive diligence and rigid self-discipline. He was in the habit of arising at five each morning to study, and his dedication to his work excluded all play and social activities. It had taken him a long time, and considerable work with a counselor, to achieve the courage to make a change in his courses. This had necessitated some freeing of his initiative and acquiring more respect for his own feelings. The teacher's contemptuous, "Don't be a quitter!" dealt a blow to his newly won courage to go after what he really wanted.

Vocational guidance people are familiar with the picture of parents bringing adolescent children for aptitude testing with the request, in effect, "Test him and tell us what he should be." This attitude leaves the adolescent very little leeway to explore, to change his mind, to seek himself in his own changing and growing world. The parental illusion, well-meant but devastating in its effect, is that there is one right way for the child to go, one right path for him to follow, and, if the experts set his feet on that path, all he need do is work hard and he will reach that one right goal with no time lost.

It is generally accepted—as an abstract theory—that learning from experience is valuable. Taking action and making changes in vocation on the basis of new knowledge is another matter, usually regarded not as "learning from experience" but as "wasting time" and "not knowing what he wants." A young man of nineteen said, "I *can't* tell my father I don't want to be a doctor, because he'll ask me, 'Then what *do* you want to be?'—and I don't *know* what I want to be." This lad felt it would create great turmoil in his family if he registered indecision. He also felt he would be hurting his father by saying he did not want to study medicine, since his father was a doctor, and the boy sensed that his father's feeling of worthwhileness was completely in terms of being a physician. The father lived for his work; the boy feared that to say he did not want to do the same work would constitute a criticism of the father. (On the unconscious level, there was more to it than this.) The result of this impasse was that the boy registered his complaint by failing his pre-medical courses, and dropped out of school in a painful state of confusion, bewilderment and humiliation.

Boys and girls of adolescent age invariably apologize when they "admit" that they "still don't know what they are going to be." It is astounding to realize that these youngsters feel it incumbent on them to know the world before they have seen it, and to be aware of their own personalities and powers without experience and without ever having been encouraged or helped to study themselves, to know themselves as persons.

Perhaps the young law student, after he has had the opportunity to explore his real self, with all his hidden wishes and hidden fears, will find he really does want to study law after all. But what a difference there is now—to go ahead out of free choice, knowing and deciding that *he* wants to study law, no matter what anyone else expects of him. He has made a choice, for which he takes responsibility, and the self-affirmation exercised in making his choice gives him great pleasure. His work, unhampered by the effects of the former slavery-defiancy pattern, will now be an expression of himself. His assertive and creative energies are liberated to flow into his purposeful study activity.

IT's AN INNER RESISTANCE

"Johnny is not responding to our tutoring. I have a feeling he is resisting. His parents always put too much pressure on him, and now he is resisting them. He wants to defeat them. He is being contrary, defiant, uncoöperative. But he's so foolish to cut off his nose to spite his face. Doesn't he realize it's his own life that's at stake. Defeating his parents won't help him any, nor do him any good."

The adolescent boy is being "negative." Why does he cling so stubbornly to his "negativism?" If our understanding of the boy stops here, we are indeed defeated, and so is the boy.

The words "resistance," "negativism," "defiancy," "stubbornness," "spite"—all these words (like "lazy") are pawns being pushed back and forth across a chessboard. They are busy words, much in use, which explore no depths and explain nothing.

To understand Johnny, and to help him, it is necessary to find out what "resistance" really means in his life. Why is it apparently more vitally necessary to him to resist authority than to pass his subjects? He cannot see what it is he is doing unless he is helped to find the underlying causes of his behavior, and to overcome them with strength and new attitudes gained in a therapeutic relationship.

What is seen behaviorally as "negativism" often turns out to be a kind of "positivism" in a different context. Perhaps the adolescent boy who behaves with "resistance" cannot afford to succeed in his school work because he is playing for higher stakes. If his whole life has been one in which authority persons have made it difficult for him to establish a sense of self, his one desperate goal is to save his own life by rescuing whatever sense of self he has managed to maintain. The feeling of intactness is essential to emotional health. Academic work may represent just one tiny corner in which he fights for the feeling of intactness, and if failing academically gives him that sense of intactness, then this price must be paid. Guarding a sense of identity, of integrity, the knowledge of *who he is* is more vital to his emotional health and survival than is academic achievement. If defying the expectations of authority figures is the only way open to him for feeling like a person, then he is making the wiser choice, even though it may mean school failure.

The task in such a situation is to permit the "defiant" boy to have, as one lad so beautifully expressed it, ". . . the freedom of his failures." When he finds he is respected in his own awkward, fumbling, experimental approaches to life, free of the former prying, pushing, overzealous, overanxious, hypercritical supervision of parents and teachers, he will take courage to build on his own valid foundations— valid because they are his own. (The case of Donald in this study illustrates this struggle and presents it more clearly than can any descriptive formulation.)

Does "resistance" belong only to the adolescent? Or, rather, one may ask whether the end of adolescence is marked by chronological age or by the achievement of comparative maturity. Many "adults"— graduate students, teachers, mothers, fathers—have never finished the business of adolescence, the important chore of individuation, of seeing parents and teachers as persons and the self as a separate, grown-up human being. These old adolescents feel "like kids" all their lives. They have great trouble feeling equal to their peers, and they have an excessive respect, sometimes amounting to awe, of persons in positions of authority.

Thus it is not unusual to find a student in his thirties showing the same "resistance" to his studies as does the "defiant" sixteen-year-old boy. The older adolescent is, like the boy, trying blindly to maintain a sense of self, and his struggle may come to his awareness in a feeling that he is "up against a stone wall." He says, "I feel there is something within me that stops me, a kind of inner resistance which makes me my own worst enemy." He is confused. "It doesn't make sense. Why should I want to defeat myself?"

IT'S NEVER GOOD ENOUGH

When the little child in school spells "cat" with a "k," he does not get two-thirds credit for the "a" and the "t." He is either *all* right or *all* wrong. When the mother says to the little child, "You were bad today," the little child feels he has been *all* bad, that goodness is entirely excluded. He is one or the other, right or wrong, good or bad. He feels he cannot be both good and bad, both right and wrong at the same time. Absolutism and perfectionism rule the day.

A college student said, "I feel I have to read every word of every page of every book on every bibliography. It's slavery! If I don't do it that way, I feel I'm doing something wrong, almost as if I am doing something *bad*." To counteract this slavery, he decided that he would not read a word again until he felt like it. He stopped reading altogether for quite a long time, because it had to be all or nothing, and to give up the nothing meant taking on the tremendous burden of the all, which created unbearable anxiety.

Another student with the same conditioning reported the same feelings. He quickly saw how his pattern of reading mirrored his pattern of meeting other life challenges. He reported that when he has to buy a pair of new shoes, he searches all the stores for the best possible pair of shoes, the one best pair for him. Buying a pair of shoes becomes a test situation, as does his every life experience, and all pleasure is missing.

The phenomenon of "cramming" mentioned in "The Surface Threads" is understandable as a time mechanism for relieving the pressures of perfectionism and absolutism. When one has all semester to read a textbook in history, or economics, or accountancy, or whatever the subject may be, he feels there is no excuse for not learning *perfectly*. With oceans of time ahead of one, what reason can one have for not living up to one's standards of absolute perfection? "If, however," the student says, "I have only these eight hours remaining in which to cover this big book, then I must be practical and realize I can hope to do only so much in those eight hours. I'll be satisfied just to pass the course. I'll give up the wish for an A-plus and settle for a B-plus, since it will be remarkable for me to pass at all in the short time left for study."

In other words, when there is no longer a time freedom-of-choice, one is somewhat freed from the crushing burden of having-to-do-the-work-perfectly. One pressure is traded for another, and that should convey an idea of how dreadful the pressure of perfectionism is. The anguish of last-minute study imposed by the clock is preferred to the anguish of the self-imposed pressure of perfectionism. It is such a familiar picture: Midnight, and a big book on the desk out of which one must get at least the main ideas. The fatal moment is eight hours away. "With so little time left, all I can be expected to do is pass this test. If I just pass it, okay." That is the bargain with destiny.

Having thus negotiated with the gods, the student sometimes experiences, to his surprise, a feeling of exhilaration during this last-minute studying, provided he is not too exhausted, and if his supply of benzedrine does not run out. (It used to be coffee and caffeine tablets; now it seems to be benzedrine for last-minute magic.) Why this unexpected upsurge of exhilaration at this harrowing time? This feeling frequently has been misunderstood and has been described as the beneficial effect of anxiety; that is, "some people do better under conditions of anxiety." The writer believes that it is not anxiety that helps the student to study well at the eleventh hour; on the contrary, anxiety itself interferes with integrated activity. What seems to happen is that there is a momentary freeing from the pressure of perfectionism, an excitement at being liberated from one's own harsh standards, and thus a more intensive application of one's energies to the challenge at hand.[4]

Regard our student: A whiff of freedom, like a breath of springtime, stirs his soul. The possibility of happier days ahead gently kindles his imagination. It is now that he makes resolutions for the next semester. He says to himself, "Why did I think this text was so much to do! There's nothing to it! Here I am, quickly covering the main ideas in only eight hours. With a *whole semester* to deal with it, what I *could* have done!" Here he begins to fall into grievous error, for instead of asking himself, "Then, why didn't I? What stopped me? What *really* got in my way?" he turns his eyes towards new resolutions without new understanding, thus doomed to repeat old mistakes. "Boy, *next* semester things are going to be different! I'll tackle the text the first night I get it, not the last night I need it. I'll be all ready for finals by the end of the first week, so far as the book goes. I'll know it cold."

Thus, in the midst of the joy of newly glimpsed freedom, in a moment of relief from perfectionistic standards, shackling resolutions are made that close the door to freedom. The student promises himself he will do much better next time—no, not much better: He will do

---

[4] This picture is oversimplified for the purpose of making the one thread stand out clearly. Actually, the story of last-minute study is far more complicated, with many forces at play.

perfectly next time. As ever, the overdisciplined person seeks salvation in more discipline. Then, bewildered and unhappy during the middle of the following semester, he finds himself not able to concentrate. Naturally, he is in reaction against the crushing standards he has set up for himself. When cramming time rolls around again, he curses himself for having all semester failed to live up to his resolutions. Then the clock, on the eve of the examination, gives him a brief respite from his self-imposed burden of perfectionism.

Many students are puzzled by their own pattern of starting a task with high enthusiasm and soon losing interest. This pattern is another manifestation of the perfectionistic, absolutist conditioning. The individual begins with a dream of what he would like to do and be; the first time he fails, or thinks he has failed, in any little step on the path to the dream, he feels the dream is totally spoiled. Excitement dies and boredom arises. He loses interest in the task, or in the vocation, because it no longer holds the magic promise of making him a perfectly wonderful, or wonderfully perfect, person.

Why does he need to be this wonderful? Why does he cling to grandiose dreams of perfection? He dreams the dream of perfection because he needs it to save him from his own cruel self-criticism.[5] He was conditioned to feel that one had to be perfectly good and perfectly perfect in order to be lovable, in order to be considered a worthwhile person, in order to "count." Since his conception of perfection is impossible in reality terms, he is repeatedly facing the self-concept of being a failure.

Finally, his only escape from constant feelings of failure is to try nothing, risk nothing, want nothing. He feels bored with life, because he has not the courage to be his real self. His real self does not seem to him to be good enough to make him acceptable. Perhaps he will just stay in his room and do nothing at all, to avoid the whole painful prospect of meeting nothing but his own self-criticism, cruel, constricting, unrelenting. One young woman said, "I stayed in bed almost the whole weekend. At least for two days I felt I would avoid any chance of making mistakes."

The perfectionist is defeated before he begins, because to succeed on his terms is hopeless. His teachers, parents and friends may call

[5] The reader is referred to Karen Horney for her discussion of "the idealized image and the despised image." *Our Inner Conflicts.* New York: W. W. Norton and Co. Inc., 1945, pp. 96-114.

him "lazy," when the opposite is true: He is excessively ambitious, and his inertia is filled with desperation. His self-criticism and his compensatory strivings must be understood and their irrationality ameliorated before he can mobilize the courage to make mistakes and the resulting energy to be productive. If a student's eggs are all in one basket, that is, if his feeling of worthwhileness depends on his perfect success academically, then he must have a guarantee of success before making any efforts. He cannot afford to take chances, because too much is at stake. Writing a term paper may seem to hold the promise of magic, complete fulfillment (unreal because measured by perfectionistic standards) or the danger of complete nullification. The risk is too great, and he prefers to choose failure than to chance it. He holds onto his dream of perfection, and his activity in reality terms is paralyzed.

The word-by-word reader, making sure he is missing nothing, suffers from these fears of being nothing if he is not perfect. He shares the too prevalent misconception that it is noble to have irrationally high standards, even though they are so high that no one could possibly achieve them, and even though the constant measuring of what one really is against the vision of what one "ought" to be leaves one too heartsick and hopeless to do what one is able to do.

Despite the fact that this way of life is inefficient, the person caught in it makes a virtue of his irrational necessity in order to maintain it, since he has the illusion that in this way lies safety. Thus, a student coming for help to overcome his word-by-word reading may gradually become aware that he wants the practical advantages of giving up his crippling perfectionism and, at the same time, wants to cling to the unreal "safety" of his perfectionism.

On the surface, this pattern gives rise to what looks like paradoxical behavior. The word-by-word reader asks for help to overcome his habit; he claims he wants to read faster, with more fluency. However, when encouraged to be less "sticky" and more selective in his reading, to skip words that are not essential to the meaning, he becomes ruffled and a little resentful, petulant and defensive. The suggestion that he try to do just an adequate job, that he strive towards being average rather than remarkable, gives rise to considerable strong feeling.

Sometimes the instructor is accused of promoting carelessness, inefficiency, mediocrity, even dishonesty—as though skipping a word were immoral. The instructor is reaping the results of exposing a weakness which has been exalted into a virtue as part of a safety system. The student's lack of self-confidence makes it impossible for him to be selective, to decide what words to read and what words to skim over; he sees this fear-ridden performance rather as evidence of his being an extraordinarily good child, perfectly "clean," conscientious and thorough.[6]

The excessive carefulness, despite all the trouble it causes, has become a source of pride, and the possessor of the perfectionistic attitude would like to be praised for it. When no special rewards are forthcoming for being so good—in fact, when it is intimated that one is foolish and ineffectual when one is *that* good—there is, quite naturally, a rage reaction. One young woman, proceeding from a discussion of her word-by-word reading to a discussion of her similarly cautious mode of activity in other life areas, said, "When I think of all the years I've wasted, never expressing my real feeling, never really living, always waiting for someone to reward me someday for my goodness, I could explode, I'm so angry!"

Thus, when an instructor or remedial-reading specialist tries to change reading habits, he is trying to change a great deal more than that. All kinds of feelings are stirred up, and safety systems erected to forestall anxiety are threatened. "Help me to read fast," the students request. "But," they add, in effect, "don't take away my perfectionistic standards."

I Am Afraid to Succeed

A woman in her middle thirties had made many sacrifices for several years to save money enough for a year's leave of absence from her teaching position, so that she might come to Teachers College for a Master's Degree. As the first semester drew to a close, she found herself having crying spells, and she came to talk things over. She said she was worried that she was not of high enough calibre for graduate-school work. She was not able to concentrate on her studies or get her papers written. She said she was a poor reader, and she wanted to take an intelligence test to make sure she had the intellect necessary for advanced study.

She rated high in the superior group on the Bellevue-Wechsler Test.

---

[6] The reader who would like a more thorough understanding of this concept is referred to discussions in the psychoanalytic literature of the genesis and characteristics of the obsessive-compulsive character structure.

Though this was reassuring to her, it also was surprising. "I never believed," she said, "that I was smart, though my teachers always told me I was." It followed now that she must wonder what in the world was making it so difficult for her to do her work. "I've wanted this chance for years," she said, "and now that I'm here at last, I can't make the most of it." She began to wonder aloud, and the underlying threads came to the surface:

Grace [7] had had an unhappy childhood. Her mother died when she was a little girl. Her mother's sister came to live with Grace, her father and her baby brother, to take care of them all and, as it turned out, to terrorize them. This aunt was like a witch out of a storybook. At first Grace described her cruelties with calm and forbearance, but later she began to reexperience the emotional torment she had endured as a child, and angry tears poured.

To come quickly to the point: While still a child, she learned that her aunt was jealous of women better educated than herself. Grace became very ambitious, wanting nothing in the world so much as a higher education. She had fleeting glimpses of awareness that she was really working towards her day of revenge: She would have a Master's Degree, and her aunt would have to look up to her—a humiliating prospect for that bitter, envious woman.

This story did not go far enough, however, to account for the weeping and the inability to concentrate. Did she feel so guilty about her wish to humiliate her aunt that she must punish herself by defeating her own constructive efforts? This did not seem strong enough a wish to produce such powerful effects; there had to be more to it than that. There was. One day the fantasy spun itself out all the way: Her aunt would *drop dead* with jealousy the day Grace came home with her higher degree. This was the hope and the wish. However, since she, like most people, felt keenly the magic power of words, she feared it might really happen that her own triumph would kill her aunt. This fear gave rise to a subsequent fear: Destiny would punish her for her wish to kill. Her punishment would be death. Thus, to do her work successfully meant she would be killed, she would die!

During the session in which this fantasy emerged, Grace realized it was natural for her to have violent death wishes against her aunt, who had been so cruel to her during her entire childhood. She said, "I didn't know how *much* I hated my aunt. I was afraid to know."

[7] Names and identifying data have been changed.

This was a turning-point for her. The weeping spells ceased, and her concentration improved. With more and more understanding of her feelings about her family relationships and her relationships with fellow students, professors and the counselor, she made steady progress. She gained weight, used more make-up, bought her first red hat and began to enjoy her courses and her extracurricular activities. She was a superior student, and she was an exceptionally gentle and kind person, with fine sensitivity to the needs of children.

This is a greatly oversimplified account of a case for the purpose of highlighting one important thread: My triumph will be at another person's expense! The example may seem so striking as to be unusual. In some ways it is, since the role of an intruder aunt in a family, replacing the mother, is not usual. However, the fear that success comes at another person's expense is not unusual. If one sees it in the setting of competition between brothers and sisters, between daughter and mother, father and son, it becomes quite clear that this thread weaves through many lives.

It occurs with particular intensity in those families where it is considered unforgivable to express anger, and where rivalry is regarded as evil instead of natural. There comes to mind a family in which the mother boasted to her friends, "In *our* family we do not quarrel." The mother did not know that her little son wanted to hit his sister on the head with his baseball bat, that her daughter had a compelling impulse to push her mother down the stairs, and that both children were dreadfully paralyzed because their constructive ambitions were so loaded with the forbidden wish that their success would cause the rival to drop dead with envy. The daughter remarked to the Counselor one day, "No wonder people say, 'That'll really slay 'em!' " [8]

I AM KEEPING A SECRET BARGAIN

A graduate student unable to concentrate on her work began to explore with the Counselor some of the feelings lurking under the

---

[8] The reader may consider this example too pathological to be representative. This is not so, however. The difference between the fantasies of these persons and the average person is not in kind, but in degree of intensity. The reputation of the young woman here described is that she is "such a sweet girl" (which she is), who "could not be mean if she tried" (also true, as she turns her bad feelings against herself and suffers psychosomatically). Since her friends do not have access to her fantasies, they are not aware of what is really going on inside her.

surface, feelings holding her *real* attention, distracting her from her studies. She discovered that she felt herself bound by an unconscious bargain, and that she was in rebellion against this bargain.

Laura, the student, had very early in life made an unconscious bargain with her sister, two years her junior. The sister was small, dainty, girlish; Laura was big and heavy-boned, with features that were not quite as fine as her sister's. "I'll be the smart one, and you can be the pretty one," was the unspoken bargain Laura made, not realizing she was afraid to compete with her sister in the area of femininity.

Now, after a triumphant academic career, nearing her doctorate, Laura seemed almost deliberately to be trying to sabotage the successful completion of her work. Further insights revealed her unconscious protest against the unconscious bargain. Her sister was married and had two children. The doctoral diploma seemed a cold substitute for love and family life. A bargain that involved suppression of her own femininity was too harsh a bargain, indeed. In a last-minute rebellion against the defeat of her womanly self, she was trying to break the bargain. It was as if she were saying to herself: "If I fail to get my degree, perhaps it is not too late to win in the other arena, in the world of competition with women, as a woman."

It came to her as a shock that she *could have everything,* her academic success *and* her feminine success. She recognized that she had carried through life the feeling of being handicapped, as handicapped as though physically disfigured, perhaps even more so. With a surge of relief she understood that she need not carry this self-imposed limitation, that she could break "the bargain" without disaster or dishonor. Further psychotherapy supported Laura's efforts to grant herself both her intellectual competency and a flowering of her womanly charm.

There are many different kinds of unconscious bargains. Often a young man or woman feels that he or she is going to college *for* a parent or sibling. One nineteen-year-old college girl said despairingly, "Mother is always reminding me how much *she* wanted to go to college, and that she couldn't go. She says, 'It hurts me that you don't make the most of the opportunity.'"

This girl felt that she had made a bargain with her mother: She was accepting tuition and living expenses in return for going to college *for* her mother. The impossibility of this goal, of *being* her mother, as it were, filled her with a hopelessness that permeated all her efforts.

One day she burst out with: "The only way I can give my mother a college education is for her to go to college herself. That must be why I am always urging her to please go take some courses. I guess I want her to get her own education so there will be less of a burden on me."

When she realized that she had made an impossible bargain, and recognized how it had paralyzed her, enraged her, and filled her with hopelessness, she began to be more courageous and was able to assert to herself that she had a right to go to college for her *own* education. With increasing freedom to be herself, her energy for study increased, and her concentration improved.

There is also the unconscious bargain made by the one physically healthy child in a family in which the other children have been damaged by illness or accident. This child is afraid to succeed because his success would seem so unfair to those who are not able to compete with him. It is as though he has made a bargain with them: "I won't press my advantage of being the healthy one. I'll give myself the handicap of not really trying. In exchange for my health, I'll pay the price of failing in school." [9]

I'D RATHER BE LOVED THAN SUCCESSFUL

This is a variation of the thread discussed directly above. It is another "unconscious bargain," another formulation of the fear of achievement. This attitude, "I'd rather be loved than be successful," is found in persons so intolerant of their own competitiveness that they feel no one will love them if their competitiveness is discovered. "If I fail," said one student, "I am no threat to anyone. If I am not a threat, they will like me."

Many years ago, Stuart A. Courtis at the University of Michigan introduced exercises in cooperation for students in the field of education. The writer recalls a discussion with a fellow student with whom one of the exercises was being carried out. Both wondered whether cooperation necessitated the complete obliteration of competitiveness. It seemed a goal impossible of attainment. Now, picking up that discussion at the present time, the writer believes that intolerance for natural competitiveness tends to inhibit natural capacities for cooperation. Perhaps an example will serve to make the point:

Consider a woman whose turn it is to entertain her bridge club.

[9] Also, he is afraid to risk making mistakes, because, being well and strong, he has "absolutely no excuse" for not being perfect in his school performance.

She is preparing a luncheon for her company, and she has at least two feelings about it: On the one hand, she enjoys the prospect of giving enjoyment to her friends by serving them excellent food, beautifully prepared; on the other hand, she has a secret satisfaction in feeling that the other women will have to recognize her superiority as a cook, since she is certain no one else has served anything quite so original, so dainty, so exquisite. Should she despise herself for the latter feeling? Must she hate herself for being competitive, for wanting so much recognition? If her conscience is overscrupulous and punitive, she will hate herself for contaminating her pure feelings with competitive ones. If she hates herself a great deal, she may have to project the hatred (unconsciously) in order to endure it. That means she will feel she does not like the other women, or she will feel they do not really like her. She is afraid no one will like her if her competitiveness is exposed. She finds one reason or another for dropping out of the club. Is this constructive and cooperative? No, for now the other women have lost her altogether. Though they are spared her competitiveness, they lose her friendship, since her warmth and goodness were not excluded by her competitiveness. Everyone loses.

How much healthier it would have been for this woman to feel something like the following: Well, that's how I am. It's true I'm competing with the other girls, but I expect them to compete with me, too, and no harm done. It's probably a hangover from my competition with my mother and my sister. Anyhow, I'm not hurting anyone by my thoughts. The only effect on them is to provide them with the comfort of my hospitality. They will have the opportunity to do the same thing when I go to their houses. We all get our chance to show off. That's how we human beings are, and it isn't so bad.[10]

Let us take another example, this time in the area of education. If several students study together for an examination—as they often do when preparing for matriculation or comprehensive examinations —mutual helpfulness is not untainted by competitiveness, yet everyone profits. Each person shares his material with the others. Should each feel guilty for his secret thought that in some special way he will particularly excel on the examination? He does not begrudge the others' doing well, but he wants to express his own identity in his very

---

[10] Individuals who are excessively self-critical tend to regard many human attributes as *sub*-human, and angelic qualities as properly human and entirely possible if only one tried hard enough.

own way, to make his own mark, to carve his own initials. If he feels guilty for this wish to be himself, which he may sense as wanting to be better than the others, at the expense of the others, he may stay away from the study groups altogether, rationalizing that he gets more work done when he works alone. He misses out, both academically and socially, on what is offered by the other students. He misses the valuable experience of formulating his own ideas to communicate them to others. He misses the fun of doing things together.

FREEDOM MAKES ME ANXIOUS

A student studying for his oral examination in English literature expressed fear that he would never finish all the books in time. He was asked, "Why did you hurry to set a date for your oral examination, when you have hardly begun the reading?" He replied, "Unless I set a deadline, I'll go all to pieces and won't be able to read at all. I get nervous, depressed, anxious and terribly inefficient if I have too much freedom."

At first this sounds like a person who has been so accustomed to functioning under rigid disciplinary conditions that freedom frightens him (21). One might say he has had "too much discipline." A great deal has been written and spoken about the evil effects of too much discipline. Recently, statements are beginning to come into the literature of child psychology about the deleterious effects of too little discipline, of failure to "set limits." The use of the words "too much" and "too little" are not helpful, however. It is the quality of discipline and the personality of the disciplining person that is of importance (3). The word "discipline" itself is a fighting word; hackles rise at the sound of it, because of its traditional authoritarian connotations. The expression "setting limits" came into being to avoid these connotations.

A young man is preparing for his oral examination, unable to work without setting a deadline. Viewing the situation from the outside, an observer of the family would unhesitatingly say that his father "over-disciplined" him and his mother "spoiled" him. His father terrified him with authoritarian demands for conformity. His mother waited on him, babied him and protected him from the neighboring children.

During the process of psychotherapy, the real picture emerges: The father is a frightened man. He shouts and blusters, and his son is frightened because he can get no strength from his father. What name can one give to this father's "discipline?" The mother turns out to be shadowy, indefinite, easily bullied; however, she, in turn, bullies her son. She wins her way by weeping and begging. Can this method of intimidation be called "discipline?" Can it be called "spoiling?" If the popular notion of "spoiling" is that the child is always allowed to have his own way, then he was not "spoiled," for he was thoroughly dominated, not only by his father's weak blustering, but by his mother's tearful bullying.

In an environment so inconsistent, with a parental show of spurious strength belied by internal weakness, the boy was almost constantly in a state of anxiety, in a fog of uncertainty. He hungered for a really strong father, someone kind and consistent, who could protect him and give him a model to follow. He yearned for a mother who would not melt into tears at his every show of independence.

This young man repeatedly set up situations for himself in which he provided a structure of limits within which he tried to function with an alleviation of his confusion and anxiety. One might almost say he was trying to be a strong mother and father to himself. He said, on one occasion, "When I was a kid, it suddenly dawned on me: 'If they are so frightened of the world, who will protect me in the world?'" It turned out that setting a deadline meant to him establishing strong parents who cared about him and would take care of him adequately. The deadline became "someone who really cared"—not like his infantile parents, who were so immature that they clutched at him for support instead of being able to give him support.

Scheduling his daily activities had the same meaning for him: The schedule was a strong parent. His difficulty was that he overdid his efforts to provide structure. The systems he set up were too rigid, too exacting, and he was bound to experience reactions against them, thus throwing himself into helpless and hopeless confusion; for freedom to him meant chaos rather than an opportunity for strong self-assertion. When reading, he was so determined to remember every word he read, and so frightened that he would not remember, that he could not concentrate. Therefore, he found himself looking at pages without seeing them. This ineffectual reading would catapult him into the most distressing depressions and feelings of hopelessness.

My Desperation Leaves Me No Time for Discriminating

There is a kind of reader whose way of reading is characteristically described as follows: "He goes too fast, misses words, stumbles, loses the meaning, has to go back, starts up again at breakneck speed, rushes headlong into the material, gets lost again, stops, goes back and so on." If I were to give a name to this kind of reading, I would call it "stuttering reading."

It has long been recognized that stuttering in speech has psychogenic origins. "Stuttering reading" is perhaps closely related to speech stuttering; it demands and deserves an equal attention to underlying causation.

There is a quality of desperation in the reader who rushes and halts, speeds and stops. An observation one can make immediately is that these readers seem to be standing in their own way, and that there is in their reading some element of self-sabotage.

Another observation is that they seem to be gulping, not savoring what they take in. Why is there this great hurry? Can one hypothesize that this kind of person is so desperate for affection and for safety that he reaches frantically and grabs indiscriminately? Can one also ask whether he so fears punitive reactions to his competitiveness that he can be aggressive only surreptitiously and speedily? Questions like these point the way to an understanding of the underlying causes of reading disability.

These are some of the most important threads that emerge from below the surface when reading problems are studied carefully. The reader will recognize them in their interacting, overlapping, dynamic relationships in the case material presented in this study.

One major point will become increasingly clear when seen in the case material: Reading cannot be regarded as separate from the other behavior of an individual.

[2]

FOUR INITIAL INTERVIEWS

FOUR INITIAL INTERVIEWS are presented in this chapter. John, Mike, Sue and Betty came to the Reading Center for help with reading, yet all had problems requiring more than tutoring. The reader will be interested in seeing what "underlying threads" seem to appear in these first interviews. In addition, the reader will be interested in the problems as understood and verbally communicated by each of the four persons. The Discussion at the end of each interview will supply additional material and further ideas for the reader's consideration.

Interview with John

John was eighteen years old at the time of his first interview. His introduction to the Reading Center was through a letter he wrote asking for help. His letter excited considerable interest because, in one page, it reviewed all the symptoms that have become so familiar to those working in the Adolescent and Adult Reading Center. A copy of his letter follows:

"In the hope that you may help me in some way with my reading problem, I have made this self-diagnosis and am hereby submitting it to you.

1.—I am reading very slowly.
2.—I comprehend slowly and inadequately, and fail many times to get the salient facts.

28

3.—Frequently I must re-read words and phrases to gain complete understanding of them.

4.—I read word by word, not phrase by phrase as I should.

5.—While reading I hear my voice in my 'inner ear' reading the words.

6.—I concentrate imperfectly.

7.—When starting to read a new book I feel I must read the entire book from beginning to end, even to the extreme of reading the book jacket over and over.

8.—I encounter much difficulty with vocabulary, and when I stop to look a word up in the dictionary, I feel that I still haven't acquired the full meaning of the thought, and I must re-read the passage over many times.

9.—I fatigue quickly, and reading to me is painful. I can read only about an hour and a half at a stretch without tiring.

10.—After reading something, I feel that I have retained very little of what I have read.

I would appreciate it very much if you could help me out in some way with my reading disability.

Very truly yours,"

An appointment was arranged. John arrived an hour early. The Counselor greeted him in the waiting-room and told him to make himself comfortable. The interview follows:

C- 1: I have read the letter you sent to us, but now I would like to hear you tell me what it is you have come for.

J- 1: Well, I notice that I am reading so slowly and that I have not absorbed what I should. I can't concentrate. I try to make a picture of the word, but that doesn't help. Nothing helps. I get distracted. My mind wanders.

C- 2: Have you ever noticed what sorts of things you think about when your mind wanders away from your reading?

J- 2: (Shrugs) Well . . . I don't know. I suppose to something I have seen or something someone has said. I guess I never paid much attention to just what.

C- 3: Tell me more.

J- 3: When I do read, I feel I should get more out of it. I feel unsatisfied with my reading. I feel it's going to hold me back in my college work that I hope to do eventually.

C- 4: When did you first notice this problem?

J- 4: I've been conscious of my reading, that it wasn't what it should be. . . . This past six months it's been worse. I feel I don't know what I'm reading about. I read and read, then it's just like I didn't even read it! (Gestures despairingly.)

C- 5: Can you tell me more?

J- 5: I'm taking the course in Improvement of Reading over at General Studies, but I feel the course over there isn't doing me any good.

C- 6: How so?

J- 6: Well, all we've done is some speed tests and reading comprehension tests there.

C- 7: How many sessions has the group had thus far?

J- 7: Two.

C- 8: How can you tell so soon that they won't be helpful to you? (Laughingly)

J- 8: (Grinning) Well, it's group work.

C- 9: You don't want to do group work?

J- 9: Well, I feel my problem is so serious, you just can't do it. I feel I need individual help. Another reason I took that course is that I wanted to take a course in college and see what it's all about. I wanted to get acquainted with college work. I felt, instead of staying home, I might as well go to school one night. I work days.

C-10: That was a nice idea. Tell me, what work do you do?

J-10: I do filing in the business office of ———— (a large department store).

C-11: And do you like it?

J-11: It's not bad. I need the money.
(Silence.)

C-12: (After a few minutes) What are you thinking?

J-12: I'll go on with the course over there, but I feel it won't help me. I need individual help.

C-13: How do you gauge your problem as being more serious than that of the other students in the course?

J-13: I did very poorly on the comprehension test they gave us. The other students covered twice as much. I was very slow.

C-14: Do you know what test it was?

J-14: (Tries to remember. . . .)

C-15: Was it by any chance the Nelson-Denny Test?

J-15: Yes, that was it.

C-16: Can you recall your scores?

J-16: I think it was 64, 44, and 33. I'm not sure.

C-17: You wouldn't know whether those were your raw or percentile scores?

J-17: No, I don't. But I know I did very badly. The others did better. The thing is, I want to get myself educated, and I feel you have to do it by reading, but every time I start to read a new book, I throw it aside, because I can't remember or know what I'm reading, so I get disgusted after a few minutes and I throw it aside. Recently I read a book on reading, but it didn't do me any good. I attempted to read some textbooks, but I had trouble with them.

C-18: Tell me again . . . how long has this been going on?

J-18: Well, I guess it wasn't so bad in high school. I know when I was sixteen I finished quite a few books. Plays, and novels, and poetry. I wasn't aware of a reading difficulty, so I just went ahead without thinking about it and read one book after another. And it was all right. No trouble.

C-19: Well, what happened?

J-19: In the eighth term we took the Regents reading comprehension test. I had trouble with the vocabulary. And I had to read something over and over. After that, I couldn't read. Because once I knew I had a reading difficulty, I lost interest in reading. Then I couldn't read any more.

(Counselor murmurs sympathetically.)

Every night before I go to sleep, I try to do some reading, and I have trouble with it, and I don't understand it. I'm beginning to feel hopeless.

C-20: What have you been reading?

J-20: Right now I'm working on the preface to the dictionary.

C-21: But that's so dull!

J-21: Yes, but it's important! I feel you should do things right. I want to read, so I have to learn vocabulary. If I learn pronunciation in the preface, I could just look up a word any time and know how to pronounce it.

C-22: Tell me more.

J-22: I tried to read the Bible, but I couldn't read that either.

C-23: You certainly choose the hard way! Do you ever read novels?

J-23: No, never any more. You see, I don't want to waste time on novels. I'd like to have a well-rounded education, like learn history and things. Lately I've taken to oral reading, the plays of Shakespeare, and I enjoy it much better than silent reading. I don't understand all of it. It's hard. But the sound of it is music to my ears. I haven't done oral reading on anything else, though.

(Silence.)

C-24: What are you thinking?

J-24: It's just that I want to acquire a good education. But when it comes to reading, I try to force myself but I can't go on with it because I feel I haven't absorbed anything at all. So I would like individual help.

C-25: You shall have it.

J-25: I'll continue the other course, too. I want to see what college life is like. When I got out of high school last year, I wanted to go to college, but I said to myself, "Maybe I'm not capable of college work."

C-26: Why did you think that?

J-26: I don't know.

C-27: You must have had a reason for thinking that. What was it?

J-27: Maybe it was because of the reading. I was told by a lot of people that you had to read a lot and that you had very little time to read.

C-28: People who have gone to college like to impress others with stories of how hard they had to work.

J-28: (Smiles.) I guess so.

C-29: They frightened you.

J-29: Well, maybe. But I want so much. I have a desire. . . . I feel that I should acquire a certain basic education.

C-30: But you lack self-confidence.

J-30: That's it. And then I tell myself if I know pronunciation, if I have trouble with any word, I can look it up and stop having trouble. . . . You see, I have a desire to learn, but something is stopping me. (Looks at counselor with almost tearful entreaty.)

C-31: Yes, something is stopping you, and it makes you very unhappy.

J-31: Yes. (Stares down at his shoes and struggles for composure.)

C-32: You feel bewildered by it.

J-32: Yes, it isn't as though I don't try. I do try, and I don't know what I'm reading. And another thing: I don't even know yet what I want to be.

C-33: It takes time to settle on a vocation. Eighteen is young.

J-33: I like acting. I did some in high school, and I liked it. But I don't know. Right now I feel it's important first to get an education. It will take time. I'll go evenings. I was just able to scrape up the forty-five dollars for this one course.

C-34: I like your spirit. I think it's grand, doing that.

J-34: (Smiles.) It's quite interesting, college life. I thought it was much different.

C-35: I bet you thought it would be much harder than it is.

J-35: (Emphatically) Yes! And . . .

C-36: And what?

J-36: Well, I didn't think things were so informal as they are. I like it. I always liked this school. Everything I heard about it, I liked. But I thought it would be more strict, not so informal. (He has a pleased expression.)
(Silence.)

C-37: What are you thinking?

J-37: I feel three years of high school were wasted. I took radio. I felt I wasn't college material.

C-38: You felt that all during high school?

J-38: I wasn't getting proper marks. I was just passing. I had no interest in school.

C-39: But now you have so much interest. . . .

J-39: Well, then I was studying math, and all technical subjects. But now I became interested in reading, in social science, and all that. I never liked the technical subjects. I couldn't do it. I'm interested in English literature.

C-40: How did you happen to major in technical subjects when they did not interest you?

J-40: I went to ———. I studied radio. I wanted to go to Brooklyn Prep., but that's a pay school.

C-41: There are other schools?

J-41: (Shrugs.) I don't know now why I chose that one. Well, I do know. My parents and relatives thought it would be best for me to take up a trade and be secure in life. Not my parents—my mother. My father's dead. He's been dead nine years.

C-42: That was hard for you.

J-42: Yes, it was. . . . Well, my mother's interested in me going to school. She *wants* me to. But I have relatives in the industrial field who have made out pretty well. They convinced me—no, they didn't convince me, they advised me—to take it. The first year-and-a-half of school didn't interest me at all. That is, certain subjects.

C-43: Well . . . we have only fifteen minutes left. Suppose we get this application blank filled out now, and make arrangements for you to come here for individual help.

J-43: All right. Thank you. (He proceeded to fill out the form. He printed carefully, slowly, painfully, laboriously. When he reached the question about having been helped by other agencies, he said:) I took an aptitude test at the ———.

C-44: How did you happen to go there?

J-44: At the time, I was in bad condition. I was about to crack up.

C-45: When was that?

J-45: It was last December. I was working in a factory, and I couldn't take it. It was too monotonous. So, I had heard about this place, and I went there. Boy, what a place! (Derogatory, but with a smile.)

C-46: What do you mean?

J-46: Well, they just gave me a couple of tests and told me I'd be good at teaching or executive work. They told me I have an objective personality. I don't agree.

C-47: (Laughs.) What does that mean, and why didn't you agree?

J-47: (Smiles.) They said I work best with people. I don't agree. I don't do well with people.

C-48: Are you enjoying this interview with me?

J-48: Yes, very much. (Emphatically)

C-49: Well, I'm "people," and we're working together.

J-49: But I have the feeling, or the idea, that I don't work well with people. This is different.

C-50: I have the feeling that you are a very warm, friendly person.

Perhaps the same thing that interferes with your reading interferes with your relationships with people.

J-50: Maybe so. I'll give you an example: If I'm in an argument, I won't win the argument, I just keep quiet. I never win. And I feel I could never work with people to . . . oh, I mean, like selling things to people, and stuff like that.

C-51: I guess you feel you can't sell yourself. You just give up before trying.

J-51: It's something like that.

C-52: Well, have you thought of having some counseling as well as work in reading?

J-52: (Grinning) I did have some counseling.

C-53: Tell me about it, where and when.

J-53: It was a vocational place. They took tests. I wanted to find out my I.Q., but they never would give it to me.

C-54: You'd like to have that, wouldn't you?

J-54: Yes. I think they should at least have talked it over with me.

C-55: Would you have any objection to my writing to these two places for their test results? That would save us time.

J-55: No, go ahead. Will you tell me my I.Q.?

C-56: I won't keep you in the dark, but I wonder why you have more question about your I.Q. than I have about it . . . about you, I mean.

J-56: Well, I'd like to know. . . .

C-57: I can tell from talking with you, from hearing you express yourself, that your I.Q. is no problem. But you haven't much faith in yourself.

J-57: No, I haven't.

C-58: Would you like an opportunity to talk about it, to get clear on why you have so little self-confidence, and what is bothering you and interfering with your reading?

J-58: Yes, I would like to get down to things. They never got down to things in the other places. I'd like to get straightened out, so next fall I'd be ready to really start my education.

C-59: Good. You're on the beam.

J-59: (Laughs.) And I'd like to work on my reading, too.

C-60: Okay. Suppose we map it out this way: Suppose you begin at once, next week, to work on your reading with one of our workers. Then, just as soon as I can find the time, I'll start the counseling sessions with you. If I can't arrange it myself, I'll find you someone else. But you'll get someone. How will that be?

J-60: Thanks, that's good. I don't want to waste any time. I feel I've wasted so much time. I don't want to waste any more. . . . When I take a subway ride and I don't do any reading, I feel I've wasted time.

C-61: Well, we'll have to work that out. But now let us finish our practical arrangements, because we've run overtime.

(It was arranged that John would come to the Reading Center once a week, or more often if possible. When discussing fee, he insisted on paying no less than one dollar per session.)

J-62: (Extending his hand as he was leaving.) I really enjoyed talking to you. I want to thank you.

C-63: I enjoyed it, too. And don't get disheartened. You're on the right track, and you came to the right place.

J-63: Yes, this time I feel I came to the right place—finally!

(When saying good-bye, John's hand was quite cold and damp. He did not shake the counselor's hand; he passively placed his hand in hers.)

Discussion of the Interview with John

The first contact with John was his letter. Since it was written in his own handwriting, not typewritten, we had an opportunity to obtain some clues to his personality before he arrived at his first appointment. His handwriting, viewed from the graphologist's standpoint, showed rigidity, low self-esteem, and a very weak flow of energy. You might say that his penmanship "mumbled," and you expected that he would speak in a low voice, not loud and clear. His speech would be precise, but only in choice of words, in formulation. He would not speak energetically, nor would he be expected to move about forcefully, with a show of strong vitality.

This prediction was correct. Let us try to reconstruct the moment of meeting. John stands in the doorway—hesitant, sagging, head bowed, apologetic. He has a big shaggy head, a beautifully shaped head, but he does not hold it high. He is about six feet tall, but his sagging posture robs him of stature. He shuffles when he walks into the room, so hesitantly as to give the impression of trying not to take up any space.

He has a handsome, intelligent face, with impressive brow and keen eyes. He needs to lose the sheepish smile and flickering, evasive gaze. The face of a man appears fleetingly in the troubled face of a boy.

He wears thick eyeglasses. He is near-sighted. Is he afraid to "look," to indulge his curiosity, to take in the environment with his eyes? Past experience with cases of near-sightedness has educated us to these possibilities. Fear of looking would not be out of place in the picture as we see it thus far: the frightened handwriting, hesitant walk, sagging posture. An article by Sylvester and Kunst comes to mind, about suppression of curiosity in the causation of reading difficulty (38). With regard to immediate responsibility, we must ascertain that his eyes have been well cared for medically and his glasses properly fitted.

He crouches over in his chair. Sometimes he looks at his shoes; sometimes he seems to be examining the carpet. He picks at his fingernails. Occasionally he shrugs his heavy, well-developed shoulders. His choked voice is low and full of tension. One gets the feeling that he wants and needs to say so much more than what he is saying. He sighs, he smiles with embarrassment and self-contempt, belittling his words.

To avoid the cumbersome effect of repeating each response in order to discuss it, we shall use the method used by other researchers in counseling, of numbering each statement. This means the reader will have to turn to the interview each time, an awkward procedure but apparently unavoidable. In this interview discussion, C is for Counselor and J for John.

C-1: The purpose of doing this is to give the client an opportunity to state his conscious reasons for coming for help, so that the counselor can hear him and he can hear himself. The written word does not have the same therapeutic value as words spoken in a relationship with another person.

J-1: Compare this with his letter.

C-2: The counselor always asks this question in response to a client's statement that his mind wanders. Invariably the response, as in C-2, is that the client has never noticed the nature or content of the wanderings. The struggle always seems to be an effort to force the mind to go in a certain direction, with no trust in the unconscious to yield important information, or with a fear of facing thoughts and feelings hidden below or outside of conscious awareness. Good writers know the value of "tapping the unconscious"; they call it, "letting the characters have their head."

C-3: This is a useful response, depending on the tone in which it is spoken, which is true of all that the counselor says. If spoken pedantically, it can cut off the flow from the client. If the voice communicates interest, patience and warmth without avidity but with a cool enough respect for the client's freedom of choice, it serves to maintain the flow of self-expression.

It is a helpful response for student counselors to keep in mind. They often fear silences and fill them with questions that deflect the client from his own trend of thought. Or, they may hurry to reflect feeling when they are still in the dark as to what feeling the client is expressing. If they feel uncomfortable in a silence, this discomfort is somehow conveyed to the client and disturbs his own efforts to arrive at comfort. Later, with more experience, the counselor will not be frightened by silence. In the meantime, a response like, "Tell me more." serves as a useful mortar for holding the interview together.

C-4: This is an effort to bring out information about the causes of the stated disability. Clarification of the genesis of the reading disability may free the client from his present despair by putting emphasis on an attitude of problem solving. In other words, the counselor is, quite early in the interview, doing some structuring in the direction of trying to stimulate insights and thereby trying to pull the client out of his bog of hopelessness. She does not succeed, however, and returns again in C-18 to the same stimulus, this time with better results.

C-8: The tone of voice is especially important in this response. It is not spoken critically or accusingly, but with softness. Nor must it be spoken triumphantly, which is a danger, since the counselor had, in fact, followed a hunch and found it correct. C-9 similarly depends for its therapeutic value on the counselor's tone of voice. The inflection here can easily be a critical one, which would rob it of usefulness. As a respectful request for further enlightenment, it advances the interview in a narrative sense and does not damage the relationship that is in process of growing. A request for this sort of information is an attempt to stimulate the client to seek insight; it is not in the category of history-taking for the counselor's sake, but rather a sharing of knowledge, and an opportunity for the client to hear himself formulate the feelings within himself.

C-10: Approval from the counselor must be sincere and spontaneous, else it is sensed as patronizing and does more harm than good. Unless the counselor can scarcely hold back the approval, because it is felt so urgently, it is better left unsaid. Approval "with a purpose" is without therapeutic value. The counselor may find it useful to adopt the premise that one person's unconscious senses the other person's unconscious. Following this premise, the counselor will recognize that establishing and maintaining a healing relationship will depend largely on his own capacity for sincerity with himself, a goal perhaps never absolutely achieved but worth growing toward. If he understands this struggle within himself, he will be better oriented toward the same struggle in his client, and he will have the necessary humility toward his client's efforts when he knows, himself, what courage is required to achieve sincerity. "Autobiography is the most difficult of the arts," said one of Charles Morgan's characters in the novel, *Sparkenbroke* (48). This truth probably is recognized only by those who work aduously at self-understanding. Too often, sincerity is regarded as a moral quality to be adopted by exercise of will, rather than as a goal to be approached with persistent effort and considerable hard work.

C-12: "What are you thinking?" is another helpful tool, like "Tell me more." "What are you thinking?" is perhaps even more useful, because "Tell me more" implies a direction to the client to continue speaking in the same vein; whereas "What are you thinking?" leaves the client free to say whatever is in his mind.

J-18 and J-19: What hypothesis comes to mind in an attempt to understand what happened to John? Why was it that as soon as he discovered by objective measurement that he had "a reading difficulty" he at once lost interest in reading? What guesses can we make? On what facts can we build a tentative hypothesis?

It is possible that at one time John was a "bookworm." He relates that at sixteen he "read one book after another—plays, novels, poetry" (J-18). Every reading specialist—and many a parent—is familiar with the adolescent who reads fiction voraciously but who cannot read his school books. Even little children who "can't read" may have no trouble reading the "hard words" in a game they are playing.

As a "bookworm" John would use books to enrich his fantasy life, to facilitate his escape from self-critical attitudes into self-glorifying identification with fictional characters and situations. The fictional world provides opportunities for emotional catharsis [1] and for imaginary strength and safety.

When John read books for pleasure, he was being himself, doing a thing he wanted to do. He was finding some relief from his perfectionistic way of life. The moment reading became identified with authoritative demands for measuring up to academic standards, it was lost to him as a pleasurable activity. He states, "Once I discovered I had a reading problem, I lost interest in reading." (J-19)

Instead of saying to himself, following the Regents test, "I've been enjoying reading, so there must be something wrong with this test," he submissively bowed to the authority symbol, the objective test. Whether he was a "good reader" or a "poor reader" according to the test is irrelevant. What is striking is his immediate modification of his self-concept as a reader. He did not stand up for himself. He did not try to understand his poor performance on the basis of disinterest in the material, nor did he take into account his anxiety in a test situation. His only protest was to "lose interest in reading."

Is it possible to be submissive to a reading test without being submissive to other authority symbols? It is not likely. An attitude tends to be pervasive and to permeate a character structure. How does this idea fit in with what we know about John thus far? We have seen the rigid, frightened handwriting, without free flow of vitality; we have observed the bowed head, the apologetic posture, the almost inaudible voice. Yes, it seems likely that we can work further on this hypothesis; namely, that John has been excessively submissive to authority, that he has not established a feeling of inner authority to give him strength to be himself fearlessly. He would surely find it difficult, if not impossible, to follow Rugg's formula: "*I* say . . . what *I* see and feel . . . *my* way." (56) He must live his life trying to please others, with the same obsequiousness with which he entered this office.

What else comes to mind as we think about him? . . . Why the downward curl of the lips as he speaks of himself, so that his smile becomes self-deprecatory? If he is scornful of his own words, why? He speaks of his problems with an air of self-contempt, with very little tolerance or patience for himself. How does this fit into our picture? Let us hold this in abeyance for the moment and continue with the interview.

[1] Bibliotherapy has only limited value because neither intellectual formulations nor emotional catharsis in themselves effectively change personality.

J-20 and J-21: This is a very literal interpretation of "first things first." He says, "I feel you should do things right," and he feels that the way to improve his reading is to start with mastering the preface to the dictionary.

J-22 and J-23: Here the counselor has to be careful not to fall into the trap of a strong cultural conditioning that looks upon novels as a luxury outside "real" education. Good novels are richly educational. As an organization of life experience, a good novel surely teaches as much human psychology as does a textbook—sometimes more. Consider, for example, Charles Jackson's *The Lost Weekend,* a profound study of alcoholism (34). All the great novelists and poets and playwrights have provided a rich storehouse for the study of human nature. However, when John states earnestly that he does not want to "waste time on novels," it is tempting to regard this as a highly commendable attitude. One might get the feeling that he knows exactly where he is going, and thus fail to challenge his navigation, which is really taking him nowhere.

Perhaps John's wish to avoid novels substantiates our hypothesis that his reading of novels at age sixteen was a compensatory activity. He perhaps feels guilty about having used fiction as an escape from his life challenges. Now he would like to curtail his indulgence in fantasy, not "waste any more time," and read only what he believes will help him build real strength in a practical world. He may sense an increasing pull towards fantasy, as a result of his increasingly stringent authoritarianism in his attitude towards himself. He must not permit himself even a subway ride without forcing himself to attend to work.

John's self-deception may not be apparent to the counselor. It would be easy to make the mistake of reinforcing John's paralysis by approving and encouraging his "serious efforts," instead of challenging him to investigate why he has to be *such* a good boy. He needs to discover and understand the reasons for the excessiveness of his diligence, the grandiose quality of his goals, and the paralyzing effect of his perfectionism.

Interview with Mike

A cumulative record from Mike's school preceded him to the Reading Center. From this record, sent by a teacher who had taken a special interest in him, it was learned that the boy had perplexed his teachers all through his school career because he did not live up to his superior I.Q.

The record began early. His kindergarten teacher described Mike (on a check-list) in the following way: "He eats a good meal, but he putters; he bites his finger-nails; once in a while he loses his temper; he likes to play the drum and build with blocks; he says he is lonely if left alone at home; he sometimes has nightmares; he is fairly courteous and sometimes stubborn; he is imaginative; he is persistent and 'tries'; you can reason with him; he is very anxious to please; he has decided likes and dislikes; he is a very affectionate child, and wants to please but is mischievous; he has a good mind, but finds it difficult to concentrate at times because his interests change so frequently."

His third-grade teacher wrote: "Work habits improving; cheerful disposition." Fourth grade: "Very popular with his classmates; honest; does not lie to save himself; never really gets down to work." Fifth grade: "Extremely lazy as far as school-work is concerned; very likable and helpful in extracurricular activities." Sixth grade: "Winsome ways and quite tactful in handling others."

Out of the cumulative record fluttered a piece of notebook paper on which Mike at age ten had laboriously written to his teacher, "I am going to do my work on time frome now on. I also am going to try to do better work for the reast of the year." This was carefully dated and signed.

When he was eleven years old, his teacher wrote about him: "Very pleasing personality; superior ability; lowest ability is reading; highest abilities are reasoning, arithmetic, induction, seeing opposites; very good in dramatics; his poor reading affects all his school work; he lacks concentrative power, yet has superior ability! He has many reading complexes. . . . Personality plus . . . ! His reading shows regressions, confusions, and he complains that his neck hurts. . . . He frowns when reading. . . . He states that he 'tries to keep up and to read fast, but makes mistakes.'"

The following year several interviews were held with the parents, and his teacher wrote: "The parents have tried to cooperate with the reading situation, and we have accomplished something, but Michael must continue to help himself. I believe he has taken a liking for reading now which will help."

When he was fourteen, a report was sent home that Mike was "Very weak in composition, and also had no book report." The parents wrote back, "What book was he to have in?" The same year, another report said, "Mike seems to be lost in English work, especially grammar. I feel he could do better if he took more time and ACTUALLY WORKED! He spends so much time telling what he can't do, he wastes the time he could be doing what he should." The parents' reply: "If you have a grammar book, will you please send it home with Mike. He should do extra work in this at home. Do not accept his home work when done carelessly. We will see that it is done over again. Thanks for your interest."

Mike was fifteen when he came to the Reading Center. He was failing four subjects, and one of his teachers, who had faith in the boy and great affection for him, sent him to us.

Mike was standing in a little hallway instead of sitting comfortably in the waiting-room when the counselor arrived. He smiled a shy, embarrassed, charming smile. He appeared much younger than his fifteen years. His small stature and peaked, almost elfin, face constituted a childlike rather than adolescent appearance. Walking down the hall to the interviewing room, Mike walked with a swagger, perhaps hoping to appear older, bigger, tougher, more athletic? He spoke with a swagger, too, pretending to take lightly matters which kept him close to tears. During the interview, the counselor occasionally caught on his face a strained look of pain and helplessness. He held his head at a jaunty angle and smiled almost continuously, trying to maintain composure. His eyes filled with tears from time to time.

The secretary had given Mike an application form to fill out while waiting for the counselor, since he had arrived almost an hour ahead of the scheduled appointment. He had written: "I want help with reading and spelling, and thinking before I do things. I do things and then think later. I want to find out how to study. I'd like to study." He also said that he had once had a year of tutoring in reading.

C- 1: Have you any idea why you are here?
M- 1: Yes.
C- 2: Tell me about it. Let's hear it from you.
M- 2: So I'll learn how to read better.
C- 3: You feel that's your problem?

M- 3: I guess so.

C- 4: What's the problem as *you* see it? People come here with problems . . . what's yours?

M- 4: I have a lot of problems.

C- 5: Want to tell me?

M- 5: Can't pass in school.
(Silence.)

C- 6: Tell me about it.

M- 6: I failed.

C- 7: When?

M- 7: Last report card.

C- 8: Is this the first time it ever happened to you?

M- 8: Yeah. First time I ever failed *four.* I've failed English before. Never failed four.

C- 9: Do you mind if this interview is recorded?

M- 9: No.

C-10: Thank you. Now tell me, do you have any idea why it happened?

M-10: Well, I just didn't get the tests good. (Sounds extremely depressed and barely enunciates.) Didn't know the work.

C-11: Do you have trouble concentrating when you're reading? Can you remember what you read?

M-11: Well, I just read. I didn't remember everything word for word.

C-12: Nobody's expected to do that, are they? Everybody forgets a lot of what they learn. People learn to prepare for tests, and then they are expected to forget a lot afterward. That's how it is.

M-12: I don't know English . . . words. They put them on the board and they tell you to change them into adjectives and stuff like that. I know nouns, but I don't know the types of nouns.

C-13: Um-hum. You need grammar.

M-13: I don't speak clearly.

C-14: You don't speak clearly?

M-14: No. I get all mixed up when I talk. I don't know why. When I talk, words come out that I don't mean to say. It just comes out that way. I ought to think before I talk.

C-15: You mean you get nervous.

M-15: No, I don't get nervous. I get all mixed up. Talking sometimes about something that don't have to do with anything. Change and be on another subject. It just comes out when it comes in my mind.

C-16: Tell me more.

M-16: That's all.

(Silence.)

C-17: What are you thinking?

M-17: Nothin'.

C-18: Is there anything new in your life that hasn't been there before, since this is the first time this has happened to you.

M-18: I don't know. (Thinks.) It might be moving to a new school.

C-19: You changed your school?

M-19: Moved into senior high school.

C-20: How do you feel about the change?

M-20: It's a lot freer than in the other school. There you had to be in the room when the bell rang and the doors closed.

C-21: Ummm. Is that right! (Sharing his tone.)

M-21: Yeah.

(Counselor offers Mike gum. He at first refuses, then accepts when Counselor says she is going to chew some, too.)

M-22: Thanks.

C-22: You're welcome. . . . Do you have the same friends in the new school as in the old one?

M-23: Well, the same, but they're just in some classes. Not home-room.

C-23: Well, tell me more. Tell me what things seem to be making a difference.

M-24: Actually, I was failing in English until I came to the story part, and I had a good imagination, so I wrote a good story. So I passed. That's the only way I got by. (Speaks with self-contempt.)

C-24: That's worth something, isn't it?

M-25: Well, the thing is, when it comes to spelling I don't get the spelling right. Red marks all over the paper.

C-25: We can help you with your spelling. But spelling isn't the most important thing. When you get to be a big successful man you can hire a secretary to correct your spelling.

M-26: I don't know whether I'll be a big successful man.

C-26: Sure you will. You're bright enough.

M-27: Everybody tells me I've got the brains. . . .

C-27: But you don't believe it?

M-28: No.

(Silence.)

C-28: What are you thinking?

M-29: My Dad wants me to get all 90's. I tell him it's impossible.

C-29: He's ambitious for you.

M-30: Oh, yeah. He can't figure out why he's so smart and I'm so dumb.

C-30: How do *you* figure it?

M-31: What?

C-31: I said, how do *you* figure it?

M-32: Why I'm dumb?

C-32: You just said your father can't figure it out. Wasn't that what you said?

M-33: I figure that he's so smart and I'm so dumb, and I can't figure out why.

C-33: Oh, I thought you said *he* can't figure it out. *You* can't figure it out. Does your father *call* you dumb?

M-34: Nah.

C-34: No. You call yourself dumb. When did you start doing that to yourself?

M-35: When? The first grade.

C-35: What happened in the first grade?

M-36: I was always in the third group in reading. I wasn't smart. I didn't know nothing. Knew 'rithmetic pretty good. English, nah.

C-36: You know, it's interesting how often that goes together. People who like arithmetic so often don't care much for spelling and English. . . . Please tell me more about you in the first grade.

M-37: They had one, two and three as far as our ability went. Like some could read fast, they would be in the first class. Every time the teacher gave a spelling test, I failed.

C-37: Umm. (Sympathetically.) Tell me more.

M-38: About what?

C-38: Oh, anything that comes into your mind. All about what's bothering you, so we can find out what's going on, what's cooking.

M-39: I don't know anything that's bothering me. I just don't want to disappoint my father.

C-39: That must be a worry to you.

M-40: He wants me to go to college. But I don't think I'm smart enough. . . . Really, I'm not too fond of school. I like to be outside. (Apologetically.)

C-40: Well, that's natural for a boy your age.

M-41: Some kids just keep their heads in a book.

C-41: That isn't so good either, is it. It is important for you to be outdoors at your age. You're growing. Studying isn't the most important thing at fifteen. To be healthy is the most important thing at fifteen, when your body is growing in all directions.

M-42: Yes. But I'm supposed to pass in school.

C-42: How much time do you put in on your school work?

M-43: An hour on each subject.

C-43: A day?

M-44: Yes.

C-44: That's quite a lot.

M-45: Oh, yes . . . ! About three hours a day. Last week one of the teachers was absent, so I only did two hours.

C-45: Do you have a gang you go with outdoors? Friends?

M-46: Yeah, a few. The gang hangs around with one guy. He has a car.

C-46: Big deal.

M-47: Yeah.
(Silence.)

C-47: What are you thinking?

M-48: Nuthin'. (Friendly but depressed in tone.)

C-48: You're under some pressure apparently, to please your Pop.

M-49: Oh, yeah. . . . And the kids tease me about my big brother. He teaches. He teaches in my school.

C-49: In your school?

M-50: Yeah. And my father teaches in a college.

C-50: Tell me more.

M-51: Well, nuthin'. . . . The kids just tease me about it.

C-51: Why do they do that?

M-52: I don't know why. Probably to suit themselves.

C-52: What do they say?

M-53: Oh . . . I say some funny things, and then they come back and keep on talkin' along. . . . I don't know how to explain. Just kiddin' around.

C-53: They like you.

M-54: I don't know. I don't know whether they like me or not.

M-55: The teachers bother me, too. Nag. They say, "You should be a smart, smart fellow, because your big brother is so smart."

C-55: It's not fair, to put that pressure on you.

M-56: I just tell them that as generations go down they get dumber and dumber. My brothers got ninety and eighty; my sisters were seventy and eighty; and I'm seventy and sixty. They don't really care much anyhow. Just give 'em reasons why I'm so dumb and don't pass.

C-56: You yourself feel that you are not smart.

M-57: Oh, I probably could be smart, but I don't want to spend time studying.

C-57: I don't think you should spend more than three hours a day studying. I think that's too much as it is. That gives you very little time to be outside, doesn't it?

M-58: Well, I work and then come home. Maybe I play ball if I finish my work fast enough. Then I take care of my paper route and come home and listen to the radio a little bit. After I eat I go upstairs for the rest of the night. If I get done studying at nine or nine-thirty I'll listen again, maybe to a half-hour program.

C-58: Tell me some more.

M-59: I was thinkin' that I don't think I want to go to college anyhow. I don't even know what I want yet. I been tryin' to get some pointers on farming; I'd like maybe a dairy farm, or a chicken farm. I'd like to work on trees, too, maybe that tree surgery stuff. I *like* it—to be out in the air and not be cooped up in a little office!

C-59: Have you had any experience with farms?

M-60: (Brightening.) Oh, yeah! My uncle has a swell place. I go up summers and help around. Fill silo and do things around. Odds and ends. I haven't done anything big. Just helped around. I like it.

C-60: It sounds wonderful. Have you talked it over with your family?

M-61: They say if I want that, it's okay. They want to put me in something I want to be.

C-61: So you would not feel you would be disappointing your parents if you didn't go to college.

M-62: I don't know. I just hope my father don't expect nothin' from me. I don't want to be a teacher or anything like that. Or an office big-business man.

C-62: Yes.

M-63: I want a little house and farm.

C-63: I think that sounds lovely. Every person has to choose his own life, doesn't he?

M-64: (Thoughtfully.) Yeah. . . .

C-64: No matter what his parents want.

M-65: Oh, they don't interfere much.

C-65: But somehow you have the feeling you want to do what would please them.

M-66: Well . . . my big brother was so smart. They figure I should be smart like that brother. My other brother, he's an airplane mechanic.

C-66: What about your sisters?

M-67: They both work in offices. Type. Stuff like that.

C-67: So, with the exception of your big brother who teaches, the other children all work with their hands. So, you wouldn't be so different. I'm a little puzzled. Where do you get the feeling that more is expected of you?

M-68: I guess it's the teachers that nag—want me to be like the brother who teaches.

C-68: And I guess there's something inside yourself that's nagging you about it, too.

M-69: (Thoughtfully.) Yeah. . . .

C-69: Tell you what. We'll talk about it some more. Right now, let's hear you read something, so we'll get some idea of how you read. Okay?

M-70: Yeah.

(Counselor administers the Strang oral reading paragraphs. Mike reads the first one fluently and accurately.)

C-70: Good. Do you remember now what it was that you read? Can you tell me what it said?

M-71: (Mike shows good comprehension of the paragraph.)

C-71: Good. Let's try another.

M-72: All right.

(Mike reads both the second and third paragraphs with accurate pronunciation and good comprehension. Counselor used the content of the third paragraph to stimulate further discussion. The paragraph dealt with the growing use of psychological and guidance clinics in meeting human problems.)

C-72: Very good reading, Mike. Now tell me what that was all about.

M-73: Well, it tells how a person like me can try to find out what's wrong. If they could find out what's wrong, they could make him ready for his future life.

C-73: Very good.

(Long pause.)

Would you like that kind of help? Are there problems in your life you'd like to have solved—that is, have help solving?

M-74: Oh, a few. But I like to solve them myself, but . . .

(Silence.)

C-74: What are you thinking?

M-75: Well, I oughta solve my own problems.

C-75: Everybody likes to . . . but sometimes it takes more courage to get help when you want it or need it. It doesn't hurt to talk things over with someone else . . . don't you think that's true?

M-76: Oh, I don't know. I mean, it's okay to talk to a friend. To have a buddy to talk to. But none of my friends listen when I talk. . . . I mean, I've fooled around so much, now you can't be serious. They say I'm stupid. (Tearful.)

C-76: That's a problem. Because you need to be taken seriously. Everyone needs to be taken seriously. And if you get into the habit of doing the joking business, so that nobody takes you seriously, it's hard to get out of it.

M-77: Yeah. But everything I say myself I almost laugh at. I can't blame anyone else for that.

C-77: In other words, you need to learn to take yourself seriously, don't you.

M-78: Yeah.

C-78: Don't you feel you're *worth* taking seriously? Perhaps you have some question about that?

M-79: I . . . well . . . I shouldn't judge myself. I should be taken seriously by someone else where it's up to them whether they take me seriously.

C-79: It's important that you take yourself seriously . . . that you have good respect for yourself as a young man. . . . Right?

M-80: Yeah. . . . (Thinking about it.)

C-80: You're a very *cute* boy, and I suppose you've gotten used to being treated as the cute little boy, haven't you?

M-81: I guess so. (Thoughtful agreement.)

C-81: The cute little kid.

M-82: (Smiles sheepishly.) It don't work no more.

C-82: You're lucky it doesn't. You wouldn't want to be a cute kid all your life, would you?

M-83: No . . . I used to be such a stupid kid when I was in the sixth grade, fifth grade. . . .

C-83: Who called you stupid?

M-84: Myself. I mean, I wasn't *stupid,* but I used to do funny things and people would laugh at me. I thought I was something big.

C-84: You mean you were the class clown.

M-85: Yeah! The teachers started calling me "show-off" and everything like that. I'd just get mad. But I don't fool around like I used to. I learned to be quiet.

C-85: And at home you're the youngest. . . . Did they treat you like a cute little kid at home?

M-86: I don't know.

C-86: It's hard to be the youngest in the family. I was the youngest in my family, and for years I was called "the baby."

M-87: Oh, they call me "baby."

C-87: Doesn't that make you angry?

M-88: Well, I just tell them to lay off. When we had our dog, I used to say, "The dog's the baby, I ain't no baby!"

C-88: (Laughs heartily.) I did the same thing exactly!

M-89: I mean, it doesn't bother me. (Shrugs.)

C-89: You feel you can shrug that one off.

M-90: Yeah. There has to be a baby in the family, no matter who it is.

C-90: Well, I guess we'll have to talk about it in our next meeting. Want to give me your address so I can write you a note about another appointment . . . ? Our time is not only up but well over.

M-91: (Mike gives address.)

C-91: Do your parents know you came here today?

M-92: My father brought me down.

C-92: Before you leave, I want you to know that anything you say to me is considered confidential. I will never tell your father or mother or teachers anything you tell me unless I get your permission first. It's between you and me, and therefore you can feel free to tell me anything you want. Okay?

M-93: Well, what I said today I'd probably not mind. . . . I mean, I could tell anybody. . . .

C-93: You haven't told me any secrets, you mean . . . but you might sometime want to, so I want you to know that you will be treated as a young man whose confidence is to be respected. Understood?

M-94: (Smiles.) Yeah.

C-94: How would you feel about going to a school where your brother isn't teaching?

M-95: Oh, I don't know. It's just the same. When I was in school where he wasn't teaching, but they knew he was a teacher anyhow, they used to say, "I'm going to tell your brother about this." And if I did something wrong, "I'm going to bring this up to your brother." They used to say that down in the old school.

C-95: Goodness! What a thing to do . . . ! Oh, someone wants this room, so now we must stop. . . . Do you want to come back again and talk some more?

M-96: I don't care. (Voice is cheerful and louder than before.)

C-96: You don't have to unless you want to.

M-97: I *want* to get straightened out.

C-97: All right. Then you do want to come back. Instead of my writing you a note, let's go to my office now and look at my calendar and make an appointment.

M-98: Okay.

Discussion of the Interview with Mike

This is the kind of interview that student counselors find discouraging. They almost tearfully protest to their supervisors, "The boy wouldn't say anything. No matter what I did, he wouldn't open up." It is tempting, under such circumstances, to give up the aim of establishing a therapeutic relationship and flee to the certainty of exercises, tests and reading materials. To have done so with Mike would have been a mistake; he has had all the teaching and tutoring that one young lad can tolerate.

What are the criteria that immediately establish the fact that Mike needs psychotherapeutic help? His I.Q. is superior, yet he failed academically. This says at once that there is more to his failure than can be met with drill work. A boy with a much lower Intelligence Quotient might need assistance in picking up study techniques, or in learning vocabulary; but with his fine intelligence, Mike ought not to require tutoring for these simple procedures. Very early in his school record, he was in trouble with his teachers for what they called "laziness"— a word that, like a smoke-screen, hides whatever difficulties are causing inefficient living.

When so little is offered verbally, it becomes especially important to watch for clues—the spoken and the non-spoken. The tension in Mike's face, the tears springing to his eyes, the exaggerated swagger, the look of bewilderment that came and went like a cloud over his face . . . . these tell a story. One wonders how he feels about his small stature, his childlike appearance. One wonders what started the "tough guy" facade, and what perpetuates it. His statement that he "gets all mixed up when he talks" calls for attention and clarification. Does he mean he has trouble with impulsiveness? Why does he feel he "ought to think before talking?" (M-14 and M-15)

It is an interesting commentary on the teaching of English, that Mike speaks of his "good imagination" with contempt. He says he can write a good story, but that he gets "red marks all over the paper" because of poor spelling. (M-24, M-25) How did it happen that the two were not kept separate? Why could he not feel proud of his story-writing ability, and keep this uncontaminated by his sense of failure in his spelling? Though spelling must be taught in a context, so that the purpose of communication is served by good spelling, thus giving purpose and meaning to the learning of words, still there ought to be some provision made for story-writing in which spelling is not corrected.

M-27, 29, 30, 36: These responses begin to reveal the perplexity and unhappiness of an adolescent boy who has superior intelligence but is unable to mobilize his energies to use his intelligence effectively for academic purposes. In M-39 he speaks key words, "I don't want to disappoint my father." He is in difficulty over wanting to be himself but also wanting to please his father in his father's terms. He is apologetic about expressing his own interests. (M-40, M-41)

He has a great deal to live up to. (M-49, M-50) Perhaps he feels, unconsciously, that he would rather not even try competing with these scholars in his family, that the competition is too great.

M-51 to M-54 gives some indication that he is not happy in his relationships with his friends, either. Later in the interview, from M-76 through M-85, there is further clarification of Mike's feeling that he is caught in a way of life which is not fulfilling to him; one gets the impression that he needs help to extricate himself from his old ways and to build new ones.

M-55 gives a clear picture of how innocently, yet devastatingly teachers may reinforce a student's fear of competition, believing they are stimulating him to greater effort, but in reality only heaping more burdens upon him.

M-59 through M-62 convey the story of the emotional trial Mike has been living through. He becomes quite animated when talking about his dream of doing outdoor work, but shortly afterwards he expresses the unhappy thought that perhaps following his dream will be a disappointment for his father. "I just hope my father don't expect nothin' from me." M-63 through M-69 air this problem further.

C-69 was a mistake. When the counselor read this interview, she was shocked to find that she had changed the subject at this point, when it would have been so much better to let the interview continue the way it was going. In an effort to reconstruct her reasons for introducing reading here, the only possible explanation the counselor can find is the following one:

When working with an adolescent, the counselor always makes it a practice to include at least ten minutes of reading work, for one reason: When the boy or girl goes home, he or she will be asked by the mother or father, "What did you do at the Reading Center?" He needs something specific to say, such as, "We practiced reading out loud," or "I read and she timed me," or, "I worked on vocabulary." To say, "We talked," leads to the next question, "What did you talk about?" How can he remember what they talked about, when it was nothing very specific? Or, he may feel reluctant to repeat what he talked about, if he talked about embarrassing things like worrying about not disappointing his father.

One cannot help an adolescent unless he continues coming for help, and he will not be able to do so unless his parents send him. If parents send adolescent children for help with reading, they may become impatient with reports of "talk," not knowing that this talk paves the way for more efficient study. They know of reading help in terms of tutoring, and it is a good idea to satisfy the parent by including a little work with reading each time, until the adolescent has had a chance to know the counselor, to feel safe with her, to like working with her, and finally to approve of a visit with the parents, at which time the counselor's method of work can be clarified to the parents.

By this time, the adolescent will be so interested in his work with the counselor that he will want to continue it, counteracting any doubts the parents may have and reassuring the parents that something worthwhile is being achieved. This is important, since the mother or father sometimes has unconscious jealousy of the "intruder," which is consciously expressed as doubts in the efficacy of the treatment. It is the counselor's responsibility to make matters clear to them, to help them, and to win them over to a state of mind that will be helpful to the adolescent.

Everything the counselor does should have one guiding purpose: to help the adolescent boy or girl who is coming to her for help. Therefore, whether communicating with the school, or the teacher, or the parents, the manner in which it is done should be carefully worked into the treatment relationship in a way that makes it part of the treatment. For example, there is a world of difference between seeing a parent at the adolescent's request, and seeing a parent completely independently of the adolescent's knowledge or interest. If done in the latter way, the conference with the parent seems to the adolescent, when he finds out about it, to be just another version of the old, old story of parent-teacher get-together to talk him over, without their having any interest in his ideas. (The Case of Donald, presented later in this study, is a good illustration of how a conference with a parent can grow out of a boy's own wishes.)

Sometimes the adolescent would like the counselor to see the parents at once, without delay. This request in itself calls for its part in therapy. A young man of nineteen said, at his third visit to the Counselor, "*You* see my parents and tell them *it's not my fault* that things have gone wrong. Tell them they should leave me alone and let me make up my own mind about things." The Counselor encouraged him to make a list, which she wrote down, of things he wanted her to tell his parents. Then she raised the question of his inability and unwillingness to tell them these things himself. She suggested they wait a few weeks and work on the problem of his fears to speak up for himself. She promised to back him up and to support him in his efforts by seeing the parents directly after he had talked to them himself. She said to him, "*I* don't need the experience of talking to your parents in order to strengthen myself; therefore, I do not want to rob you of the opportunity to strengthen yourself by doing your own talking." This made sense to him, and he agreed to wait a while and try to discover why he felt so helpless in their presence. The complaint, so familiar in reading cases, sprang to his lips, "It's like talking to a stone wall."

Written reports back and forth, from reading clinic to school, ought not to be documents hidden from the adolescents about whom they are written. The writer will never forget the look on the face of a fourteen-year-old boy when she said to him, "I have a report from your school about you. Want to pull your chair around and read it with me?" He looked stricken with surprise, then recovered and said eagerly, "Yeah!"

When a report is to be written to a parent or teacher, who is better equipped to help write it than the person about whom the letter is being written? He should have a part in thinking through what is important to communicate and what he would prefer not to have revealed. This activity becomes part of the therapy.

To return to Mike, from whom we digressed to explain why the counselor interrupted his valuable trend of thought: Mike suffered a great deal from lack of privacy throughout his school life. His teachers by-passed him to deal *about* him with his father and his brother, since both were in the academic world. The counselor felt it especially important in his case to keep his relationship with her completely his own, to do with as he pleased. She therefore gave him some reading work to provide him with something to talk about if questioned by his father, and thus make it easier for him to keep to himself, if he so wished, the more personal discussion that had taken place.

Returning to the interview: It is interesting to see the change in rhythm in Mike's speech as the interview progresses. His sentences become lengthier and clearer, less elliptic. M-95 is a long, complete expression spoken more soberly and more carefully than anything he has said thus far. Apparently he is beginning to take himself more seriously.

Finally, with M-97, he formulates his purpose in planning to return: "I want to get straightened out." He has come a long way from his initial request, that he wants to come, "So I'll learn how to read better."

Interview with Sue

When the Counselor arrived, she found Sue sitting at a table in the waiting-room, deeply engrossed in a book about a horse. Sue was so interested in her book that she did not notice anyone standing beside her until the Counselor said, "Hello there, now." She quickly looked up, somewhat startled, as though jarred out of deep concentration, then she smiled brightly and said, "Hello!"

At the time of this interview, Sue was twelve years old, but she looked like nine. This was partly because she was so petite and partly because of the way she was dressed. It was a cold winter afternoon, but Sue wore a little girl's cotton dress with a tiny round collar and a sash tied in a bow in the back. She wore ankle sox and scuffed brown oxfords, which were suitable to her age. Her hair-do, however, like her dress, added to her childlike appearance. Her hair, dark and straight, was cut quite short, was parted in the center and was worn in bangs—the classic Buster Brown coiffure. Her tiny, up-turned nose and her freckles completed her "pixie" look. When she smiled, her whole face became radiant, and she showed small, pearly teeth, almost hidden by heavy braces.

On the way to the sound-recording room Sue chatted easily with the Counselor about the book she had been reading while waiting. The sound-recording room was too cold for a cotton dress, so the Counselor took Sue back to her office. As soon as they were seated, Sue asked,

S- 1: Do you want me to read for you?
C- 1: Would you like to?
S- 2: Sure.

It became obvious at the start that Sue's emphasis was on comprehension. Whenever she missed a word, which was not often, she realized by the time she reached the end of the sentence that something was wrong, and she went back to re-read. Her high degree of intelligence rapidly became apparent. Her manner was brisk, matter-of-fact, business-like. At one point she whisked a white card off the desk and held the card under each line as she read.

C- 2: What's the card for?

S- 3: I have to do this, or I'll skip something. When I get to the end of the line, I might not go to the right place. (She reads on.) Shouldn't there be a comma here?

C- 3: Yes, you're right. You're a good grammarian, aren't you.

S- 4: (Smiling.) What's *that*?

C- 4: It means you know your punctuation. Nobody can fool you on where commas belong!

S- 5: (Explains quite expansively why she thought there had to be a comma there. She seems to be having a good enough time, but it seems as though she is putting on a performance.)

C- 5: Tell me, why did you come here today?

S- 6: My Daddy told me to.

C- 6: Did you know what you were coming here for?

S- 7: Sure. To get some help with my reading.

C- 7: Do you need help with your reading?

S- 8: Well, lots of times I read for pleasure, and I like that, but Mother gets after me to write a book report for extra credit, and I don't want to. I think it's silly!

C- 8: So! Why does she want you to get extra credit?

S- 9: They give you extra credit if you write extra book reports, and she just thinks I ought to. But I'd rather spend the time reading other books than writing book reports.
(She sits quietly, with her head down and a pouting expression.)

C- 9: Tell me some more.

S-10: I sometimes can't pronounce a word. I read one word at a time, too. I think I should look ahead, and not do just one word at a time.

C-10: You feel you want help with those two things?

S-11: Yes!
(Sue's way of saying "yes" has a special quality. She expresses agreement with great emphasis, almost with relief, as if to say, "*Thank heavens* you know exactly what I mean!" Every "yes" in this interview carried this emphasis.)

C-11: So you yourself want some help.

S-12: Yes, I do.

C-12: That's good. You know, it's hard to help people unless they themselves want help. We always like to settle that first, right off the bat.

(Sue looked at the counselor thoughtfully and examiningly. The counselor felt that Sue liked being talked to as an adult. At this point, Sue, who had been watching the counselor taking shorthand notes, asked:)

S-13: What's *that*?

C-13: Shorthand. I'm taking notes of what you say and what I say.

S-14: Oh!

C-14: Forgive me for not asking your permission first. Is it all right with you?

S-15: (Beamingly.) You have my permission!

C-15: Thank you. It helps me to have notes. Didn't you ever see shorthand before?

S-16: No! Sometimes I write letters for words—like, I'll write "a" for "and." Is that what you mean?

C-16: Yes, exactly. You've made up your own system of shorthand. The system I am using was invented by someone named "Gregg." Would you like to see a little bit how it works?

S-17: Oh, *yes!*

(Counselor showed Sue the shorthand signs for several words, and Sue seemed to enjoy this.)

C-17: Well, tell me some more about yourself. Introduce me!

S-18: (Smiling.) What do you want to know?

C-18: Well . . . what school do you go to, what grade are you in, what do you think of your teachers . . . you know, all that.

S-19: Well, I'm in the seventh grade, and I go to ————. Our math teacher won't explain anything to us, and she yells all the time, and you just can't understand anything at all.

C-19: Heavens!

S-20: Yes! She's just awful! Sometimes I can do my work fast, while listening to the radio, but . . . I don't know. Our English teacher is wonderful, but she doesn't keep us interested. I think she doesn't do her homework. She has to look around for her books, and she never knows where anything is. She's reading *Oliver Twist* to us, and the words are so big.

C-20: When I saw you reading out there in the other room, I got the feeling that you like to read.

S-21: I do like to read. In fact, I just love it. But sometimes I get a very dull book, so I put it away behind the other books in the bookcase. Then Mother says (mimicking), "Where is that book you were reading," and I tell her I didn't like that book, and that I like another book I'm reading much better. But she says, "You should *finish* it!"

C-21: And you'd rather read books that are more interesting.

S-22: *Yes!*

C-22: I agree with you.

S-23: My brother can get away with anything, but not me!

C-23: How old is your brother?

S-24: He's twenty-four, and he's getting his Ph.D. in philosophy this year.

C-24: Do you have other brothers?

S-25: No, just him.

C-25: Sisters?

S-26: Nope.

C-26: So, your brother can get away with things, but you can't.

S-27: (Heatedly.) Boy, that's right! I want to wear my hair long, but my mother won't let me. I want it to grow down to my shoulders, and curl it, but she says I have to wear it short. And I don't like it short!

C-27: Do you tell your mother how you would like to wear your hair? Do you talk it over?

S-28: Well, I can't do much about it.

C-28: Are you timid about speaking up for what you want?

S-29: It's hard. (Smiles shyly at counselor.) My mother and my brother don't think I'm shy. But I really am shy. (She says this as though confiding a secret.)

C-29: I believe you. By the way, perhaps I should tell you, in case you were wondering, I will keep everything you tell me a secret, and I won't talk at all to your parents unless I have your permission. If it's something you would like me to do, I'll do it—if you feel I can help you out at all by talking to them. But that will be all up to you. And they'll never see these notes.

S-30: (With vigorous big smile and beaming eyes.) I give you my permission!

C-30: Thank you. Now go on and tell me all your troubles.

S-31: (Beginning quickly to list her troubles) Well, my hair is *awful.*

It won't stay in place, and I have to wet it to make it stay in place.

C-31: I know what you mean. I have the same trouble.

S-32: Well, if you wet it, that helps. Just wet it.

C-32: Thank you, I'll try that.

S-33: And I bite my fingernails. (Holding up her hands to counselor and watching counselor's face closely.)

C-33: (Smiling) You do a good job of it, anyway!

S-34: Don't you think it's *awful* of me to do it?

C-34: No. But I suppose you'd like to let them grow and put nail polish on, and you get mad at yourself for biting them off.

S-35. That's *right*!

C-35: Okay, that's all right. Just say to yourself, "I'm not such a bad girl for biting my nails. Lots of people bite their nails." Then maybe you'll gradually not have to do it anymore. (Counselor was here following the principle of, "Forgive yourself your sins, else you must sin again.")

S-36. And I also have a habit of not eating on time.

C-36: What do you mean?

S-37: Well, I can eat an awful lot. I can eat a lot in the afternoon and then eat again for supper. My mother thinks I shouldn't eat between meals.

C-37: You mean she's afraid you'll spoil your supper.

S-38: Yes! But I don't! I can eat all the time!

C-38: Your mother kind of babies you, doesn't she?

S-39: *Yes!* And she makes all my clothes, and the other girls' mothers buy their clothes, and I'd like to buy my clothes, too. And I don't like my shoes. I want to wear loafers, like all the kids do, but Mother says (mimicking), "They'll ruin your feet." But *all* the kids wear loafers, so why can't I?

C-39: Sounds reasonable to me. A girl wants to be like the other girls, and not be different, isn't that it?

S-40: (She gazes at counselor with a wondering and tender expression and then says slowly and softly) Yes, I want to be like the others.
(Silence)

C-40: What are you thinking?

S-41: I'm afraid I'm a "goody-goody."

C-41: How come?

S-42: Well, the kids do things, but I don't. And they have parties, and most of the time they don't ask me. . . . And there is one girl, Alice, and she is always making fun of me and teasing me. She'll say, "Do you think *you're* pretty?" (Sits quietly.)

C-42: You wish you didn't have those freckles and that you didn't have to wear those braces on your teeth, isn't that right?

S-43: Oh, *yes!*

C-43: But the braces won't be on your teeth forever. . . .

S-44: Oh, no. The dentist is very nice. He says my teeth will be all right—maybe by next year.

C-44: Good. . . . So . . . you've had a heart-ache about how you look, haven't you?

S-45: Yes.

C-45: But you know, don't you, that you are very pretty. You have an adorable nose and an unusually pretty mouth, and a most charming smile.

S-46: (With a warm smile.) Thank you. (Thinks a moment.) I wish I could have a clothing allowance. I think I would do better.

C-46: You'd like to select your own clothes.

S-47: Oh, I would! My mother never likes what I like. And it's hard to tell her I would rather buy my clothes. She goes to a lot of trouble to make them.

C-47: You're beginning to be a young lady, and you'll want to develop the strength to express your wishes and your taste in a more grown-up way.

S-48: My mother acts like I'm still a baby.

C-48: Mothers often do that. She doesn't realize that you are growing up. Would you like us to have a talk with her and see how she feels about all that?

S-49: Oh, yes!

C-49: Eventually, you will want to develop the courage to speak for yourself, but maybe at this point we can give you a helping hand.

S-50: (Begins to weep, but holds back.)

C-50: You want so much to cry. Go ahead, it's good to cry. Don't hold back.

S-51: (Trembles and weeps, but makes no sound.)

C-51: (Hands Sue a handkerchief.) My goodness, you don't make any noise when you cry. When I cry, you can hear me a block away.

S-52: (Sobbing and laughing.) It's my marks, too! Alice says to me, "What marks did you get?" And she makes fun of me because I get bad marks.

C-52: She isn't nice, is she?

S-53: No!

C-53: She isn't nice at all. I guess you'd like to tell her to mind her own business.

S-54: It wouldn't do any good. And I feel awful when I bring my marks home, too. But tutoring helps.
(Sits thinking.)
I think I would do *much* better with a clothing allowance.

C-54: Are you on any sort of allowance now?

S-55. I get thirty-five cents a week. I pay five cents a week for club dues, and the rest for candy and things.
(The hour was going over the allotted time, and counselor had to draw the interview to a close.)

C-55: Well, there are lots of things to straighten out, aren't there.

S-56: (Laughs.) *Yes!*

C-56: Would you like to come here once a week to talk about things, and also to work on your reading?

S-57: Yes, I would! I wish we could have a different day, though. Because today I don't miss any classes.

C-57: You'd rather miss classes?

S-58: Yes, I would! (Both laugh.)

C-58: I must explain to you that I usually see everyone for the first time, and then I ask someone else to go on from there. Which would you rather talk to, a man or a woman?

S-59: Either one. But if it's a man, I hope it's a handsome one!

C-59: I'll do my best for you.

S-60: My brother is good-looking.

C-60: How does he treat you?

S-61: He's nice to me. The other night I asked my mother if I could have my friends in while I was washing the dishes. My mother said no. But after she went out, my brother said to go ahead and have my friends in but not to tell my mother.

C-61: Then your brother is a pal.

S-62: Yes, he is.

C-62: That's good. . . . I wish I could hear more about him, but we just don't have the time. And I wish I could go on working with you myself, because I like you so much.

S-63: (Beaming.) Thank you. I wish you could, too.

C-63: Believe me, I would if I had the time. But I haven't the time, so I have to give you up. I'll find someone real nice, and I'll give that person your name and address and then he or she will write to you next week to make another appointment with you. Okay?

S-64: Yes!

C-64: In the meantime, just don't worry, if you can manage not to. Try to have a lot of fun, and be hopeful. We're going to stand by you and give you all the help we can.

S-65: Thank you! I'll try.

C-65: Good-bye now. You'll hear from us next week.

S-66: Good-bye.

Discussion of the Interview with Sue

The Counselor's first impression of Sue was of a little girl so deeply engrossed in reading a book that she was quite unconcerned about the other people moving about in the waiting room. Such rapt attention to a book surely indicates that she is able to find pleasure in reading. Why, then, has she been sent to a reading clinic? The way she is dressed, making her look like a little child, is the first clue to possible trouble. Dressed this way, she undoubtedly feels out of place among her peers.

She takes the initiative to begin the interview. She is brisk and practical, not particularly threatened by this new adult, this tutor. She has had tutors before, and she knows what to do with them and how to perform for them. Her voice is clear and direct, not apologetic, not timid, not warm, not curious, not really interested—she will go through the motions and get this thing over with. She has no expectation of her own interests or wishes being consulted, and thus she appears surprised when the counselor (in C-5, 6 and 7) stimulates her to consider why she has come here.

While it is important to ask adults to formulate their purpose in coming for help, it is especially necessary to do so when interviewing an adolescent. Almost always the adolescents are sent by parents or teachers or both; rarely are their wishes consulted. They do not come, therefore, with the feeling of having an active voice in a constructive project, but rather with apathetic obedience to authority figures. The reading specialist is to them just an extension of school personnel, and they accept without protest, and without interest, this new assignment.

Sue's cool disinterest in what, to her, was so obviously just another school chore, made it imperative to quickly turn the interview into an experience involving her own wishes and feelings. The way she dressed revealed that she was not being consulted at home, perhaps that she was not being taken seriously. Her responses to the counselor's questions early in the interview (for example, S-4, 6, 7, 8) carry a note of flippancy—brittle, pseudo-sophisticated, and without real emotional investment. She is not quick to believe that this new "teacher" really cares about her answers to the questions asked, and she tosses them back with a slightly cynical, though polite air. The counselor wonders what unhappiness is being concealed by this flippant exterior.

After the counselor's sober offer of information, "It's hard to help people unless they themselves want help," Sue looked at her searchingly, the first sign of recognizing her as a person, not as an abstract symbol of authority. Immediately afterwards, she felt free to express curiosity, asking about the notes the counselor was taking. In C-14, the counselor is sincerely asking to be forgiven, since ordinarily she does ask permission to take notes, but this time had neglected to do so.

S-15: One would have to hear Sue's voice and to see her face as she spoke these words, to get the full value of them as they expressed her reaction to suddenly being put into a position of authority. Her chin went up, her shoulders straightened, her eyes beamed. Like a queen, she pronounced evenly and proudly the words: *"You have my permission!"* One would guess, from her great pleasure at this unexpected power, that she had not had much freedom at home to express her feelings.

S-17 through S-26 carry the interview forward rapidly, revealing a great deal about Sue and about her reading. This material seems to call for no additional comment.

With S-27 the interview begins to touch on matters really vital to Sue, and her manner becomes more serious, less flippant. In S-28 and S-29 she confesses feelings of helplessness, and one begins to find the areas of unhappiness under the brittle pose.

C-30: The counselor senses that Sue is ready and eager to unburden herself, and she formulates for her the main opportunity of the interview, a chance to "tell her troubles."

Responses S-31 through S-41 show very rapid movement and corroborate the counselor's feeling that Sue was eager to speak freely. It is regrettable that the reader cannot see and hear Sue solemnly and quickly make an inventory of her troubles; it was such an abrupt change from her impersonal flippancy to her deeply personal sharing of her secret misgivings.

Reports that came in later from Sue's school told of her habitual clowning. In this interview with Sue, an unhappy little girl emerges from beneath the clowning facade. As soon as she is taken seriously, her real feelings come out. How can one explain the clowning? Perhaps she clowns to give her classmates *reason* to laugh at her, so that they will not laugh in contempt—mirroring her own feeling that she is in some way laughable. A sentence spoken by a young man similarly given to clowning may describe Sue's behavior, too. He said, "I spread a net of humor to catch me if I fall." Sue apparently succeeds in covering her real feelings; she states quite clearly that others do not believe she is shy, but that she *is* shy. If she continues always hiding her real feelings she must become more and more lonely, separating her inner self from others.

C-33, 34 and 35 merit discussion because these three responses are examples of a basic therapeutic attitude: Alleviate the pressures of a too-severe moral judgment in the client. Every clinician knows the healing power of self-forgiveness. People unfamiliar with it tend to counter at once with this objection: "We *must have standards,* else how will we do what is right and good?" Many readers probably were upset by the counselor's statement to Sue, "You are not a bad girl for biting your finger nails." They may feel that this constitutes encouraging her to continue biting them, but this is not so. Alleviating guilt helps to free an individual from a compulsive habit. Clinically and pragmatically, the quotation from the writings of the Chassidim, a medieval religious sect, is true and sound: "Forgive yourself your sins lest you repeat them." [2]

C-38 and C-39: In these responses, the counselor supports Sue against an unreasonable component in the mother's discipline, and

---

[2] To understand how nail biting involves moral judgment, it is necessary to be aware of its unconscious significance to the individual caught in this "bad habit." For a discussion of nail biting, see (44).

tries to help Sue formulate the meaning of the mother's behavior by the interpretation, "She kind of babies you."

S-50: Why does Sue start to weep just at this time, not before this, but now? The sentence, "We can give you a helping hand," sets her off. One can only theorize about it, but, based on clinical experience, one may guess that she weeps when this help is offered because she feels like a *bad girl* who does not deserve help. She perhaps has the feeling she is wicked for having harbored secret rage against her mother; now, instead of being punished or scolded for her "bad feelings" she is being offered help, and she is overwhelmed by what seems like undeserved kindness.

S-61: One can be thankful for the big brother who softens the mother's rigid discipline by taking the little girl's part. Yet, on the other hand, Sue may feel separated from her mother by these secrets with her brother, thus adding to her feeling of loneliness. A girl needs to resolve her quarrel with her mother. She needs to be able to fight with her openly and then to make up with her, and to find qualities in her to admire and with which to identify. Thus, in working with a girl of any age one must permit and encourage free expression of all feelings, including resentment, toward the mother, but must not let her leave the therapeutic relationship until she has "made up with" her mother, or with the memory of her mother if the parent is dead. "Unfinished business" between mother and daughter leads to continued unhappiness, with inability to relate well to men.

It is especially important that counselors be quite clear about their relationships with their own parents, else they are in danger of using their adolescent client or student as a battleground on which to fight a parent-surrogate. The effect is harmful for the young person in the counselor's care, for it means being separated from the parent instead of arriving at a better relationship with the parent. Indeed, sometimes counselors are so hostile to the parents of their adolescent clients that they are accusatory instead of understanding in their conferences with parents, thus achieving nothing and often aggravating the parents' difficulties. This may be the reason psychologists working in schools are sometimes referred to as "parent-eaters."

Interview with Betty

The counselor's first impression of Betty was of a slim, shy girl, of medium height, with beautiful eyes, wavy hair, and a fair complexion.

She appeared younger than an eighteen-year-old college freshman, and she blushed frequently.

B- 1: (She seems restless, and now giggles nervously.) Well, I guess you know why I'm here—from what I told that man. (Referring to the intake interview.)

C- 1: I hope you won't mind repeating it to me. I like to be told all over again.

B- 2: (Laughs.) Okay. Well, I'm doing well in everything except political science. I finally passed the political science test. It was a big event.
(Her speech is very rapid, with a quality of breathlessness, as though she is struggling against tearfulness.)
I'd just like to learn to read faster.

C- 2: Tell me more.

B- 3: What do you want me to tell you?

C- 3: About yourself.

B- 4: I'm at ———— College, but you know that.

C- 4: Go on.

B- 5: Well, I came here because of my political science course. I couldn't manage to learn anything there. I think I know the root of my difficulty. As a child I never read books. I never had the patience to sit down and read. I never did my homework, either. In elementary school, I passed everything except history and geography. In high school, I learned a little how to study. In high school I always passed everything. I had teachers who gave high marks. The teacher I have now is very cold. Half the class is flunking. She gives out zeros. Every time she asks a question and you can't answer it, she gives out zeros. Back in high school, as I went on, I picked up quite a lot. I taught myself to study. Now I can sit down and study. I never used to be able to. I used to be the kind of kid who would run around. I'd take out books just to fill out my library cards. (Giggles.)

C- 5: What's the matter?

B- 6: It was so silly. Just because all the kids had library cards, and I'd feel foolish with an empty card . . . so, I'd take out books, let them always lay around for two weeks, and then take them back again. I never read them. Now I do my reading school-work at home. I try to read where no one is walking around, distracting me. Today at the library I couldn't concentrate, it was too noisy. . . . I used to have my own room, but my aunt moved in with us, and I had to give her my room. (Sits quietly.)

C- 6: What are you thinking?

B- 7: I'm thinking of my finals. That's what bothers me now. At midterm I got a 52 in political science, a "C" in English, and a B— in French. My political science teacher won't mark on the curve. I'm not terribly interested in the subject. I never have been. I force myself more or less to want to do it. Regardless of what I read, I read slowly.

C- 7: Are your eyes in good condition? Have you had them examined recently?

B- 8: I went to an eye doctor and got these glasses. I suppose they are all right. (Shrugs.) Regardless of what I read, I *always* read slowly, as I just told you. That bothers me. Now I am so wrapped up in the two reading courses, I don't have time for anything else.

B- 9: (Thoughtful.) My sister is four years older than I am. (Begins to choke up with tears.) There was always a lot of difference between us. (She weeps hysterically and is unable to speak for a few minutes. Then:) I don't know why I am crying.

C- 9: We'll have to find out, won't we.

B-10: Yes. (She struggles to speak.) When I was a little girl . . . (sob) . . . she was a big girl. She was so busy, she just was never home. (Betty continues to weep and to squeeze out words between sobs.) She went to City College. I rarely saw her. I couldn't get a chance to talk to her if I wanted to. And somehow she always *smiled* when I talked to her. (This is said with considerable anger.) It's as if she was saying that her little sister is growing up! Now, finally, everyone accepts a little bit that I'm growing up.

C-10: You feel that no one takes you seriously.

B-11: That's just it! (Very indignant and tearful.) I'm *sick* of it . . . ! But now she and I are getting closer together in age. I don't talk to her much. She comes over once in a while. Once a week. Sometimes she stays for weekends.

C-11: She lives away from home?

B-12: Oh, I didn't tell you? She has a job as a laboratory technician at ———— (out of town). But she doesn't get home until late evening Fridays, so I don't get much time to talk to her. And I should tell you about my mother and father. They get along, yet they don't. (At this point, fresh sobs shake her so thoroughly that she is unable to speak for several moments.) Why am I crying like this! I didn't expect to cry. (She says this apologetically.)

C-12: Why do you apologize for crying? You know, you have to break eggs to make an omelet.

B-13: (Smiles pathetically, her eyes full of tears.) I see what you mean. But I didn't realize I felt like crying. As far back as I can remember, there were always arguments in our house. They never meant anything, but they always existed. Sometimes for a week or so my parents didn't talk to each other. My father is a very hot-tempered man. The sort of work he is doing is not too good for him. He's a salesman in a store, and the strain of it seems to tire him very much. He seems to be nervous. There are so many difficulties, it makes him nervous. My mother isn't very well. She is a nervous person, too. She has never told me what's wrong with her. She is close to fifty years old, so she might be having menopause, but she won't talk to *me* about it. With her, sex is a "hush-hush" matter.

C-13: How old is your father?

B-14: I think he is fifty-four. . . . As a matter of fact, my mother and father have quieted down lately. But little things keep happening. For example, I was going to help her with the house. I cleaned and polished the floors around the rugs, then I vacuumed the rugs and the furniture. Instead of telling me how nice it looked, she said I should've vacuumed first and polished after—because that's what she always does. What difference did it make! Why couldn't she let me do it my own way! (Fresh tears.) Right now I'm always seeming to do something wrong at home. Even when I *know* I'm right, they won't give me the benefit of the doubt. My father will say I *don't know.* They always had a lot of arguments, and in front of me. (Sobs.) When I was eight, I practically got *sick* because they were fighting in front of me. I begged my mother to stop it. I *told* her they were making me feel sick. My mother said, "It's none of your business." (Several minutes go by in silence while Betty struggles to control her sobbing.) Another thing: I never *had* anyone. No friends, no one to talk to. And I couldn't talk to my parents. And I couldn't talk to my sister. I've always had a desire to have companions, I guess.

C-14: I guess you've been troubled by the feeling of somehow being *different*?

B-15: Yes! I felt there must be something *wrong* with me, because I never *had* anybody. (Smiles timidly at counselor.)

C-15: Well, we've used up our time. So we'll go on next time, shall we . . . ? Next week, same hour, same place.

B-16: Oh, I forgot! When am I supposed to pay you? And how much?

(Counselor discussed with Betty the problem of fee. Since the family has very little money, a fifty-cent fee was decided upon as being appropriate to her means.)

Discussion of the First Interview with Betty

B-1: Betty had been seen by someone else, who had referred her to the counselor. She had been quite tense and tearful in the other interview, and it was apparent that she needed counseling help.[3]

B-5: The reading problem is a long-standing one, dating back to elementary school. However, in high school she managed to pass all her courses. One wonders whether in high school she really had teachers "who gave high marks," or whether these teachers were just warm and encouraging, as opposed to her present political science teacher, who, says Betty, is "very cold." What is wrong with this teacher, that "half the class is flunking?" She seems to be quite threatening, for, "every time she asks a question and you can't answer it, she gives out zeros."

Does this teacher remind Betty of someone else in her life who is "cold" to her, or is the teacher really cold to all her students? What effect does a "cold" teacher have on almost any student? Is it easy to perform for a critical supervisor? Is it pleasant to *give* to a cold, pun-

---

[3] A letter from her school described her as being "too emotional." With regard to some implications of the phrase "too emotional," the reader is referred to a new book by Arthur T. Jersild (36).

ishing teacher? Is one stimulated to take chances and think fearlessly and spontaneously with a teacher who is quick to penalize one for errors?

The counselor is reminded of an article, published in *The New York Times* some years ago, describing the techniques of collaboration used by the playwrights Lindsay and Crouse. In this article, the two writers are quoted as saying, in effect, that they would find it very difficult to write if they were not so accepting and uncritical of each other's ideas. By tolerating each other's awkwardness and exploratory mistakes, they encouraged each other's spontaneity and creativity and were able to function productively as a team. If Betty's teacher were not so intolerant of error, her class not only would enjoy political science more, but undoubtedly would function more efficiently as students.

B-6: Betty "took out books just to fill out her library card." This reveals the usual wish to "be like the other kids." However, she must have had feelings of inadequacy about just going through the motions of doing what the others did. They really read books; she only pretended. This would not give her a true feeling of being like the others. She would feel sheepish about the pretense and still feel apart from the group who really did read their books. One wonders if Betty did not feel "different" from the other children in areas quite apart from reading, and whether this game with the library books was only a symbol of a larger picture of loneliness.

Betty's inability to concentrate at the library probably has causes other than the one she states. She feels she is distracted by people walking around, and by noise.[4] While some people are startled out of concentration by any little noise, others utilize noises for their "distraction value." Many parents cannot understand how their adolescent children can study with the radio going, yet this external noise may provide a shell for an inner area of quiet and concentrated thought.

In Betty's case one gets the feeling that the noise at the library is not the cause of her inability to study there. She has told us that as a child she "never had the patience to sit down and read," and that she "used to be the kind of kid who would run around." Now one must wait for more information to fill out the picture. Thus far, she gives the impression of restlessness and depressiveness.

---

[4] An interesting study might be made of why some people study best in solitude, and some require an atmosphere of activity.

B-10: The statement: "Somehow she always *smiled* when I talked to her," gives a possible clue to a conflict that may be going on in Betty. She perhaps wants to remain a lovable little baby-girl, and get the smiles that go to a baby; and, on the other hand, she dislikes being a toy to the grown-ups and would like to get the respect and admiration that go to a young lady. She wants to feel the power of adulthood, but she is attracted to being forever a precious toy. Thus, the sister's smile stirs up rage because it "rubs in" the conflict. If Betty did not *want* to remain a baby, she might not interpret the smile as one that implies she *is* a baby.

It is noteworthy, in the light of her wish to be considered "grown-up," that she came to the third interview looking like fourteen instead of eighteen, with her hair flowing down over her shoulders, and wearing slacks and sandals. If she had no conflict about wanting to be accepted as adult, she might have a more mature hair-do, perhaps wear high heels.

C-13: This is an inappropriate response by the counselor. It showed that at this point she was not really following Betty, but had paused to think about Betty's father. It was particularly unfortunate to make an error like this at this point, because Betty wanted and needed to talk about sex. When the counselor deflected her from it, instead of reflecting her feeling about her mother's keeping sex a "hush-hush" matter, Betty did not return to the subject again until the very last interview.

B-14: This long and informative outpouring of Betty's feelings gives the impression of a very lonely girl who has carried tremendous, pent-up pressure for a long time. She has had no one to turn to. Her parents criticize her and will not give her credit for doing things her way. Her sister ignored her and was somehow unavailable to her. As she says, "I never *had* anyone."

B-15: When parents do not respect a child as a person in her own right, she gets the feeling she does not *deserve* better treatment, for she has had no way to build a strong sense of self on which to stand firmly and evaluate the parents' attitude toward her. Instead, she feels, "There must be something wrong with me." She extends this feeling to her relationship with her peers, and she is afraid to make overtures of friendship. She does not feel "good enough."

C-15: Such abrupt endings to interviews are very troublesome. This would have been a nice time to continue a few minutes, for Betty was arriving at some helpful thoughts. However, in a clinic where rooms are reserved by the hour, a knock on the door suddenly determines the ending of the session. The counselor discussed the fee with Betty while walking down the hall, escorting her to the room where she would be paying her fees.

[3]

THE CASE OF DONALD

IN THIS CHAPTER, the reader will have the opportunity of reading the complete case of Donald, including nine interviews with the boy, one interview with his mother and a letter received from Donald several years after he left the Reading Center. As in Chapter Two, a section entitled Discussion will succeed each interview.

First Interview with Donald

Donald, age fifteen, arrived at the Reading Center with his father. Both father and son made an attractive appearance, being good-looking and well-groomed. The counselor introduced Donald's father to another worker, and then proceeded to interview Donald.

C- 1: Before we begin, I must ask you: Do you have any objection to my taking notes?

D- 1: It's okay.

C- 2: Notes are helpful. If I keep notes, I won't have to depend entirely on memory. But of course I wouldn't think of doing so without your permission.

D- 2: I don't mind.

C- 3: Thank you. Now tell me, why are you here?

D- 3: (Laughs.) I have a problem about reading.

C- 4: Was it your idea to come here?

D- 4: No. It was my mother's idea, and my father's. They think it will help me later.

C- 5: Is coming here something you want to do?

D- 5: No. Right now I don't come here because I *want* to. I guess it's because they told me to come.

C- 6: You mean, you're doing it only to please your parents.

D- 6: Well, they've told me all through my life that I'm not a good reader. But I don't notice it in my school work. It doesn't handicap me now. They think that later I'll be handicapped.

C- 7: What do *you* think?

D- 7: I don't know. I suppose they're right. I know that in arithmetic problems I would write the wrong things because I wouldn't read the directions right.

C- 8: Was this something you became aware of yourself?

D- 8: Well, no. I used to bring my homework to my father to be checked, and he told me I wasn't reading the directions right.

C- 9: Could you tell me more about that?

D- 9: I would do my lesson, he would correct my mistakes, then I'd copy it over to hand in.

(The counselor smiles, and Donald returns the smile, somewhat sheepishly.)

D-10: I guess my teacher wouldn't like to know about that. (He looks at counselor questioningly and apprehensively.)

C-10: She won't learn it from me, because you know that everything you tell me is confidential.

D-11: I don't do that now anymore, anyhow. If you give the impression you can do that well, then you're worse off the next semester. The teacher I have now wants us to hand in our papers without anybody correcting them first. So we can learn.

(Silence.)

C-11: What else do you want to tell me?

D-12: Well, they say I'm a slow reader.

C-12: And what do *you* say?

D-13: I guess I'm a little slower than average, but I don't think I'm handicapped. When I read a book, I might not be able to recite every fact out of it, but I can get enough of it.

C-13: Would I be correct in assuming that you are coming here to please your parents?

D-14: (Grins.) I told them I wasn't too keen on coming, but the adviser at school advised me to do it, too. I figured if they all showed so much interest in me, it probably would be good to do it.

C-14: What did your adviser tell you?

D-15: She didn't tell me anything. She spoke to my mother.

C-15: So you are coming here reluctantly.

D-16: Yes. I don't enjoy coming all the way up here. It's a long trip. And I don't feel it's entirely necessary. I told my parents it doesn't hamper me now, but they say that later on it will handicap me a lot. They say I don't read thoroughly. I sometimes bring my homework to them, and they say I have the wrong thing. I know that when I try to read faster, I miss some words. And sometimes I have my mind on something else, so I rush, so I can get to do that thing I'm thinking about.

C-16: Like what, for example?

D-17: I have a workshop in the garage, and I like to repair things, fix things.

C-17: What else do you do for fun?

D-18: All us boys have workshops, and we go to each other's houses and watch each other fix things.

C-18: Sounds like fun. What else do you do?

D-19: We play baseball and football. You know. (Sits quietly and smiles at counselor.)

C-19: What else do you want to tell me?

D-20: I guess I am a slow reader. I can read faster when I read to myself, but when I read aloud in front of the class, I feel self-conscious, and then I rush and I miss words and have to go back over them. (Thoughtful.) I can't memorize easily, either. That's hard.

C-20: Do you mean that you yourself want to get some help, aside from what your parents feel about it?

D-21: Yes, I think I'd like to try it. I think I'll take a chance and see what happens.

C-21: Good. I guess we still have time today to do something with an oral reading test. Would you like to do that?

D-22: Sure. I have a tough time reading out loud.

Counselor took from her desk a copy of Dr. Strang's *Examiner's Reading Diagnostic Record for High School and College*

Students (64), and handed the booklet to Donald, so that he could write his name on the cover. When counselor offered her pen, Donald accepted it, looked at it, returned it, and then took out his own pen, a Parker 51 identical to counselor's pen. He filled in the required information without delay and was then given the first test paragraph, with verbal instructions to read it aloud and try to remember what he read. Donald read aloud at 150 words per minute, with quite choppy cadence and poor phrasing. He omitted two small words, but these omissions did not affect his comprehension, which was excellent. In fact, his comprehension was good enough to permit him to think analytically about the material. The paragraph told of a test used in India for determining guilt; if rice remained dry in the accused's mouth, it meant that fear, caused by his guilt, had stopped the flow of saliva. Instead of just repeating this story, Donald criticized it, as follows: "Even if you were not guilty, you might be nervous, and that would stop the saliva, so that you might get the wrong person." Counselor complimented Donald for his critical approach to the material and told him she was in agreement, that it was possible for one to be fearful whether guilty or not guilty. Counselor had noticed, incidentally, that Donald's mouth, by the sound of his speech while reading, seemed to be dry.

C-22: Is your mouth dry right now?

D-23: (Laughs.) I guess so. I guess it's because it's hot in here.

C-23: Are you scared?

D-24: (Grins.) Reading out loud always makes me self-conscious. But I'm not scared.

C-24: Your reading of that paragraph really was not slow. Were you aware of how you were reading as you read?

D-25: As I read, I felt I was racing, and trying to go fast makes me skip words.

C-25: Shall we do another one?

D-26: Sure.

The second paragraph presented more of a challenge, using symbolic language to describe a geological phenomenon. Donald tried to rush through it, but skipped three or four words—

unimportant words, not essential to the context. He went back to correct his errors. His comprehension of the material was adequate but stated falteringly.

C-26: How did you feel as you read that one?

D-27: As I got to the end, I thought to myself, "I don't remember a thing I just read." Also, I tried to race, but I missed words and had to go back.

C-27: You thought you would not remember, but you did remember very well. Would you like to go over it again, with me?

Counselor read the paragraph to Donald this time, and both discussed its meaning.

C-28: You didn't particularly care for this paragraph, did you?

D-28: No. It was too . . . general. I liked the other one because it told me something new; it was descriptive; it was interesting.

C-29: What reading have you been doing lately that you like?

D-29: Just school work. Do you want me to tell you what subjects I have?

C-30: Yes, I would like to know what you're studying.

D-30: Well, I have five majors. That's the most you can take. Social studies, English, science and algebra. And mechanical drawing. Two weeks ago I changed my program from four majors to five. I told my adviser I wanted to take shop, but it was too late in the year to start in shop. She talked about mechanical drawing, so I took that.

C-31: Do you like your program?

D-31: It's okay. Sometimes I have my mother check my English. And when I write letters I never read them over afterwards. You know, sometimes you make silly mistakes, typographical errors, but I don't have the patience to look it over. I just don't have the patience.

C-32: Well, we can talk about all those things as we go along. By the way, you know it might be a good thing for you to consider just how much *you* want to come, not just to please others. Come back only if you yourself want to.

D-32: I want to. I want to take a chance at it and see what happens.

C-33: It will be your own responsibility, and the work we do together will be yours. The records I keep will not be available to your parents or anyone, not without your permission. If your parents come, they will talk to one of the other people here. Are you planning to come here alone next time, or with your father?

D-33: No, I'll come by myself.

C-34: I'll see you next week at the same time, then. . . . Tell me, did you learn anything interesting today?

D-34: (Smiles.) Yes, I didn't read so very slow.

Discussion of the First Interview with Donald

C-1 and C-2: Verbatim records are necessary for purposes of research and teaching. Differences of opinion exist, however, regarding the effect on both counselor and client of obtaining a verbatim record. Some counselors feel it in no way interferes with their own performance or the freedom of the client; others feel it is impossible to achieve good rapport or spontaneity while the interview is being recorded. It is important to weigh the value of verbatim records against the possible hindrance to a particular client's thinking and feeling or to a counselor's effective functioning.

If some record has to be had in fairly verbatim form, as for a study of this nature, or for students learning the techniques of counseling, it is sometimes easier for the client to see notes being written than to have recordings made. One young woman, when asked her preference, said, "Oh, you can take all the notes you like; I could always deny I said those things. But I could not very well deny my own voice on a phonograph record."

In the case of another young woman, the counselor used a recording machine, with her consent, for five sessions. As this client entered the room for the sixth counseling hour, she said, looking at the machine, "Are we going to use that *again* today?" The counselor said, "Why do you ask?" She replied, "Well, I feel like *really* talking today." The machine was disconnected, and the interview was far more personal and meaningful than the previous ones had been. Her previous consent to the use of the machine had been an expression of her submissiveness, not *real* consent.

C-4 through C-15; and C-20, C-32, C-33: The counselor's immediate impression of Donald was of reluctancy and withdrawal. His tone of voice was flat and noncommittal; his replies to her questions were cryptic; and he looked at her guardedly, with a sulky expression. The counselor lost no time in going directly to the matter of chief importance: To convey to him that her only interest was in helping him establish *his* goals. This is a new idea to him. It is hard for him to believe that the counselor wants to strengthen *his* sense of self, that she is more concerned with his needs than her own, or the clinic's, or the school's, or his parents'. The reader will discover, in following the subsequent interviews (Chapter III), that Donald did not completely trust her for a long time. It seemed incredible to him that any adult would encourage him to express his own point of view, and support him in his efforts to develop a point of view, without the intrusion of wishes extraneous to his own.

C-14 and C-15: Teachers and parents usually underestimate the competency of children to discuss their own attitudes and problems. Conferences are held *about* children, without benefit of the children's participation. Highlighting the effect of this "by-passing" of children, the counselor recalls the most destructive example of it in her experience: The parents of a sixteen-year-old girl would sit at the dinner table with her and communicate with each other *about* her. The mother would say to the father, "Do you think Dorothy would like more salad?" The father would reply to the mother, "Yes, she would, and some more meat, too." After a few months of therapy, this crushed and bewildered young girl was able to cry out at them, "For heaven's sake, *I'm* sitting *right here*! Ask *me* if *I* want something!"

A contrasting story is told by Dr. James Clark Moloney, a psychoanalyst who was stationed in Okinawa during the war as a Commander in the United States Navy. One day Dr. Moloney wanted to take a picture of a four-year-old girl in a red dress. She refused to pose for the picture. Dr. Moloney appealed to her father, expecting that he would order the child to stand still. The father took the child aside for a quiet conference. Then he returned to Dr. Moloney and said, "I'm sorry, she does not want to have her picture taken." [1]

C-17 and C-18: The counselor's asking, "What else?" is not very good. It has a rushing, pushing quality, possibly sending Donald away from what he is talking about to "something *else*." C-17 and C-18 ought to have been just a pleasant murmur, or "Tell me more," or a reflection of his feeling, which probably would have been, "You don't feel really interested in telling me these things, do you?"

D-20 and D-21: This is the beginning of Donald's taking responsi-

---

[1] Heard in a lecture by Dr. Moloney on the subject of the low incidence of neuroses among the Okinawans.

bility himself for coming to the Reading Center. "I think I'll take a chance and see what happens," is an amusing formulation of his attitude. It's as if he is holding back a little bit, not too ready to go all the way in believing this to be *his* choice. He's being cautious; he is not giving up his reluctancy quite so easily. He does not really trust the counselor yet. She might still turn out to be an extension of the long arm of authority.

C-27: This is important. It occurs so frequently that students who consider themselves poor readers are not aware of how much they remember. They do not realize that one observes a great deal without being conscious of the act of observing. They make the mistake of regarding conscious knowledge as total knowledge. It is like looking at an iceberg jutting out of the water, and saying, "That is the whole iceberg," not taking into account the large proportion of the iceberg lying below the surface.

D-30: It is too bad that Donald was not permitted to take "shop" when he wanted it, even though it was late in the year. Why must he take mechanical drawing, when it is shop that he wants? The two meet quite different needs.

It seems that the guidance of students in choice of subjects ranges on a continuum from excellent, where the guidance really tries to meet the students' needs and interests within the framework of the curriculum, though it is still old-fashioned and not growing out of individual interests, to horrifying, where students are plunged into a nightmare of unnecessarily trying to fit themselves into work wholly alien to their gifts and inclinations. The counselor remembers a high-school boy who had lived for a year in a fever of misery, trying to pass courses in radio. He showed the Counselor his notebook of material related to the radio work and said despairingly, "I have to pass exams on this stuff, and I don't understand any of it, and I didn't want to take it in the first place." This young man could have had a fine time in high school. He had a profound understanding of literature, and a great love for writing. He wanted to work on the school newspaper, but the long hours he had to put into the radio work, in order to pass the courses, robbed him of the chance to develop as a young journalist.

D-34: Donald's smile is important. He said verbally to the counselor that the interesting thing he had learned today was that he "didn't read so very slow." Actually, he knows he learned much more than that, and he says this with his smile. He knows he has found an ally, and he knows that she knows how he feels about certain things. This was the beginning of a good therapeutic relationship, in which Donald expressed his affection for the counselor by sly and humorous teasing, accompanied always by this characteristic warm smile.

Second Interview with Donald

Donald arrived right on time. He asked if he might remove his jacket because he was warm. He moved chairs into place for both counselor and himself.

C- 1: Before we get started, and before I forget: Do you think you could plan to spend two hours here next time?

D- 1: (Thoughtfully.) I guess so.

C- 2: I want to do something with you that may take two hours. We may be through in an hour, but, just in case. . . .

D- 2: Okay.

C- 3: Now tell me, what sort of week did you have?

D- 3: (Shrugs.) Okay.

C- 4: That tells me a lot. (Laughs.)

D- 4: (Laughs.) Well, nothing happened. Just went to school, and the usual stuff.

C- 5: Did you want to come here today?

D- 5: No.

C- 6: Then why did you come?

D- 6: I had an appointment. (Looks at counselor reprovingly.)

C- 7: I don't understand. I thought we had said you would not come here today unless it was something you wanted to do.

D- 7: Well, my folks expected me to come.

C- 8: And that's the only reason you came.

D- 8: No . . . I guess so. . . . They always win.

C- 9: If I did not feel I had a problem about reading, I would not go all the way to New York to a reading clinic.

D- 9: Well, I guess I'm afraid they might be right. That even though I don't have a problem now, I might have one later. So I'd rather get it over with now.

C-10: What do you mean when you say your parents "always win?"

D-10: I guess they're usually right. In the long run. (Silence.)

C-11: What else do you want to tell me?

D-11: I don't know. (Laughs, somewhat sheepishly.)

C-12: Let's fool around with these. (Counselor takes out a few of Henry Murray's Thematic Apperception Test cards.) This is a sort of game. I'll show you pictures, and you make up stories about them.

D-12: How do you mean?

C-13: Well, suppose you tell me about the present situation in the picture, what led up to it, and what will happen next and in the future.

D-13: (Appears interested as he looks at Card I, which is a picture of a small boy and a violin.)
He's probably supposed to be practicing. But he's kind of dreary and just thinking about it. He's probably thinking about the long time he'll have to finish out his practicing, and dreading it. . . . Now do I do the past?

C-14: Yes, if you like.

D-14: Well, I'd say that he wanted to grow up to be a good violinist, and he wanted just to do that and not practice. But, like everyone else, he has to practice.
Can I give two versions?

C-15: Anything you like.

D-15: Well, the other version would be that his parents thought he should take it up. He didn't approve of that so much, so he's just sitting and thinking about it. Then, when his father or mother comes in and tells him to start practicing, he'll probably have to do it. . . . He's just thinking about how he'll have to finish out his practicing for the days to come . . . why he has to practice so long.

C-16: What mood would you say he has?

D-16: Well, *dreary.* And he's kind of mad, I'd say. He's angry, much more angry than happy.

C-17: (As counselor took Card I from him, she asked): Do you like doing this?

D-17: I don't know.

C-18: If *you* don't know, who does?

D-18: (Looks at counselor with surprise, then grins.)
It's okay, I guess.
(Picks up the next card, a farm scene.)
Well, I suppose this is a picture of a huge farm. In some

western state. Right next to a lake. The family consists of a mother, father and daughter. The father is ploughing the fields, the mother is standing, looking at the skies. There is also a horse there, helping with the ploughing. And the daughter has to go to some kind of school.

Now, the past: They were a fairly poor family, but the father and mother wanted their child to get the best schooling possible and to grow up to be better than they were. The child doesn't like that so much. She wishes she could stay home and help at home, but she's off to school and doesn't seem to be so happy about it.

Now, the future: The mother and father will probably go on living like now, and if their intentions come true, the girl will go through school, grow up, get married and, if she is lucky, she'll either have a place in the city or enough money to have a nicer farm, if that's what she wants.

C-19: (Places both cards on the desk before Donald.) Is there anything in either card and your stories that would remind you of anything in your own life?

D-19: Yeah—this one. (Card I.) I used to play the violin once. I suppose I felt the same way he does. I don't remember if it was my idea or not. I suppose I was about the same age, but that was so long ago I can't remember how old I was.

C-20: (Laughing.) My, my, what an old man!

D-20: (Laughs.) Well, I have a lot to think about these days! Well, I don't remember how old I was. But I remember I felt very dreary about practicing. I took piano before I took violin, and after. I didn't enjoy it. Then I took flute, which I enjoyed. I played in the band in school. I didn't like the band. It wasn't a good band, so two years ago I dropped them all. (Sits quietly thinking.)

C-21: What are you thinking about?

D-21: I was just wondering if I'd ever want to play the flute again. I can't tell.

C-22: Were you thinking of being a musician?

D-22: I had an idea I'd like to be a mechanical engineer.

C-23: And?

D-23: Well, I'm planning it. I'm going to be it. . . . (Silence.)

C-24: What are you thinking?

D-24: I can't remember if I wanted to take the violin myself or if it was their idea.

(Thoughtful silence.)

C-25: You mentioned a moment ago that you have "a lot of things to think about these days." What, for instance?

D-25: (Laughs.) Oh, you know. Just everything in normal life. Everybody has a lot to think of. (Smiles teasingly at counselor.)

C-26: Okay for you, you don't want to tell me. Here. (Hands Donald Card 6BM, a picture of a young man and a white-haired woman.)

D-26: (Seeming to warm up to the task.) Well. . . . (He makes himself comfortable, folding his legs in a relaxed manner.) Well, this is probably taking place in a foyer of a house. That's the son and mother standing next to the window. He's probably decided he wants to do something that's against his mother's wishes. He's trying to think of what to say, so she won't be too stunned or too surprised. He's probably let a little of it out and is trying to think of what to say next. He probably wants to go into some business, or on a trip, or marry some certain person. And, whatever it is, he probably had it planned ever since he could remember, and he probably wants it so bad. . . . (Pause) But his mother had something else planned, and finally the time came when he wanted to do it, and this is the moment when he is telling her. He will probably think of some way to tell her so that she won't be too unhappy . . . and he'll go ahead and do it. If his conscience doesn't hurt him . . . if he thinks it's sensible. (Silence.)

C-27: What are you thinking?

D-27: Well, if he thinks that she'll be happy later, and that he'll make progress, then he should go ahead and do it. But if he doesn't think it will get him anywhere, he won't do it.

C-28: Do you feel he has to take his chances?

D-28: Yes, and so he's not taking *her* advice.

C-29: Does that remind you of anything in your life?

D-29: Well, yes. My mother and I have always been on good terms. Once in a while she wants me to do things for her, and I'm not keen on it, but I go ahead and do it. And it's usually better in the end. Like when she wanted me to go to a certain party. Naturally, I had to go, but I was dead set against it. But I went, and it turned out okay.

C-30: Why was it you didn't want to go?

D-30: The boy who was giving the party was not the same kind of boy I am. . . . Oh, I just wanted to do something else, I guess.

C-31: Don't you like parties?

D-31: Oh, they're all right.

C-32: What about girls?

D-32: I don't have any girl friend now. This is the first year I've been without one.

C-33: How come?

D-33: I don't know. It's funny, because I usually do have one. I haven't gone dating at all this fall—but I did this summer. I get along with them all right, but I guess I have my mind all on school for a change. I don't know. . . . We just don't talk about girls now.

C-34: You mean you and the boys?

D-34: Yeah. (Quiet.)

C-35: What else do you want to tell me?

D-35: Nothing.

C-36: Well, then, how about this picture. (Card 3BM)

D-36: If this picture is what I think it is, it sounds kind of stupid. What's this thing on the floor?

C-37: Whatever you think it is.

D-37: Well, I'll say that's a girl there, and she got mad at one of her boy friends and shot him, and that's her gun on the floor. She just blew up, and now she's crying over spilt milk. What led up to it, I suppose, is that the boy friend was a crook, and he belonged to a gang, and he married her, and they didn't get along too well together, and they had fights once in a while. This time it was a very big fight. She bawled him out and then shot him. Then she realized what she had done, and she is crying. She'll probably be arrested and done away with.

C-38: What do you think they quarrelled about?

D-38: I don't know. Maybe he went out with other girls, and she wasn't too happy about it. Maybe she wanted him to quit the gang, and he didn't want to. Or maybe they had their own little gang, and she was the boss, and he did something wrong, so she punished him. Yeah, that's a better story. (He becomes quite interested and animated.) He wasn't anything, and she taught him to be a good crook. (Laughs.) One day he killed a man, so she shot him because he wasn't supposed to go that far. And then she was arrested and done away with. (Laughs.) That sounds like a radio program.

C-39: You enjoy the radio programs?

D-39: Well, I listen whenever I get a chance, to pass time away.

C-40: Do you also read to pass time away?

D-40: (Quite fiercely.) No, I *don't* read to pass time away! Sometimes I read only if I have to, or if I want to. Sometimes I get so interested in a book, I read all night. Once I got so interested in a book, I skipped gym class to read it.

C-41: That must have been a wonderful book.

D-41: It was. I'm not reading any book at the moment, but I like adventure stories. Did you read *Mutiny on the Bounty*?

C-42: No, but I saw the movie.

D-42: I liked that book. The same authors wrote *No More Gas,* but that wasn't so good. But *Mutiny on the Bounty* was very good. I like that kind of story. One book I used to like in the sixth or seventh grade was *The Boy Aviators.* I loved those. It was a series.

C-43: Yes, I know what you mean. I read a series at the same age. I think it was *The Corner-House Girls* or something like that. It's great fun.

D-43: My mother says I have to be pushed to go to the library for a book. But I don't mind reading if I get started and get interested. It's the thought of starting it. I think of all the other things I'd rather do instead. There was a point last year when, if I didn't read a whole book every two weeks, I didn't get my allowance.

In my family they read all the time. My mother and father read three or four books every week. Mother sits down and reads all day. My eyes get tired. I get so I can't see what I'm reading.

Do you think it's right for them to take away my allowance if I don't read?

C-44: What's their purpose in doing so?

D-44: To make me read.

C-45: Does it make you like to read?

D-45: No.

C-46: If you tell a child he cannot have dessert until he eats his spinach, does that make him like spinach?

D-46: No! It's like taking medicine! I wish you'd tell that to my parents!

C-47: Why don't you tell them yourself?

D-47: It wouldn't do any good. They always win.

C-48: That seems to be a problem, then, doesn't it?

D-48: What?

C-49: That you feel you can't get anywhere in talking to your parents, that you feel you have to have me speak for you.

D-49: I suppose so. I always give in. They always win.

C-50: I won't speak to them for you because it's more important for us to work out the problem of why you can't approach them yourself. Don't you think so?

D-50: Well, can I quote you to them?

C-51: Why not?

D-51: Okay! I'll tell them what you said.

C-52: Okay. Shall we stop here?

(As Donald put on his jacket, he showed counselor the inside pocket where he had a comic book.)

D-52: This is what I read on the train, but I don't dare let my father see it. They don't like me to read comic books.

C-53: Whenever I read a paper, I always read the funnies first. What do you think of *Superman*?

D-53: *Superman* is my favorite!

(Donald was laughing with pleasure as he waved good-bye from the hallway.)

Discussion of the Second Interview with Donald

C-5 through D-10: The counselor feels that her most important responsibility to Donald is to help him get rid of his excessive conformity. His submissive attitude amounts almost to lethargy, making him appear dull except for the occasional sparkle that lights his eyes momentarily when his interest is aroused. She therefore uses every opportunity to stimulate him to assert his own thoughts, opinions and wishes. Thus, she asks him again why he finds himself doing something he really does not want to do.

C-12: The Thematic Apperception Cards were introduced to facilitate free association. The significance of the material that emerged seems to be quite obvious, not requiring comment.

D-16: This seemed to the counselor to express very well her own impression of how Donald was feeling: "Dreary. And kind of mad. He's angry, much more angry than happy."

D-20: The same feeling is repeated. "I felt very dreary about practicing."

C-26 through D-38: The developments here provide a good example of how useful the Thematic Apperception Cards can be in stimulating the emergence of helpful associations.

D-40: The counselor was pleased by the fervor of Donald's self-expression. It showed genuine feeling and more real interest in communicating to the counselor.

D-40 through D-43: Donald has plenty of interest in reading. He "once got so interested in a book, he skipped gym class to read it."

There is a nice long outpouring of feeling here, ending with his question, "Do you think it's right for them to take away my allowance if I don't read?"

C-44 through D-46: This exchange of ideas is more fruitful than just a "No" answer to Donald's question. It helps him to understand why "No" is the reasonable answer, and he can give that answer himself.

D-46 through D-51: It is quite clear that the channels of communication are closed between Donald and his parents. He feels hopeless about expressing himself to them. "I always give in. They always win."

D-52: Donald's confidence and trust in the counselor are growing. He shares with her the secret of his comic books.

Third Interview with Donald

D- 1: (Rushing into the room.) Am I going to be here for one hour or two hours today? I have to let my father know.

C- 1: We may finish in less than two hours, but I think we had better leave ourselves enough time, so let's say two hours.

D- 2: I'll go phone him and be right back.

C- 2: Do you know where to find the telephones?

D- 3: Yes, right downstairs.

(Donald hurried out and returned in about ten minutes.)

I'm sorry to keep you waiting. He wanted to know how long I'd be here, so I had to phone him.

C- 3: Counselor explained it is difficult to know how much time to allow for the Rorschach technique, because everyone takes his own time. Counselor went on to prepare Donald for the Rorschach, explaining it is not a "test" in the usual sense of the word, but rather a way of seeing how the person reacts to various stimuli and situations.

She explained that there is no possibility of failing this "test" or of getting a high "grade;" that there is no reward for speed, no penalty for going slowly. Just as ten people looking at one cloud in the sky will see ten different images, so everyone looking at these ten inkblots sees something different; therefore, anything he wants to say about them is acceptable, and he is not supposed to try to figure out any "correct answers" because there are none. Donald, when asked, said he had no questions, and the Rorschach was then administered. It required almost two hours. Afterwards:

D- 4: How will this help my reading? I don't see what inkblots have got to do with it.

C- 4: When you read, how much of you is doing the reading?

D- 5: You mean, not just my eyes, but my whole body. *All* of me!

C- 5: Would you say, then, that *all* of you might have bearing on your reading problem?

D- 6: Sure . . . only I thought we didn't decide yet that I had a reading problem, that it was my father's and mother's idea. (Smiles at counselor, as though sharing a secret joke.)

C- 6: (Smiling in return.) I'll explain the Rorschach to you when we have more time. I've kept you so late, I really must let you go now.

D- 7: (Putting on his coat.) Okay. But you forgot to ask me today. (Smiles broadly.)

C- 7: You mean, I forgot to ask whether *you* wanted to come here today?

D- 8: Yes. I was waiting for it. (Obviously teasing.)

C- 8: All right, I'll ask you now. Did you want to come here today?

D- 9: No! (Banteringly, playing a game.)

C- 9: Now I think you're making fun of me!

D-10: Well, I was waiting for you to ask me, that's all.

C-10: Why?

D-11: I don't know. (Smiles.)

(Counselor and Donald leave the counseling room. In the hall, Donald asks:)

D-12: Is it five o'clock next week?

C-12: That's right.

(He departs cheerfully.)

Discussion of the Third Interview with Donald

D-7 through D-12: Donald is warming up to the counselor and is beginning to enjoy these sessions. His teasing has a mature and sophisticated quality; he is quite openly expressing affection.

SUMMARY OF THE RORSCHACH FINDINGS:

This boy's responses to the Rorschach cards reveal a fine intelligence with good capacity for abstract thinking, but his performance is uneven because of emotional difficulties. Someone or something in his environment must be conditioning him to inhibit his spontaneity. He is very much stimulated by life's challenges, but he holds back his responsiveness. He must experience considerable fatigue as a result of this conflict: being very stimulated and struggling to repress his excitement. The danger here is that if he continues to feel hopeless about achieving self-expression without losing love, he may give up the struggle. He now has the capacity to develop into a person who can live warmly, richly, and with sparkle; but he is becoming flat and forlorn and hopeless. There is still enough vitality and aggression left to mobilize energy for a good fight. He needs to have pressures lifted and a chance to develop his own real interests with a sense of dignity and importance. If he is helped to integrate his energies in the pursuit of his own goals, he undoubtedly will develop vigorously, because there is a volcano of energy being held back by his fear of his own emotional responsiveness.

Fourth Interview with Donald

Donald came in looking rather glum today.

C- 1: How did you feel about coming here today?

D- 1: (Shrugs.) Okay.

C- 2: What did you do this week that was interesting?

D- 2: Nothing.

C- 3: Nothing?

D- 3: No, nothing.

C- 4: If you had a chance to talk about something that particularly interests you, what would you talk about?

D- 4: I don't know.

C- 5: What about your shop?

D- 5: I suppose so.

C- 6: What would you tell me?

D- 6: About what I did. What I'm going to start making in a little while, I'll have to read for. I'm going to make model planes— all the models. (All of this is said with very little interest, as though wearily complying with the demands of one more adult.)

C- 7: That sounds interesting, but you don't sound interested.

D- 7: Aw, it's all right.

C- 8: Would you be interested in making up some more stories to these cards? (The Thematic Apperception Test.)

D- 8: Okay. (Picks up the Card 8BM)
It looks to me like they're going to murder someone, and the boy is just standing by, looking. Or, there could be some gang. They are going to try to operate on him. What led up to it was, he was sick. He got a bullet in him, or something. In the future: Well, the operation will be okay—if they don't kill him. (Smiles.)

C- 9: Why might they kill him?

D- 9: They might kill him if they can't get him well. If they can't cure him.
(He picks up Card 5, the next one on the desk.)
This probably is some wife or something that put out flowers on the table. She is going into the room to be sure they're still there. She probably wanted to please her husband, or to make the house look nice. The flowers will stay there until they die.

C-10: What do you think of that woman?

D-10: Aw, she's an old maid!

C-11: I thought I heard you say she had a husband.

D-11: Well, there are people like that around. She acts like an old maid. She sticks around the house, cleans it up. She's the snooty type, not very friendly.

C-12: Do you know any woman like her?

D-12: Nope.

C-13: She doesn't remind you of anyone?

D-13: Nope.

(Counselor's further efforts to get associations to both cards were unsuccessful.)

D-14: (In response to Card 7BM)

It just looks to me like a father looking over his son. He probably did something wrong, and was pulled into court, and he was in a cell. His father is a very well-known person. He is looking at the boy and thinking. What led up to it is that the boy did the crime. The future is that the father is going to get him out.

C-15: How does the boy feel?

D-15: The boy feels terrible.

C-16: Tell me more.

D-16: There's nothing more to tell.

(Counselor's attempts to get personal associations to this card were unsuccessful.)

C-17: Would you like to get an objective test of your reading ability?

D-17: Yes, I would.

(Counselor administered the Stanford Advanced Reading Test, Form D. Donald finished both sections with considerable time to spare.)

C-18: Did you find the test interesting?

D-18: It was okay.

C-19: You're so dejected today. What's the trouble?

D-19: I guess I just resent coming here. To me it's just a great big nuisance! (Spoken with considerable feeling.)

C-20: Then you have definitely decided that you do not need any help?

D-20: I don't know. At school they say I need help. My mother says I *have* to come.

C-21: Perhaps I ought to have a talk with your parents and suggest that they leave you alone?

D-21: (His face lights up.) Well, wait and see how I come out on this test today. I'll come next week, anyhow.

(As Donald left, he gave counselor the first bright smile of the day and said, "I hope you have a nice Thanksgiving.")

Discussion of the Fourth Interview with Donald

The challenges of this interview were not too skillfully met by the counselor. Donald should have been asked right at the start, "Why so glum today?" Trying to stimulate his interest was not good. Reflecting his feeling would have been more to the point. Finally she resorts to the Thematic Apperception Test and to a reading test. Near the end of the interview the counselor says what she ought to have said at the beginning: "You're so dejected today. What's the trouble?"

Fifth Interview with Donald

Donald arrives right on time and says hello rather cheerfully.

C- 1: What would you like to tell me today?

D- 1: Nothing special.

C- 2: Would you like to go over the test you took last week?

D- 2: Yes, I would.

C- 3: You came out well. You were in your right age and class groups. Perhaps your school demands higher calibre work than the average school, and so they consider you a little bit beneath the standards they want upheld.

D- 3: (With great pride.) It's one of the best schools in the country!

C- 4: Would you like me to communicate with them, so that we can pool our knowledge to help you? I'll give them my findings, and I'll ask them for their test results and other observations.

D- 4: Sure, I don't mind.

C- 5: Your mother did not give her signature authorizing us to write to the school for information.

D- 5: Shall I bring a note from her?

C- 6: Would you?

D- 6: Sure, I'll bring one next week.

Counselor and Donald went over the Stanford Test in minute detail, discussing it in every way that occurred to them. Donald was very interested in the method of scoring, and he chuckled particularly over the vocabulary errors. He reached for the dictionary to look up synonyms from time to time, and showed the most spontaneous interest to date.

At one point he said, "You know, I have trouble relating things." He selected one of the paragraphs of the comprehension test and said, "You see, I couldn't relate this word to this one." Counselor observed him going over some of the paragraphs he had missed and noticed that if the right answer did not come to him immediately, as if by magic, he at once gave up. Counselor told him of this observation and asked him if he had noticed it himself. "Yes, but you either know it or you don't," he replied. Counselor showed him how it is possible to go more slowly and look for context clues, and to reason out relationships within the material, rather than to give up at once if one does not have the right answer immediately. Counselor and Donald together practiced the reasoning-out approach on the paragraphs he had missed.

D- 7: (After test was set aside.) We're reading quite a book at school right now.

C- 7: What is it?

D- 8: The *Odyssey*! (Scornfully.) My teacher says Ulysses was a kind of Superman. It's true—he is, kind of. But why do we have to read something with all those hard names? I can't remember those names. They ought to put it in modern times, then it would be interesting.

C- 8: You have a good idea there. In fact, that's just what some people are doing with books.

D- 9: You mean they re-write them and make them modern?

C- 9: Well, they make them easier to read.

D-10: That's a good idea. They should do that more. People ask you what kind of books you like to read. I never can say. There's no one kind. It depends on the way they are written. I can't tell what kind I'll like until I start reading it. Then I can tell if I like the way it is written.

C-10: You look for literary flavor, don't you?

D-11: (Appears pleased.) I guess you'd call it that. I just finished reading *Gentlemen's Agreement,* and I want to see the movie. Have you seen the movie yet?

C-11: No. I want to see it, too. I hear it's very good. Was the book good?

D-12: Yeah, it was swell.

C-12: Tell me more.

D-13: Well, I liked *The Yearling*. It was a good picture, too. Did you see the picture?

C-13: I saw it twice. Cried both times.

D-14: Me, too! I mean, I saw it twice. Wasn't it good, though? And the book was *wonderful*. (He says this in a dreamy, wistful voice.) There oughta be more books like *that*. That was not only a good story, but I liked the way it was written. It was beautiful. There was another book something like it, but not so good. And it was a movie, too. I can't think of the name of it. About a horse.

C-14: Do you mean *Flicka*?

D-15: Oh, *yes*! *Flicka*! Did you see that picture?

C-15: No, I missed that one.

D-16: Too bad! Don't worry, though. It really wasn't as good as *The Yearling*. (He speaks these words very comfortingly, showing deep empathy for counselor's feeling of regret at having missed *Flicka*.)

(Picking up an adventure story, one of several books counselor had put on the desk.)

This book looks pretty good. I like adventure stories.

C-16: We have about fifteen minutes left. Would you like to read some of that book, and I'll read this one?

D-17: Okay. (Opened book, but went on talking instead of reading.) It's fun to read when you find something really interesting and well written.

C-17: Writers should find out what kinds of books people your age want to read, and write books like that. For example, I seem to remember hearing somewhere about adolescent boys and girls wanting more books written about people their own age, doing the kinds of things they themselves are doing.

D-18: That's *right*! There really aren't any books like that. It's hard to find books that you really like to read.

(Donald spent the rest of the hour talking about *Mutiny on the Bounty* and *The Yearling*. His mood seemed nostalgic as he recalled favorite episodes in the latter. The counselor told him the experiences she had had with *The Yearling* when teaching high school in a small town.)

Discussion of the Fifth Interview with Donald

D-6: Donald reaches for the dictionary, chuckles over his errors, and shows plenty of spontaneous interest—when it is *his* self that he is building; by now he is fairly convinced that the counselor is "on his side."

His statement, "You either know or you don't," is an interesting reflection of education's emphasis on absolute accuracy. Education impresses upon children the *need to be right,* and they grow up under the tyranny of immediacy and unrelenting accuracy. There is desperation in the rushing to be right, with the accompanying fear of being hurled down the abyss of rejection if one is *wrong* instead of *right.* Therefore, Donald feels that one either knows or does not know, almost by magic, and without the trust in his own good mind to stay with a problem and reason it out.

D-10 through D-18: Donald's interests in books reveal good taste and deep emotional experiencing. The nostalgia he feels for *The Yearling* may grow out of a longing for a similar father-son relationship.

Sixth Interview with Donald

Walking down the hall, on the way to the counseling room, the counselor stopped with Donald to show him the one-way-vision room. Donald seemed to be excited by it, and gave the counselor the scientific explanation for being able to see through the glass on one side and being confronted by a mirror on the other side.

D- 1: You really mean you didn't know what made it work like that?

C- 1: No, I didn't.

D- 2: Gosh. . . . (Smiling and fingering a book on the desk.) I've been pretty sick. About two weeks before school closed, I had laryngitis. It got worse. I went to the doctor for some kind of treatment. Then I went home and went to bed. I thought I was going to die. I really thought so. (Looks at counselor almost surreptitiously, and searchingly—to see if she believes and sympathizes.)

C- 2: That's a very unhappy experience. I'm sorry to hear you had all that discomfort and trouble.

D- 3: (Perks up.) Yes, it was pretty bad. I was up all night, coughing. We were all up. Finally we got a big steam thing, the kind they use in hospitals. It lasted seventy-five hours. That helped.

So. . . . (Sighing.) I got four weeks vacation, but it didn't do me any good. . . . I made a wooden box for plants, but it didn't come out exactly right. One side is off by about one-eighth of an inch.

C- 3: Does that bother you very much?

D- 4: Well, it shows I didn't measure right, or something. It isn't *right,* I know that.

C- 4: That seems to matter to you quite a lot, doesn't it?

D- 5: Yes, it does seem to bother me.

C- 5: Here you make a useful thing, a nice wooden box for plants, but instead of being able to enjoy what you've done, you are concerned about one-eighth-of-an-inch of mistake.

D- 6: I guess I'm that way about a lot of things. My school notebook is always neat. Most people's notebooks are not neat. . . .

C- 6: How is that?

D- 7: I don't know. I just like it neat. I don't see why other people can't keep theirs neat. It's so easy. . . . I could make you a box for plants. I have an electric saw now, so yours will be better than mine.

C- 7: Thank you. I'd love that.

D- 8: Well, what'll we talk about? There is really nothing new to tell you. Just school. It's not so bad. (He seems lackadaisical. He picks up a book on planes that was lying on the desk.) I'd like to look at this, because I'm building model planes. Shall I read out loud to you?

C- 8: Thank you. That would be nice.

D- 9: Where shall I start?

C- 9: Wherever you'd like to start.

(Donald reads aloud from the book on airplanes, stopping only to point out pictures he found amusing. His phrasing was at first poor, but when counselor suggested he read according to the meaning, he claimed he knew how to phrase very well, and he did proceed to read with much better expression.)

D-10: This is interesting.

(He shows a great deal more warmth and interest tonight than formerly. The rest of the session was devoted to the book. At one time counselor showed Donald how to make a little gadget, a card with slots to remind him of phrasing. Counselor suggested, however, that, although gadgets were fun, it was really better to try to read according to meaning. He responded affably.)

Discussion of the Sixth Interview with Donald

D-2 and D-3: Donald makes a rather pathetic plea for affection, watching the counselor closely to see if she really cares that he has been ill.

He is distressed by a mistake amounting to one-eighth of an inch; he says, "It didn't come out exactly right." Instead of feeling pleased and proud that he has constructed a useful object, he is all too aware of a tiny error. In his next responses (D-5 and D-6), he gives further evidence of his over-concern for exactness. The need to be absolutely right, neat, clean, exact, is a slavery to goals antagonistic to creativity, spontaneity and joy in living. He has been conditioned to be "too good," and this conditioning robs him of a free-flowing expression of his creative energies. (It is interesting to see how his concern for neatness and exactness fits the Rorschach findings.)

D-7: He wants to make a plant box for the counselor, and this one "will be better." Nothing more was ever heard about this box, and the counselor wonders if perhaps he never considered his gift "good enough." Perhaps he did not make one, fearing it would not turn out *exactly right*. These are necessarily only conjectures, since no facts about it are available.

Seventh Interview with Donald

Donald's parents came to the Reading Center today, and they were seen by another interviewer while Donald had his usual session with the counselor.

D- 1: Wasn't this a terrible week? I mean, all the terrible weather. . . . Say, do you write down every word I say?

C- 1: How do you feel about it?

D- 2: (Shrugs.) Aw, I don't know. It seems funny.

C- 2: I won't take notes today if you would rather I didn't. We have to keep records, but you know that the records are confidential.

D- 3: Aw, it's all right. (He seems very bored, but his eyes watch counselor carefully.)

C- 3: Perhaps you are wondering about this because your parents are here tonight. Were you wondering if we would show them your record?

D- 4: But you don't, do you?

C- 4: No.

D- 5: How does that other person know what to tell my parents? She doesn't know me.

C- 5: I had a very careful discussion with her, about you, so that she *would* know what to say to them. . . . It's no secret. Would you like to know what she and I talked about?

D- 6: (His face lights up with a big smile.) Yeah!

C- 6: Well, to make a long story short, after going over our interviews—yours and mine—she and I decided that perhaps your parents were putting too much pressure on you, and that you needed more leeway to work out your own goals and your own way of doing things.

D- 7: Is that what she's going to tell them?

C- 7: Yes.

D- 8: Gosh. (Grins.) I hope it does some good, but I bet it doesn't.

C- 8: You are pessimistic.

D- 9: Well, I know my parents. I don't think they'll stop doing what they've always been doing. It isn't so easy. They want me to be smarter than I am.

C- 9: You do have excellent intelligence, but they don't give you room to use it as you choose.

D-10: How can you tell that I have "excellent intelligence?"

C-10: From talking to you, and from the Rorschach Test.

D-11: You mean those inkblots?

C-11: Yes.

D-12: Tell me something about it. How do you find things out from the inkblots?

C-12: It's complicated and it requires a great deal of study and practice, but maybe I can give you some idea about it. Here is this magazine, for instance. Look at the cover. We can use that picture as we would an inkblot picture, since I don't have the cards here. Most of the space is taken up by this big red airplane, isn't it. Right. Way off here in the corner is a tiny blue airplane—you can hardly see it. Now, what would you say about a person who would look at this picture and say, "The first thing I notice is a little blue airplane?"

D-13: I'd say he pays too much attention to something that isn't important, and he neglects the most important thing.

C-13: Wonderful! That's an excellent interpretation. What else would you say?

D-14: He might be a person who is going too far away from his environment—he is going far away into a little world of his own.

C-14: Good! Do you see how bright you are? You got the main ideas immediately.

D-15: (Chuckles.) That's an interesting test, isn't it. What did you find out about me?

C-15: Well, it showed that you are very intelligent, but that you don't particularly enjoy your intelligence because you always have the feeling you could have done better. So, even when you do beautifully, you have a sense of failure and you keep trying to do more and more to make up for it.

D-16: I know what you mean. Because I know my parents always said to me, "You can do better." So I guess I always feel that way.

C-16: Then you know what I'm talking about.

D-17: Yes, but I'll tell you what bothers me. It's hard to explain. . . . You see, it's like this. My mother will nag me and nag me about getting my work done, so I do it. I ask her to stop bothering me, that then I'll do better. But once she did stop, and my marks went down. I think it's because they've got me so used to being told what to do that then I sink down if they stop telling. But she didn't stop for a long enough time. Do you know what I mean? I mean that if she stopped nagging for a long enough time, that would give me time to learn how to do it without being nagged. Oh, it's hard to explain.

C-17: You are right about what you've just said. I understand it. Let me try to give you another example, to see if I understand it as you mean it. Suppose a little baby is spoon-fed all the time, so it doesn't get any practice handling a spoon. Then suddenly the parents say, "Okay, now you can feed yourself." The baby will need a period of learning how to handle the spoon, and he may make an awful mess of things, but, if everybody has patience, after a while he has learned how to feed himself quite well.

D-18: Yes, that's a good example. That's just how I feel about it. I might mess around for a while, but in the long run it would be better for me. My mother is always telling me how brilliant she was at my age, and how she always knew how to do everything. And my father was terribly smart, too. So, all right, I'm not as smart as they are. I know the whole trouble in a nutshell: They expect too much of me.

C-18: That's a pretty good size-up, I'd say.

D-19: I like talking this way. I'd like to keep coming here—but not for tutoring in reading. Not for tutoring. But I *would* like to come if we could talk this way every time.

C-19: I think that would be a good idea.

D-20: But I don't think my parents will let me come unless it's for tutoring.

C-20: Why not wait and see what the outcome is of tonight's conference?

D-21: Okay.

Discussion of the Seventh Interview with Donald

This is perhaps the best interview thus far. Donald and the counselor have a really good talk, and Donald ends up saying, "I like talking this way." (D-19)

D-1 through D-4: This is an example of how verbal consent may be given (submissively) to the recording of interviews without emotional consent. Donald does not like the idea of the counselor's "writing down every word" he says. He probably has never liked it, but has not had the courage to voice his dislike. It is a good sign of progress that he can tell the counselor now how he feels about it, and can ask for reassurance that the notes will not be shown to his parents.

D-5 through D-9: Several times in this study, the counselor has pointed out the importance of including the adolescent in the discussion of his problems and plans, instead of "talking around him." In this exchange with Donald, there is one more instance of the very real value of "letting him in on" the conference about him. The counselor will always remember the look on his face and the delight in his voice as he said, "Yeah!"

D-13 through D-17: This is vivid evidence of Donald's really fine mind.

C-17 through C-19: Donald and the counselor have a meaningful talk. Donald feels more hopeful and is beginning to expend more energy in the direction of establishing his own goals. The lethargy is disappearing; the vitality and sparkle are increasing.

Eighth Interview with Donald

D- 1: I paid ten dollars today.

C- 1: Thank you. That's fine.

D- 2: I had a talk with my parents. They said I had some good points . . . but I don't know if it helped. Mother said I could come here to talk to you if I wanted to. I asked her if she would come to see you. She said she would. They had arguments to everything I said, although they admitted I had some good points.

C- 2: Why do you want your mother to see me?

D- 3: I feel you could tell them better than I can. They had arguments to everything, and I couldn't explain as well as you can.

C- 3: I'll be glad to see your mother if that's what you want, but I wonder if it wouldn't be better for you to have the experience of standing up for yourself.

D- 4: If you saw her just once, it might help. You see, I explained to them that if they keep on directing me all through high school, I would probably drop down when I got to college. It would be better for me to have the practice now, in high school, of directing myself. But they said that if I were left to lead my own life now, later I might regret it and blame them. They said they knew exactly what they were doing. I wish you would tell them not to be so terribly concerned about my school work. I gathered that the person who saw them didn't tell them that. They were talking about my going to summer school. . . . The other day my friends were saying that I was being henpecked because I am so bossed by my mother. But my mother says I have a lot of privileges, more than most kids of my age. . . . I was pretty nervous talking to them. We had an argument, my father and I, and so I went upstairs and said I wanted to have a talk with them. (As he says this, Donald pulls at the hair on the side of his head, rhythmically, and slaps his head several times.) I don't know who won. It was never exactly finished. It was the first time I said I wanted to have a talk with them. They seemed to be nice for the rest of the day.

C- 4: That was a real achievement.

D- 5: (Smiles.) (Thoughtful.) I wonder—may I borrow twenty-five cents? I came out without enough money today.

C- 5: Okay. Here you are.

D- 6: Thanks. I'll tell you what happened. (Grins mischievously.) I bought a comic book, and then I realized I didn't have enough money on me. I would have had to walk home from the station. (Laughs.)

C- 6: What is it?

D- 7: I was just thinking of a crook relating all his tales, the way I come and relate all my troubles to you. That comes from listening to stories on the radio, I guess. You know, I used to get bad dreams every night. Finally I found that if I went to bed a certain way, I didn't have the bad dreams.

C- 7: Tell me about it.

D- 8: Well, it's hard to explain. But, if I would lie first on one side, then on the other side, I wouldn't have the bad dreams; otherwise, I'd have them every night. I don't seem to have them lately. It's funny—when you are wide awake, you can't just dream; then you have to *think* of it. Then you make up a dream.

C- 8: Yes, that is called a "fantasy." When you're asleep, it's a dream; when you're awake, it's a daydream or fantasy.

D- 9: Oh, yeah! That's right—daydreams.

C- 9: Can you remember them?

D-10: No, I just remember I used to get bad dreams every night, but I don't get them anymore.

C-10: I may be mistaken, but your talking about lying in certain positions in bed makes me wonder if you were having some difficulty about masturbation. It's just a hunch.

D-11: (Looks up alertly.) What do you mean?

C-11: Well, young people whose bodies are growing have to have time to get used to the changes that take place. When boys and girls start maturing sexually, they may feel like masturbating but be afraid to if they don't know it's okay to go right ahead and masturbate if they feel like it.

D-12: Oh-h-h-h. . . . (Softly, smiling and playing with a pencil, which he gently rolls on the blotter on the desk.)

C-12: How about it? Has anybody told you "the facts of life?"

D-13: Well . . . no . . . but I know.

C-13: How do you know, and what do you know, and what else would you *like* to know? Now's your chance.

D-14: (Laughs.) Well, you know. . . . The boys talk about it, so I think I know everything I should know.

C-14: Do you know there's no harm in masturbating?

D-15: Yes, I think I heard that.

C-15: Well, in case you are not sure, I'll tell you now: Everybody masturbates at one time or another, and there's no more harm in it than in scratching your ear if it itches—only, masturbation is more fun.

(Counselor and Donald both laugh.)

D-16: It seems I remember my father talked to me about it once . . . but I can't remember it very well.

C-16: Well, someday you will be a grown man with sons of your own, and you'll be able to tell them it's okay to masturbate. And you will thereby save them a lot of anxiety.

D-17: Gosh. . . . (Smiles at counselor.) Say, do you think you could see my mother soon?

C-17: Well, I won't be here next week, but I could see her the next time. How about bringing her with you then, and I could see you for a half-hour and see her for a half-hour.

D-18: I wish you could see her sooner.

C-18: What's the big rush?

D-19: (Grins.) I guess I'm scared. We get our report cards next Monday, and I'm afraid my marks won't be as good as they want them to be. The last marks we had were just regular marks, but these marks were based on tests.

C-19: What is it you would like me to do to help you?

D-20: If you could talk to her before I get my report card, she might not get so terribly upset.

C-20: Well, suppose I see her on Monday—that's the same day you get your report card. Would that help?

D-21: Yes, thanks, that would be swell. I just don't like to see her getting so terribly concerned over my marks.

(Donald fell silent at this point, and kept glancing surreptitiously at counselor.)

C-21: There is something else you want to tell me.

D-22: Nope, my mind is a blank. (Grins.)

C-22: That's impossible. There's always something doing in a person's noggin.

D-23: Well, I'll tell you. (Long pause, then very serious and deliberate speech, while he gazes searchingly into counselor's face.) I didn't trust you this week. I didn't trust you because my parents didn't say to me the things you said that other person was going to say to them. So I felt I couldn't trust you.

C-23: I can understand your feelings. Now, let's see if we can understand what accounts for the discrepancy.

D-24: Well, they just didn't say much about having to leave me alone and all that. They said I could come talk to you, but that I should get help with my study habits, and that I might come to summer school. You didn't say anything to me about that.

C-24: People usually are not able to remember everything that takes place in an interview. They tend to remember the things that appeal to them the most, or that somehow are most important to them, in one way or another.

D-25: I see what you mean. To my parents, it still would be most important that I get help with my studying, to improve my marks. Yes, I can see that.

C-25: I'm glad you spoke of it. You see how important it is to come out with things you are thinking. We can thrash things out and then maybe you won't be carrying unnecessary emotional burdens.

D-26: Yes, that's very good. . . . Oh, by the way, I brought that letter. You know, you needed a letter from my parents in order to write to school about me.

C-26: Thank you. I'm glad to get it. Are you sure it's okay with you that I write to your school for test results? That just means I won't have to give you the same tests all over again.

D-27: Sure, it's okay. . . . What'll we talk about now?

C-27: What would you like to talk about?

D-28: I don't know—anything.

C-28: I should wait until you think of something, but it occurs to me that we haven't discussed something we ought to discuss.

D-29: (Smiles.) What?

C-29: Well, we talk about marks, and studying, and all that, but we forget to find out whether you are getting enough exercise, rest, fresh air. You're an adolescent. That means you are doing a lot of growing, and you need plenty of rest and outdoors.

D-30: It's true that I'm always getting sleepy. On Sundays, for example, I just eat, sleep, eat again, sleep again. I talk, go outside and play around, then go to sleep again. I might do a little work in the shop—anything. But I do sleep a lot.

C-30: Do you have a hearty appetite, too, to help you grow?

D-31: Yeah, I think I eat enough. (He picks up the book on planes that is lying on the desk.) Here's that book again. I told you, I'm making model planes.

C-31: Yes.

D-32: Shall we read some more of this?

C-32: That would be fun.

(Donald spends the brief remaining time reading to counselor.)

Discussion of the Eighth Interview with Donald

One of the most important developments in this interview is Donald's courageous statement to the counselor that he did not trust her (D-23). The relationship between them might have been less therapeutic if he had not been able to tell her his doubts. By bringing them out into the open, he made it possible to clear up the misunderstanding and retrieve his trust of her.

More than this was accomplished, however. At one time Donald might have said, "Who am I to trust or not trust?" Now he sees his importance. He sees that it is of concern to this adult that *he,* the evolving person, does not trust. When he challenges, his challenge is honored, and he is given an answer equal to his challenge. He is not told, "Trust me because I say so."

It was essential for Donald to get it settled in his mind that *the counselor consistently supports his efforts at self-affirmation.*[2] In this hour his plea is, in effect: "Help me get my parents off my back. Don't line up with them to burden me with their demands for high marks, for summer school, for studying harder, for living up to their academic standards." Perhaps he feared the counselor was also bent on imposing standards of her own.

[2] The reader will be aware of the frequent repetition of this theme. It is what Polonius told Laertes: "To thine own self be true." Though self-knowledge must forever be incomplete, one can, while trying to expand self-understanding, strive to be true to as much as one does know of one's self.

It was fortunate that the counselor pursued the meaning of the expression on the boy's face. If she had accepted the response, "My mind is a blank," and had turned to reading exercises or had introduced another subject, this development might have been lost, and Donald might have left the interview with feelings of distrust.

D-2 through D-4: Donald has found the courage to open the channels of communication between himself and his parents. Since he is beginning to find value in his own self, he is beginning to have a base from which to communicate with his parents. The counselor supports his efforts to build such a base.

D-5 and D-6: This is another example of Donald's growing courage. He is able to ask the counselor for some money, and he is not afraid to confess to her that he spent his bus fare on a comic book. He has the courage to reveal an impractical act for which he is willing to take responsibility.

D-7 through D-10: Donald volunteers material of an increasingly personal nature.

Why does Donald refer to himself as "a crook?" (D-7) If he feels he deserves to be called a "crook," then he is feeling guilty. There may be many sources of guilt feelings. For one thing, he is accustomed to repressing his self-assertion and honoring his parents' attitude of, "We'll think for you, since we know what is best for you." Affirming his own feelings and asserting his own ideas represent to Donald defiance of his parents' wishes. It makes him feel "like a crook" to secretly enjoy self-assertion or even fantasies of self-assertion. Talking to the counselor, therefore, seems to him a guilty conspiracy in which she encourages him to think for himself and speak for himself. Eventually Donald will learn that self-affirmation and self-assertion are mature types of behavior and do not constitute defiance of authority. At this point, however, it seems to Donald that it is wicked to stand up for his own ideas; it makes him feel "like a crook."

One must ask the question: Do the parents of adolescents really "know best?" Even if they do, the adolescent needs more to be encouraged to believe in his own wishes and capacities than to be given correct solutions to problems and a blueprint of how to live. His own gropings, with all their awkwardness, add more to his real stature—his sense of worth, his self-affirmation, his individuation—than do the accumulation of superimposed skills and knowledge. The boy is what he *is,* not what he *knows.* What he is, influences what he knows, so that what he knows becomes a part of what he is, and the person and his knowledge become integrated.

For what other reasons does Donald feel "like a crook?" When he introduces the subject of bad dreams and of lying in bed in certain ways to ward off these bad dreams, this suggests to the clinician that the boy may be feeling guilty about masturbation and masturbation fantasies. In reading over the interview, the counselor had some question as to whether giving reassurance about masturbation was in line with the development of the interview. It seems to be brought in rather abruptly. However, although one cannot be certain that Donald was referring to masturbation and masturbation fantasies, it is worthwhile to take a chance on the clue suggested by his ritualistic way of warding off his bad dreams.

Reassuring an adolescent boy that masturbation is appropriate to his age (it would not be appropriate if he were old enough for heterosexual relationships) may be helpful. If he does not know that masturbation is normal and inevitable in adolescent boys, telling him about it may relieve him of an enormous burden of doubt, guilt and confusion.

When masturbation is excessive to the point of becoming a compulsion, it is being used to alleviate anxiety, but guilt about the masturbation generates even more anxiety.

Without knowing the content of Donald's fantasies, one does not know what was going on in him. Also, we do not have any statements regarding his attitudes toward masturbation. Thus, one can only hypothesize as follows: Perhaps Donald's repressed self-assertion led to guilt, anxiety and fear of punishment or loss of his parents' love; for he had the wish to assert himself but felt it was dangerous to do so.[3] Perhaps masturbation carried with it the fantasy of reassuring himself: "If *they* won't love me and let me be important, then *I* will love myself." But, since this is an escapist technique, it leads to an increased feeling of failure and degradation: "I'm no good because of my fantasies and because of masturbation." This would make him feel more guilty, more lonely, more separated from the persons to whom he needs to feel close. With increased anxiety, there is an increased need for self-comforting activity, and a subsequent snowballing of guilt and confusion. The more guilty he feels, the more compulsive and exces-

[3] The Rorschach symbolism is interesting in this regard. He said about the bat which is popularly seen in flight: "It looks better dead."

sive the masturbation becomes. One should not confuse this compulsive, excessive masturbation with the normal, healthy masturbatory activity of the adolescent who is not driven by anxiety to excesses in self-comforting.[4]

The paradox is that reassurance about the innocence of normal adolescent masturbation does not increase the desire to masturbate; on the contrary, the alleviation of guilt-feelings frees the individual to feel worthy of human companionship and to need less self-comforting. Instead of launching him into a life-time of auto-erotism, the absolving of his guilt-feelings about masturbation helps him to love others, and he becomes more, rather than less, inclined to develop social relationships.[5]

Another question may be asked: Should the counselor have suggested that the father discuss masturbation with Donald? Under favorable conditions, yes. Donald and his father needed to improve their relationship with each other. However, from the report submitted by the worker who had interviewed the father at the initial meeting, it was thought that Donald's father might not feel free enough to really help Donald accept his own sexual impulses without guilt. The father was tense, worried that Donald would not get to Harvard and concerned that his son showed signs of being "lazy." Despite his obvious intelligence, he evidenced little understanding of the importance of encouraging his son to take on manly responsibilities. For example, he asked that the bills for the boy's treatment be sent to his office, "so that Donald won't have to bother with paying for his interviews."

It was, therefore, not unsound for the counselor to discuss masturbation with Donald during his interview with her, rather than leave it to the father, who seemed emotionally unprepared to face this problem with his son at the time. It would not have been therapeutically defensible to postpone an opportunity to alleviate guilt feelings when the boy appeared to be under considerable pressure.

[4] Where the individual is driven by anxiety to excessive, compulsive needs for seeking self-comforting, his channels for this may not be confined to excessive sexual masturbation, but may include other compulsive excessive activities, such as the following: chain-smoking, alcohol-drinking, drug-addiction, coffee-drinking, candy-eating, indulging in too many movies, spending too many hours listening to music, nail-biting, pulling at hair, picking at face and fingers, and many other compulsions.

[5] Donald wrote in his follow-up letter that during the year after therapy he "rather went overboard on social activities." This is an important item, since increased sociability is a sign of successful therapy.

D-17 through D-21: This is a vivid description of the pressure under which Donald has been living. He is extremely uncomfortable at the thought of seeing his mother become upset over his report card.

What is the justification for the counselor's apparent inconsistency? She earlier had said she would not see Donald's parents, that it was better for him to face them himself. Now she agrees to speak to Donald's mother for him. The explanation is that Donald has made the effort; he did try to handle the situation himself. Now he needs support from the person who has been helping him develop a base of operations. To deny him this support would be not only purposeless but unkind. He is up against difficult opposition, and to ask him to batter himself against adult barriers with his immature, adolescent and fairly new self-assertion is asking too much. A helping hand is needed and is given.

Interview with Donald's Mother

This interview was with Donald's mother, an attractive woman, youthful in appearance and tastefully dressed. She arrived ten minutes late, breathless, apologetic, but rather vigorously on the defensive. She at once took the lead in the discussion, as follows:

M- 1: I'm glad of a chance to talk to you because I'm sure Donald has not told you the whole story but just his side of it. He's been complaining lately that we are not letting him be independent; but you see, his best friends are seventeen years old, and he's just fifteen. We can't let him do everything his friends do because they are *older* than he is. For example, they are able to drive, but you *can't* let him drive until he is sixteen. It's quite true that he drives beautifully, and last summer we let him drive on the Island, but we can't let him drive in the city until he is sixteen. Isn't that true?

C- 1: You are quite right—and I imagine Donald accepts that, doesn't he?

M- 2: As a matter of fact, he *is* reasonable about that. He knows we can't let him drive until he is sixteen. Of course, he was delighted when we allowed him to drive last summer. He just had a wonderful time with that. . . . Oh . . . (Reaching into her pocketbook.) He wanted me to show you his report card. He got it today.

C- 2: What do you think of it?

M- 3: Well, I know he can do a great deal better than *that*, but I'm surprised he could do that well on the amount of studying he did. All his friends were studying, but he did *not* study one bit.

C- 3: This is really an adequate report card, isn't it?

M- 4: (Bristling.) Well, obviously! But it's a pity when you think how much better he is capable of doing.

C- 4: There may be other areas in his life right now that have more real importance to him than his report card.

M- 5: It's just human nature to want your son to do well! How is he going to get into a good college unless he makes a record in high school?

C- 5: Is Donald worrying about college?

M- 6: If he is, he certainly doesn't show it.

C- 6: Perhaps everything would work out better if you could avoid putting pressure on him.

M- 7: I never put pressure on him.

C- 7: But perhaps you are yourself under pressure to see him achieve high grades in school, and he feels that.

M- 8: Well, yes. I take that back. That is the one place where my husband and I have both put pressure on him. We want him to study and do as well as he can.

C- 8: (Counselor suggested that perhaps other factors in the boy's life were more important at present than scholastic achievement. For example, his emotional development is of great importance, as is his physical growth. Just as a fifteen-year-old boy needs exercise, fresh air, fun, rest and good food, he needs room for emotional experimentation and expansion. He needs a chance to develop his own goals and purposes, which may be very simple and immediate in the beginning. If left alone to take responsibility and initiative on his own, he will learn to direct and use his energies to better advantage, and he will gain his manhood.

While counselor was talking in this vein, Mrs. ——— kept commenting, "Well, obviously," or, "That's just human nature, isn't it?" These remarks, spoken with an aggressive air, seemed to be attempts, conscious or otherwise, to belittle everything the counselor was saying. At the same time, these remarks made by Mrs. ——— seemed to represent an effort at showing that she already knew everything the counselor was trying to communicate. Therefore, finally:)

C- 9: I don't know why I'm saying all this. It's clear to me that I am just repeating information that you already have. But I am grateful to you for coming to get acquainted with me today, anyhow.

M- 9: I came because I wanted to help my son. But I don't happen to care for the psychologists I know.

C-10: Why is that?

M-10: Well, psychologists should be well-trained. So many of them are not!

C-11: I completely agree with you. If your son goes to a psychologist for help, you have a right to know that psychologist's training. Now, if you like, I'll be very pleased to tell you in detail about my years of training.

M-11: (Taken aback.) No, no. That's all right. He likes you, and that's a good thing. He is always so shy and undemonstrative. I just have not cared about the psychologists I've known. They try to tell everybody else how to live, but they often don't know how to themselves.

C-12: I wonder why you are on the defensive with me. I am not a "parent-eater."

M-12: I am *not* defensive; I'm feeling my way.

C-13: With a chip on your shoulder, just a little bit?

M-13: No! As I say, I would not be here if I did not want to help my son, so why should I have a chip on my shoulder. Wouldn't that be silly?

C-14: Many facts often seem silly. I think you are defending yourself by attacking me because you think you are being scolded in some way. I am not scolding you. I wanted to see you to get your help in trying to help Donald.

M-14: Well, he does like you. Lately, when he tells us things, I can just hear *you* talking. He seems to remember every word you tell him.

C-15: Just the same, I am not promising to achieve anything spectacular. In fact, he may decide he doesn't want to come here at all. If he decides that, we have to leave it up to him. If you insist that he come, his coming here will not be worth much.

M-15: Oh, of course! I understand that.

C-16: But you did *not* understand that, because you were insisting that he come here. Isn't that true?

M-16: Well, that was the fault of his school and his teachers. They definitely said he needs help with his reading.

C-17: I think it would be a good idea to take his part. Even if it happens to be incorrect, it is more important for him to feel that he has a soft, loving mama who has faith in his judgment. This is more important than to follow out academic instructions.

M-17: (Warmly.) Well, I'm glad to know that! I did not always agree with his teachers. In fact, I think he has some pretty terrible teachers, but I felt I had to back them up. Now, if you say I should back *him* up, I'll know what to do. . . . But the thing I don't understand is that he always seemed to have such a good relationship with me. He is always doing things for me around the house. He spends his allowance to buy little ornaments and things for the house. In fact, (smiling) I wish he were less close to me, and closer to his father. Those two are a clash of temperaments. (Laughs.) The other day his father was unable to fix a clock. Donald said, "Let me try it." His father insisted he could not do it, that the clock would have to be taken in for repair, but Donald kept asking, "Let me *try* it," so finally his father let him try it—and don't you think he fixed it? He certainly did! . . . Sometimes he seems to be like a man in the house, not a boy. He is always fixing things for me around the house. He even tells me not to worry when he sees that something is upsetting me.

C-18: He does seem older than fifteen. Tell me, does he spend much time with friends, outdoors?

M-18: Not enough. He stays shut up in that shop of his every free minute. Or else he is helping around the house in some way. Donald has always been *good,* maybe *too* good. As a baby, you could dump him into his play-pen and he'd just stay there for twenty-four hours if you left him. He never complains. But recently he has been showing some temper.

C-19: Blame me for that, not him. I've been egging him on to "fight for his rights."

M-19: (Laughs.) Oh, then that explains it. Because Donald never used to show any temper.

C-20: He is a firecracker, but he uses a lot of his energy controlling it. It would be better for him to let it out, to fight openly. Perhaps he is afraid of losing your affection if he shows his temper.

M-20: Yes, I don't believe in holding everything in.

C-21: I'm glad you feel that way. My own feeling is that it will be healthier for him to be a little scrappier than he has been. His tendency is to feel hopeless about fulfilling what is expected of him. He tends to flatten himself out instead of becoming indignant. He doesn't think in terms of what *he* wants, and, therefore, he cannot develop a sense of self. If he continues to try hopelessly to fulfill what is expected of him, he may just give up altogether and let others "do" for him. Then he'll be just a shadow, not a person.

M-21: You know, I have felt he hides away in his shop too much. That's what you mean, isn't it?

C-22: Yes, that's part of it. He makes a little world for himself there because that's one spot where he can use initiative and make his own goals. If he could feel stronger in relationship to you and to his father, he perhaps would not need to spend so much time away from you.

M-22: I must tell you, he was really wonderful the day he had a long talk with us. He told you about it, didn't he? Well, of course I could just hear *you* talking. He understood so clearly what you told him. I almost wept because he was so kind about it. He said, "You are making the mistake of trying to live my life for me. But of course that's unconscious on your part; you don't realize that you are doing that." My husband said, "Oh yes! We know what we are doing; we're guiding you." He told us why it would be better to let him guide himself. He used an example about letting a baby learn to feed itself. He got that from you, didn't he? Well, he had it all very clearly in mind. It was the first time he ever talked to us like that. We were very touched.

C-23: Being a parent is quite a career, isn't it.

M-23: (Laughs.) You can say that again! You never know when you are doing the best thing for them.

C-24: Parents of adolescents have to be flexible sounding boards for them. This period has sometimes been called "the adolescent crisis"—when they have a wish to be independent, but, since they are still, in large part, children, they do not have adult tools for independence, and they are afraid of their own wish to be on their own. So, they project onto their parents their own fear of being altogether independent, and they shout at their parents, "*You* won't let me be independent." Actually, they feel some comfort in the fact that their parents won't let them go *all* out for independence before they are ready. . . . If you just respect his point of view, let him talk out how he feels and, about his schoolwork, take it for granted that he knows how much he needs to study . . . you know?

M-24: (After listening attentively to the above.) We certainly *have* nagged him about studying. We thought it was necessary. His father, particularly, has felt Donald could do so much better. But we won't do *that* any more.

C-25: Good. Well, we've used up our time, I'm sorry to say.

M-25: I want you to know this has been very helpful, and I'm grateful to you.

C-26: (Laughing.) We started off on the wrong foot, but I think we understand each other now.

M-26: Yes, this has been most worthwhile for me.

C-27: I've enjoyed it very much. Will I have the pleasure of seeing you again?

M-27: I surely would like to come again if I may.

C-28: Please do. Any time. Just phone me and let me know you are on the way.

M-28: I'll do that. Good-bye, and thanks again.

C-29: Good-bye. And thank you for coming in.

Discussion of the Interview with Donald's Mother

In reading over this interview, the counselor had the impression that perhaps the most important lesson to be learned from it is that one must be prepared to deal constructively and therapeutically with the defensiveness, and possibly the jealousy, of the parent of an adolescent in treatment. If the counselor is easily threatened, she is not able to recognize that the mother feels threatened. The counselor must objectively throw light on the total situation from the perspective of an outsider. This does not mean that she is impartial, for her first loyalty is to the boy, who depends on her to stand by him; but she would not be helping him if she made him a battleground on which to fight his parents.

One might raise the question as to whether Donald's mother would be able to change her attitudes toward Donald without obtaining psychotherapy for herself. If Donald had been much younger, the counselor would have made the parents' psychotherapy a condition of accepting the child for treatment. However, since Donald is almost sixteen and thus close to the threshold of leaving his home to go away to college, it seems less urgent to change the parents in order to help the boy. Had Donald continued with the counselor, she would have invited his parents for interviews from time to time, always, however, with Donald's permission, and perhaps only at his request, depending upon the demands of the situation.

Most of the significant material in the interview emerges too clearly to require elaboration. However, one might comment on the statement made by Donald's mother that she and her son have "always had such a good relationship." One must not be misled by a statement such as this, for when one learns more about the relationship, one is prompted to ask the following questions: What has the mother done, or felt, or omitted to do, that has resulted in keeping Donald tied so closely to her? Why has he not been able to develop a better relationship with his father? Is it usual for an adolescent boy to spend his allowance "to buy little ornaments and things for the house?" Is he placating his mother with his gifts? These are the questions one must ask about Donald's relationship with his parents.

It is interesting to obtain information from Donald's mother that so clearly and succinctly substantiates the Rorschach findings as well as the interview material: "Donald has always been *good,* maybe *too* good."

Ninth Interview with Donald

Donald met counselor with a big smile and a warm hello.

D- 1: My mother enjoyed the talk she had with you. She liked you very much. And she's leaving me alone now, so I think everything is going to be all right.

C- 1: Why, that's wonderful.

D- 2: Yes, I feel that everything has been accomplished now, and that we can let things ride. But I would like to come see you in a month or so, to check up.

C- 2: That sounds good to me.

D- 3: Yes, the thing we wanted to accomplish was to let me be on my own. I think if they see they can trust me, I'll gain the same feeling; I mean, I'll gain confidence in myself. (Donald sits back in the armchair contentedly and beams at counselor.) Well, we accomplished what we set out to accomplish. . . . Your hair looks nice that way. I like it. (Counselor had a new hair-do.)

C- 3: Thank you. I'm glad you approve of it. I like it, too.

D- 4: Yes, it's very nice. . . . Well, that was the main thing I needed help on—to get them to let me be independent. My mother said she enjoyed talking to you. She said that you were very nice.

C- 4: I enjoyed talking to her, too. We had a good talk.

D- 5: Yes, it must have been good, because she is acting different. Now, I figure it would be a waste of your time and mine to come down here when I have no problems to talk about. But I would like to feel free to call you if I need you. Could I do that?

C- 5: You most certainly could.

D- 6: Could we make an appointment now for, say, one month from today?

C- 6: Good idea.

(Donald reaches for the calendar on the desk and tells counselor the date of the planned appointment.)

D- 7: Okay? Five o'clock? This room?

C- 7: Check.

D- 8: Then we can get together and talk things over again. (Smiles.) My mother thinks I'm satisfied with my marks, but I'm not. I want to do better.

C- 8: I hope this doesn't mean that you are going to drive yourself even harder than they have driven you!

D- 9: Aw, no. . . .

C- 9: Do you know what I mean? You don't have to be so grateful for getting what's coming to you, that then you feel you have to be twice as "good." You might feel that now you *have* to prove yourself to them, to prove you were right in asking them not to nag you.

D-10: Oh, I see. Yeah. . . . (Thoughtful.)

C-10: You really don't have to prove yourself, do you? Or do you feel that you *do* have to?

D-11: I guess I did feel that now I *have* to get good marks, to show them this way is better. I'm glad you brought that up. I wasn't aware of it.

C-11: It certainly doesn't take you long to catch on!

D-12: Well, you make things clear. My mother said she didn't really have to come talk to you, that she knew everything you told her. But I thought it would clear things up if I had her come talk to you. I think that now she'll stick to it. Because she said she thought my marks were pretty good, considering I had Regents and didn't have time to study. . . . Did she find this place all right?

C-12: Yes.

D-13: It's hard, walking on snowy sidewalks. . . . Well, she probably *didn't* know it all; she just had to say that. Anyhow, I'm sure it made it more clear to her. That's why I wanted her to come talk to you. I couldn't tell her everything the way you can.

C-13: From what she told me of the talk you had with them, you do a very good job of telling them things.

D-14: Did she tell you about it?

C-14: Yes, she was very proud. I'll tell you about our interview—all the important things, that is. (Counselor rapidly reconstructs the main points of the interview with his mother.) And, as I said, she spoke very proudly of how you dealt with them.

D-15: Of course, that was the very first time I ever talked to them— because it isn't supposed to be the child's place to tell the parents how to bring him up. A child is supposed to respect his parents.

C-15: I also believe that parents should respect children.

D-16: (Laughs.) But they don't. I tell you, though, it's *teachers* who sit on thrones. They don't really care about children.

C-16: I'm afraid that's all too true of a great many people in the teaching profession.

D-17: The teachers are so old and so lazy at our school; the children get the feeling that the teachers don't want them around at all.

C-17: That's very sad, isn't it.

D-18: It certainly is. It shouldn't be like that.

C-18: Tell me more about your teachers.

D-19: Well, some of them are nice, but there are too many that aren't so nice. For example, the ———— teacher used to bang you on the head with a blackboard eraser if you talked, or if she *thought* you were talking, even if you weren't. It didn't hurt, but it got chalk dust in your hair. Our ———— teacher frightens us by talking sarcastically. Nobody wants to recite because of the things she says. She can really make you feel embarrassed. She doesn't mind saying, "*You're* even dumber than so-and-so," and things like that, I can't even remember them all.

C-19: That's shocking! It's perfectly dreadful!

D-20: They aren't happy, and they take it out on the kids.

C-20: You are so understanding—it's really very wonderful, your capacity to sense what the other person is feeling.

D-21: (Smiles.) It's easy to talk to you.

C-21: I hope you will always remember that I am here for you to come and talk to—even years from now, if you like. And if for some reason you can't find me, remember you do know now that it is possible to find someone to share your troubles with and talk things through. Will you remember that?

D-22: (Gets up and looks out the window.) Yes, I'll remember. (Turns to counselor.) Well, I think I ought to go now, if you don't mind. There's so much snow, I might miss my train. It made me late tonight getting here, too.

C-22: Good-bye, Donald. I hope you are going to keep in touch with me. I like you, and I'd like to hear from you from time to time.

D-23: I'll see you in one month! (He smiles a big, sweet smile.) Thanks for everything so far. You helped me so much.

C-23: (Extending hand for hand shake.) I'm so glad things are turning out well. Take care of yourself.

D-24: You take care of yourself, too. Well, good night.

C-24: Good night, Donald.

(He turns and waves gaily at counselor from down the hall.)

Discussion of the Ninth Interview with Donald

Donald has come a long way since the first meeting, and in this final interview he seems to glow with pleasure and a sense of achievement. The lethargic look has quite vanished; his face and posture express hopefulness and vitality.

However, the counselor does not expect that Donald will have no more of his old problems. In C-8, C-9 and C-10, she points out to him the danger of imposing even harsher perfectionistic standards on himself than those imposed by his parents. She also takes care to make it clear to him that he may come back for more help at any time in the future.

A Follow-up Report on Donald

Donald did not return in a month. He telephoned to say that everything was all right and that he did not need to return.

The counselor wrote to Donald several years later, asking him to bring her up to date. His reply [6] follows:

"Dear —:

"I was very pleased to receive your letter. I hope you do not mind me using theme paper, but I have too much to say to use writing paper.

"During my tenth grade, I rather went overboard on social life, and took school as a side-line. I finished the tenth grade with fair grades.

"Then I decided I wanted to go to a prep school, so that I would be able to get into a good college. So I went to ———, quite a hard school, and I did not do very well in the eleventh grade. But during my senior year, I did very good work. I graduated quite near the top of the class, and I was accepted at every college I applied to except Harvard. I applied to fourteen colleges.

"I chose to come to ——— University. I feel that I made a very wise choice in coming here, because I love the school itself and am doing quite well in the work. I am in the Engineering College.

"I hope this little summary of the last few years of my educational life is what you asked for.

"Again, thanks for writing to me, and maybe someday, when I am near New York City, we can get together.

"Yours sincerely,

"Donald —."

⁶ With identifying data disguised or omitted.

[4]

THE CASE OF RALPH

THE CASE OF RALPH is presented in this chapter. In all, there were thirty-nine interviews, extending over two semesters. At the end of the chapter the reader will find a follow-up statement from Ralph received several years after his last visit to the Reading Center. As in Chapters Two and Three, each interview will be succeeded by a section entitled Discussion.

At the time of referral, Ralph, twenty years old, had just dropped out of a small college near New York because he could not keep up with the work. He had enrolled in the Improvement of Reading course because he felt his chief difficulty was his inability to read quickly and to retain what he read. His plan was to improve his reading and continue his education.

He did not join the class until the third session and thus missed the reading test. After the fifth class meeting, he informed the instructor that the work made him nervous. He could not follow the reading material of the Harvard Films, even at their slowest speed, and he could not listen to the discussion without becoming panicky. The instructor therefore referred him for individual help.

The First Interview with Ralph

Ralph was ten minutes late to the first interview. His appearance is attractive. He is tall, he has good features, light brown hair, dark eyes and a pleasant voice. He came to this interview, as to all succeeding ones, well-dressed and impeccably groomed.

123

The counselor offered him the arm-chair at the desk, so that he would not have to face the light from the big windows. The counselor took the chair at one side of the desk, making it possible for Ralph to face her or not, as he chose.

C- 1: Do you mind if I take notes?

R- 1: Not at all.

C- 2: Thank you. I find them helpful, and they will of course be confidential.

R- 2: Yes, I know.

C- 3: Miss ——— told me some things about you, but let's hear— what brings you to the Reading Clinic?

R- 3: It's the feeling I have that I am not the reader that I should be. Slowness, inability to comprehend what I read—slight difficulty in mind wandering—many times a lack of interest in what I am doing. I don't get from my reading the essential things of what I am reading.

C- 4: Your mind wanders to what kinds of things?

R- 4: To more pleasant things. At college, I'd think about the fiancée, wondering where she is, what she's doing. And little things, I can't say exactly what. Like thinking I'm thirsty and wanting to go out for a drink of water. Or that I ought to go out for coffee. I might be thinking of other things I could be doing.

C- 5: Like what?

R- 5: Oh, I guess it's mostly about my fiancée. (His voice is very low, his speech low. His face is flushed, and he puts his head down, covering his eyes with one hand.)

C- 6: What do you want to tell me?

R- 6: I don't know. (Not defiantly spoken, but puzzled.)

C- 7: You are depressed?

R- 7: Yes, a little . . . because of what has happened at college. I feel bad about stopping college.

C- 8: Do you want to tell me more about what happened?

R- 8: Yes. I was at ——— College. It's a small town, a nice campus. There was a college ruling that if you dropped a course it automatically was counted a failure. They would count it a failure, even after just one week. (His voice is tearful.)

C- 9: Tell me more.

R- 9: Well, I dropped trigonometry. It put me on probation. I was

on probation all that year and part of this year. (Stops talking.)

C-10: What career did you have in mind?

R-10: I was interested in engineering, but now I am interested in just
one thing: getting a degree. I'm putting engineering out of my
mind just now.

(Ralph related the detailed story of going to see one of his
instructors, who asked him about his study habits.)
He told me I don't belong in college because I have trouble
taking notes and studying. He gave me a booklet, "How to
Study." This booklet told me it's time to face this problem I've
had all my life. Way back in high school it was always the same
thing, always the trouble in studying, in concentrating. And
also the fact that I just didn't go fast enough. I would read for
an hour, then my eyes would blur and I couldn't read any
longer. I have glasses. I had them checked last year. As I
understand it, I have a slight astigmatism in my left eye. I could
read an hour at most before the page would start blurring. I
imagine I've always had it, but I've never read as much as
I read at college. I'd be working all day, and find myself all
out of breath just reading. I've been told—by someone who
doesn't count—that I don't know how to relax when I read.
I'm out of breath when I stop, even after just one hour. Could
it be that I'm not relaxed?

C-11: Do you have any other evidence of not being relaxed?

R-11: Yes, sometimes I feel that my coördination is tense, and my
stomach muscles are a little tense. (Sighs, and is quietly
thoughtful.)

C-12: What are you thinking?

R-12: About the fee. I don't know about how I'm supposed to pay
you.
(Counselor takes out application form.)

C-13: Suppose we let you fill in this form and get that taken care of.
(Counselor explains about range of fees and where and when
the fee is paid.)
You may pay whatever you feel you can afford. Since you are
not working right now, perhaps you would like to pay less than
the two dollars an hour you indicated here.

R-13: Oh, no. I can afford the two dollars all right. . . . What were we talking about?

C-14: What would you like to talk about?

R-14: Oh—the situation at college. Well, it was quite critical. Seeing that I was on probation, if I didn't do well enough this marking period, the college would ask me to leave. I went to see the Dean and asked him what I should do. The Dean said it was true, I'd have been asked to leave in January if my marks didn't come up this marking. Then I'd never be able to get into any other college. . . . It all happened about two weeks ago. My whole life was switched. (Smiles a wry smile.) I said, "Dean Jones, what school could I attend to find out information on this?" He said, "New York City isn't far from where you live. Go to Columbia and see what they offer you." I told him I'd go home and talk it over with Dad and Mom. When I came here, I had my first interview with the secretary. She said it wasn't too late to join a class. So I went to school last week, closed up my work there, said I might be back in February, if I was ready—whenever I am ready. And that's what the situation is. (Sits quietly, grasping arms of chair tightly.)

C-15: Don't you want to tell me what your Dad and Mom said?

R-15: (Smiles.) My father is a very well-educated person, very understanding and open-minded. He and I get along very well together. Dad saw my situation. In fact, he had something of the same situation while he was in college. He had to leave college and get extra help. So he encouraged me to leave for a while to acquire the background that I need. (Is quiet again.)

C-16: And your mother?

R-16: My mother is a person with little education but is very understanding. She would, of course, feel the same way my father feels. She is influenced by him. She feels disappointed, as he does, but they feel that everything is going to work out all right.

C-17: And you?

R-17: Yes, I know that sooner or later it will work out all right. (Silence.)

C-18: What are you thinking?

R-18: Well, I'm not sure of my plans for the future. I don't know exactly what I can do. Will I receive an I.Q. test?

C-19: If you like.

R-19: I think it would be a good idea. I'd like to know just what my standing is. For one thing, I am very confused on what I'm going to do. I'm planning to be married, but the woman is entitled to some knowledge of her security after marriage. I've always thought I'd be an engineer.

C-20: You wanted to be an engineer?

R-20: Well, it was influenced by the family, of course, Dad's being a consulting engineer. But Dad asked me to please put the idea of engineering out of my mind, out of my head. He said, "When you hear how difficult the engineering subjects are, you build up a fear, so you can't put your mind on the work that you are doing." And that's true. Many's the time I've thought, "If I can't do this work, what will I do with the harder work?" Anyhow, Dad said, "You might want to go into teaching and help people in the beginning, not to make the mistakes that you have made." I've been thinking about that quite a bit lately. I asked my fiancée last night how she'd feel if I went into teaching. She said she'd be happy so long as I'm happy. She loves me. The only difficulty I have in love is that we are so much in love with each other.

C-21: Is that a difficulty?

R-21: Well, it might be considered a difficulty if you think about your mind wandering.

C-22: You mean you have sexual fantasies?

R-22: Yes . . . I can't help it. (Apologetically.)

C-23: Isn't that normal under the circumstances, and rather pleasant?

R-23: Yes (big bright smile) . . . but when I'm supposed to be thinking of mathematics, and she is so much more pleasant to think about. . . . We are planning to be married this summer.

C-24: Did you both want to wait until summer to be married?

R-24: No, my parents wanted me to finish school first. But I can't see that. There's the problem of finances, though. Also, she'll be out of school then. That was another reason—another thing that was holding us up.

(The session was coming to an end, and counselor began to gather her things.)

R-25: Oh, just one more thing I want to tell you. I forgot to put on that sheet, where it says "high school," that I went my last three years to a military academy.

C-25: We'll add that, shall we? (Making notation.)
(Both get to their feet and prepare to leave.)

R-26: (Obviously eager to extend the interview.) Yes. You see, my parents sent me there to get me away from girls. But, it's funny —that's where I met Jane. Jane is my fiancée. But I must tell you something else: Jane helps me study. Whenever I used to call her up to go out, she would say, "Are you through with your studying?" If I would say, "No," she would tell me she wouldn't see me until I finished my studying.
(Counselor opened the door to leave. Ralph sprang to hold the door open for her.)
(His expression bright, his voice lively.) Thank you. Thank you very much. I'll see you Friday?

C-26: Yes, we'll meet Friday at the same time.

R-27: Right here?

C-27: Yes, right here. Good-bye now.

Discussion of the Interview with Ralph

The counselor's first impression of Ralph was that he seemed depressed, confused, preoccupied and very weary. He appeared ashamed to find himself in so much trouble and to be helpless in dealing with it. His soft, almost strangled, voice communicated the feeling that he was spending considerable energy to keep his despair under control. The counselor had a glimpse of a lonely young man who had had a solitary struggle for a long, long time. There was something pathetic and childlike in his helplessness, as though he were pleading: "Please tell me what is happening to me. Please help me." He seemed to be in awe of the counselor, not aware of her as a person but only as a symbol of highly idealized authority. His voice conveyed this by its expression of excessive respect and painful submissiveness. As the interview progressed, these initial impressions were reinforced.

R-4 and R-5: When Ralph's mind wanders, it goes to thoughts of his fiancée and to thoughts of going out for a drink of water or a cup of coffee. Very tentatively, one asks whether this thirst for his sweetheart and thirst for something to drink may represent a more basic thirst; namely, a thirst for his mother's affection. Holding this in mind, one will wait now to find out what Ralph's relationship with his mother has been. Has she been able to give warmth, affection, closeness? Or has it been difficult for her to feed his emotional needs, and has she left him in a state of endless hunger for her affection? If this is true, he must have a yearning to be with his mother, hoping, all unconsciously, still to get what he ought to have gotten much earlier, the warmth from her that he needs in order to grow and to become independent of her.

At this point it might be well to clarify a phenomenon that appears so very paradoxical. One often sees a child or adolescent clinging to a mother who is cool, critical, not very affectionate, perhaps even un- kind. It seems odd for him to be particularly fond of this parent, yet he must be, else why would he cling to her? The fallacy is the belief that he clings because he gets so much from her that he does not want to leave. The underlying truth is that he clings because he is still waiting and hoping for her approval, her love, her warmth. As one young woman said, "Almost anyone in the world would be nicer to me than my mother is, yet I feel I can't leave her until I change her, until I force *some* love out of her." She was not able to formulate this, how- ever, until after two years of psychotherapy. In the beginning, earlier, she described her mother as being "a good mother."

Another possible factor in this clinging is a need to be near the mother to punish her for not having given love. If the child grows up, matures, is successful, this is the mother's reward for having been a loving mother. If the child fails and has to go home and stay with his mother, this, unconsciously, is his punishment of her for not having given love. Her son's failure reflects her failure. Still another possible factor in the picture is the need to go home and protect one's mother against one's own unconscious rages and wishes for revenge. The young woman quoted above said, "If anything happened to my mother while I am not with her, it would coincide too closely with my wishes that something *should* happen to her, and I'd feel guilty, as though my wishes had come true."

This may seem to the reader like very heavy embroidery on a fragile theme. All this on the basis of his wanting to go out for coffee! It is important for the reader to get the picture of what happens in the therapist's mind the moment the client steps into the office. It is no different from what happens to anyone upon meeting a new person, but the therapist makes it his business to be aware of his own im- pressions of the other person, whereas in usual social intercourse one tends to be less scrupulous about remarking upon these impressions.

The above paragraphs written about Ralph are based on the Counselor's reactions to him from the moment of saying "Hello." Meeting him starts a process of association in the mind of the therapist; in this case, the Counselor has many associations to Ralph—to his appearance, manner, inability to concentrate, returning home to his parents, being preoccupied by thoughts of his sweetheart, and wanting to go out for coffee or water while trying to study.

Thoughts come flooding into a therapist's mind not only in response to the immediate impressions but out of past experience with other clinical cases, out of training and reading in psychotherapy, out of an accumulation of knowledge gathered from novels and human relationships and out of the manifold non-verbal clues communicated by the client.

Subsequent interviews will correct, verify, amplify and elucidate the first impressions. Certainly the therapist considers all these thoughts strictly hypothetical until they are verified many times in many interviews. Even then, the formulation in the therapist's mind may never be spoken aloud as such. It is important to make this distinction between what goes on in the free associations of the therapist and what is given to the client. Following the parallel development of interview and discussion will provide an example of this difference between what is thought and what is spoken by the therapist (50).

C-7: One of the elements of depression is repressed, unbearable rage. Ralph's depression is obvious and conscious. The counselor makes a mental note to watch for sources of rage, where it began, what perpetuates it and why he has had to repress it and accumulate it instead of paying it out in small coin.

R-10: Being told he "does not belong in college" must have been a severe blow to Ralph's self-confidence. "You do not belong," strikes at a fundamental need for belongingness, and thus carries overtones of rejection far beyond the problem of needing to learn good steady habits. It is one thing to be told: "You need to learn how to study," and quite another: "You are not college material." One problem has been contaminated by the other. The two will have to be separated and clarified for Ralph, else he will carry with him the self-doubt, "I am not good enough," and, "I do not belong in college." This quality of basic self-doubt does not belong in the same category with, "I need to learn more efficient study habits."

His difficulty with concentration is not new; it dates back to high school, and perhaps to "all his life." This corroborates the feeling the counselor had that Ralph is worn out with fighting a long, long battle.

The description of how his eyes behave when he reads indicates the importance of another eye examination, to make certain that the diagnosis of "a slight astigmatism" is correct.

Ralph finds himself "all out of breath, just reading." This is an interesting and challenging symptom.[1] What does it mean? Since he assures the counselor, later in the interview, that a fairly recent medical examination found him in excellent health, the symptom of breathlessness has to be explained in other than medical terms. It brings to mind the work by Ribble (52), who showed the relationship between "mothering" and the establishment of strong postnatal respiration. She states, "Despite the fact that oxygen is plentiful in the air, the infant continues to be in want because of the immaturity of the breathing apparatus and also because his body is adjusted to breathing by way of that highly important prenatal organ, the placenta. . . . 'Mothering' a newborn baby helps him to breathe by bringing into action certain nervous reflexes which insure proper and necessary respiration. The importance of mothering in helping the child to breathe at such a time (during the early postnatal period) can hardly be overstressed." She goes on to say that, "Good breathing determines smooth speech development and is, throughout life, closely related to both physical and mental health."

When Ralph speaks of his breathlessness, one wonders whether a habit of shallow breathing dates back to his early postnatal days. Why does he specify that *reading* makes him breathless? The counselor's association to this is a case presented by Sylvester and Kunst, who told of a boy who said, "I can't read because my mother's face is between me and the page (38)." What connection may all this have with Ralph's reading problem and breathlessness when reading? The counselor has the thought that there may be a story of a mother from whom it has been difficult to obtain closeness, intimacy, soft "mothering." Again, the reader is cautioned to remember that these are hypotheses that the counselor keeps in mind and does not speak of to Ralph.

R-12 and C-13: One might question the advisability of bringing the application blank into the interview at this point instead of setting it aside until the end of the session and encouraging Ralph to continue

[1] This symptom of breathlessness has subsequently been found in another reading case.

speaking of his tensions. The only thing to be said for introducing it here is that it follows Ralph's lead; he asked about fees, and the counselor responded to his question. It is, moreover, a mistake to regard the application blank as something apart from the interview. It can be a very useful and integral part of the interview. For example, it was important to observe with what painful, laborious care Ralph wrote, and with what strain and timidity the written characters were formed. He pondered a long time before answering the question about childhood diseases, because he could not definitely remember the exact age at which he had had one of the illnesses. Finally the counselor rescued him from this impasse by assuring him that the approximate age would suffice. This reassurance that absolute rightness was not required carried in itself a therapeutic value. It made a beginning in establishing for Ralph the fact that the counselor does not belong among those influences in his life that demand perfection.

Some useful, additional material is obtained from the application form, and, if the flow of the interview is not running along well, the material in the application form can be used as a springboard for interview discussion. In this case, however, to dwell on the written information would have meant deflecting Ralph from the things he wanted to talk about as evidenced by his going right back to the topic he had been talking about before.

It is learned from the application form that he has two sisters and no brothers, that he had a medical examination by the Army a few years previous, that there are no physical complaints except for the fact that his eyes tire quickly and that his family is Christian Scientist. (The Counselor tried subsequently to induce Ralph to get a physical examination, in order to make sure his breathlessness was given adequate medical attention, but he would not consent to it.)

In answer to the question, "Indicate how you think the Guidance Laboratory can be of assistance?" he wrote, "Show me my bad habits and how to correct them." This is the "tell me what to do" so characteristic of the helpless, dependent character structure. It also suggests an over-awareness of "bad habits," thus an over-critical attitude toward the self.

R-13 and C-14: This may seem like a small point, but it is a nice point in therapeutic technique, and one that occurs again and again. Ralph's question, "What were we talking about?" puts upon the counselor the responsibility for carrying the continuity of the interview. The counselor considers it more therapeutic for Ralph to carry that responsibility himself, for thus she is not encouraging his submissiveness nor his dependency. By saying, "What would you like to talk about?" she shifts the initiative from herself to him, and puts emphasis on his making a choice. It is important to recognize the emotional quality and meaning of this maneuver: On the face of it, it may look like rejection. He asks for something, and she refuses to give it. But she gives him something better than what he asked for; she gives him what he—the healthiest part of him—is *really*, or unconsciously, asking for. She gives him a vote of confidence and an opportunity for self-assertion. She gives him a chance to do what he would *like* to do, beginning at once the important therapy of freeing him from blind obedience to authority, from the concept of "*ought* to do." This is a small step, but it is one of the multiple small steps to self-confidence and independence. An example may clarify this further: Instead of rushing to tie a child's shoe laces, because this is swifter and more efficient, a good mother waits patiently while the child awkwardly experiments with the operation himself. In this way she does not rob him of one of the many, many little experiences that finally add up to self-assurance.

R-15 and R-16: The description of his parents does not fit the picture of what Ralph seems to be as he is thus far revealed. It is not likely that Ralph would be this helpless or despondent if his parents had not failed him in some fundamental way. This does not mean "blaming" the parents. If they failed him, they could not help it, it was part of failing themselves; but fail him they must have, else he would not find himself in his present state. One must wait to find out what they are truly like, and whether Ralph is protecting them consciously or self-deceptively. One gets the impression that Ralph is a passive child, idealizing the authority persons in his life and repressing his defiance, hiding from himself his criticism of those on whom he depends for love and emotional support. The more one needs to depend on another person, the more one tends to idealize that person, to make him worth depending on. The counselor's role here is patience and watchful waiting. It is too early for anything more. Perhaps when Ralph has had a chance to shift some of his dependency from his parents to her, he will feel less afraid to criticize them, to face his real feelings towards them.

R-17: This is spoken without much conviction. It is an effort to be brave and hopeful, but he has doubt about it. This is further evidenced by his next response: In R-18 he shows some question about his intelligence, and he has this confused with several other things, with his choice of a vocation and with his relationship to his future wife. (See R-19.)

This is an interesting example of how self-doubt can permeate every area of one's life. He speaks with equal perplexity and urgency about his studying, his ability to concentrate, his intelligence, his ability to provide financial security for his future wife and his choice of a vocation. Granted that these are logically interrelated, there is an underlying attitude of anxiety that colors his approach to each and all of these areas.

Against a background of clinical experience, one is prepared to see, in addition to the verbalized problems, indications of a possible sexual disturbance. He is perhaps more deeply concerned about providing sexual adequacy to his marriage than financial security. It is well known that in men the sexual pattern and creative work pattern reflect each other. In other words, the causes of sexual impotency would be expressed in impotency in scholastic productivity. Both kinds of impotency are symptomatic of an underlying disturbance in self-confidence, and, instead of treating the symptoms, one tries to reach the underlying disturbance. Then, both kinds of impotency are cleared up simultaneously. It is interesting to note that Ralph introduces very quickly his doubts about his ability to provide for a wife. It is as though he unconsciously "knows" that his school problems and his sexual problems are linked together by a common cause, and he presents them more clearly than he realizes.

R-20: The father and the instructor have both told Ralph he is not capable or competent. The instructor said he did not belong in college; the father said he did not belong in engineering, and that he has "made mistakes." Now the task is to arrive at an evaluation of his capacities based on his own feelings after he builds some self-confidence and can overcome the negative propaganda to which he has been subjected. It is becoming increasingly clear that he does not feel strong enough to make choices. He does not know what he wants because he is confronted with his self-doubts no matter which way he turns.

C-21 through C-23: This is an interesting and good development, leading to Ralph's first smile of the interview (See R-23). When the counselor assured Ralph that it is not shameful—on the contrary, pleasant—to have sexual fantasies, he suddenly became more lively in manner. The counselor's attitude toward his sexual preoccupations seemed to break the ice for him; it was perhaps just at this point that he started to be aware of something new and different in this counseling environment. Perhaps he had a feeling that here he could feel safe in unburdening himself, because his voice became louder and more vital, his appearance more spirited, and he wanted to prolong the interview, as though he had found something good to which he wanted to cling.

R-24: The parents' wish that their son finish school before marrying is the usual attitude in our society. However, in recent years more and more parents have recognized that the standard, "You must be able to support yourself before you marry," is an arbitrary hurdle, not really an indication of preparedness for marriage. Providing an allowance to one's child for the duration of his education has little to do with whether he is single or married. He is apt to study more effectively if his sexual life is a happy one, and he can begin to support himself and his wife—with her help, if she loves him—after graduation from college. The counselor felt the impact of Ralph's helplessness here. It was apparent that he was quite unable to fight for what he wanted, or even to formulate clearly his point of view.

R-25: This is a puzzle—why Ralph forgot to write on the application blank that he went to a military academy, and why he suddenly thought of it at the end of the interview.

R-26: Here Ralph gives us some information that is very helpful: His parents sent him to a military academy to get him away from girls. Now the picture is beginning to fill out a little bit. His parents, instead of rejoicing that their adolescent son was making the normal adjustment to heterosexuality and was showing an interest in girls, rushed him away from girls. What were they afraid of? Why did they feel it necessary to deprive him of female companionship?

What is learned about Jane? She will not let him have fun until he is through studying. Why doesn't she leave this up to him? This makes one suspect that Jane is like his mother, or that his mother is like Jane—no fun until studying is finished. Work and fun are separate entities. He secretly resents this, one would guess, and does not know he resents it.

At the start of this interview, Ralph spoke very slowly and almost inaudibly; near the end of the interview he spoke with animation and wanted to continue talking. At the beginning, he avoided the counselor's eyes and stared down at the floor; at the end, he looked directly at the counselor. This has been a good interview.

Second Interview with Ralph

The second meeting with Ralph was devoted to an eye examination using the Keystone Visual Survey Telebinocular.

Ralph was interested in the machine and was friendly and cooperative. The test indicated that Ralph's eyes, even with glasses, were not functioning properly, and counselor recommended that he see a physician for a thorough eye examination. He said he would go back to the man who had prescribed his glasses, but, because of his Christian Science beliefs, he did not wish to consult a physician.

For the same reason, it was not possible to obtain a medical report on Ralph's general physical condition.

Third Interview with Ralph

This was a two hour session, with Rorschach test administered by counselor. As counselor set out the materials, Ralph began talking:

R- 1:   Jane did a Stanford-Binet test on me the other night. She said I had 126 or 130 I.Q.

C- 1:   That's an eminently adequate I.Q. How did you happen to take the test?

R- 2:   Well, I was talking to her about school here, and that I thought I would sometimes get an I.Q. test. She said she could give me one. I said, "Sure, there's nothing we can lose." So last Saturday we went up to my room. She was very strict about the whole thing. (Laughing.) She wouldn't let me cheat. Not that I wanted to. It was just a joking manner I had at the time.

Here the Rorschach was given. In the remaining half-hour, the following interview took place:

R- 3:   I spoke to the optometrist this morning. He said that my eyes are quite all right. He said my eyes would tire because of lack of proper reading habits. He told me to go to the Reading Clinic at Columbia (laughs) and that they do good work and could help me. He didn't know that I've been coming here. (Chuckles with pleasure, as though sharing a joke with counselor.) He knows me from when I was a little boy, and he told me of an incident, and I then remembered it. He said that my trouble goes way back to the second grade—that he remembers that my mother asked the school not to pass me because she felt I didn't have good reading habits. So I must have been having trouble with reading way back there. He said, "You had the same problem back at that time. It wasn't corrected then, and it should have been."

C- 3: In the second grade your mother asked your teacher to keep you back a grade?

R- 4: Yes. My teacher wanted to pass me. I remember I had a good report card, but my mother insisted I ought not pass.

C- 4: How did you feel about it?

R- 5: I remember I felt pretty bad. All my friends passed, and I didn't. My marks were good, but she felt I wasn't a good reader. She would make me sit at the table and read to her aloud every night. And I didn't like it too much. She wanted me to read, but sometimes I would find her sound asleep while I was reading to her, or she would bawl me out if I didn't get something right. So it would make me terribly nervous. It was the same in arithmetic. She'd have the answers on the back of the cards, and she'd look at the answers herself.

C- 5: I wonder if you didn't feel betrayed by your mother—because she went to your school and told your teacher not to pass you.

R- 6: I must have because I still can feel how terribly hurt I was by it. It seems to me I had an inferiority complex after that. I felt I *had* to do something to prove myself, so I turned to athletics, and finally I could beat the others in skating and tennis. With my dad—well, I still can't feel I can get as close to my father as I would like to. I can no more go out and take a walk with Dad . . . ! It's just impossible. I finally wrote him a letter last year saying there is a barrier between us like a brick wall. I told him I wanted to be able to talk to him. There isn't a man on earth I couldn't talk to easier than my dad. That goes way back, too. I remember when I was a little kid,

I'd be making model planes, but if I heard him coming into the room, I'd have to hide them until he went away again. I couldn't work on them if he was around. (Sits quietly.)

C- 6: (After a brief wait.) Tell me more.

R- 7: Sometimes he objects to my visiting my fiancée so much. But my family is beginning to see I'm a man, and they've got to let me do what I want! (Defiantly.) I don't know. . . . I'd like to get things worked out with my folks, but there's that barrier. I just remembered something else about my mother. I was a little kid. . . . I remember sitting in class. . . . It was a room in the basement. And I looked up out of the window and suddenly saw my mother walking up to the school. I began to shake all over, I was so scared. She walked right into the class room, didn't say a word to the teacher or anybody, walked right to my seat, and began to beat me. I can still hear the teacher pleading with her, "Please don't beat that little boy!"

C- 7: What was it all about?

R- 8: The teacher was keeping me after school to help me with my spelling, and my mother thought it was to punish me. So she came to punish me, too.

C- 8: So, again you felt betrayed by your mother.

R- 9: I was awful scared, I know that.

C- 9: Isn't it customary for little children to go to their mothers for support and safety and understanding?

R-10: I see what you mean. I was scared of her instead of feeling she would understand. (His face is flushed.)

C-10: You must have been enraged. That was unfair treatment.

R-11: I know I felt pretty terrible.

C-11: I wonder if you have let yourself see your rage.

R-12: Well, what can I do about it now? It's in the past. It wouldn't do any good to go back there now and tell her.
I feel worried about one thing right now. I don't want anything to interfere with my marriage with Jane.

C-12: Are you afraid anything will?

R-13: Well, not knowing what work I'm going to do, and all that, and leaving college. And I keep thinking about her, wondering where she is and what she is doing.

C-13: Wondering where she is and what she is doing?

R-14: Yes, I can't seem to get her out of my mind. (Quite agitated.)

C-14: Are you afraid she also will not be your pal—like your mother?

R-15: Gosh, I wouldn't be able to stand it if she let me down!

C-15: I think I'll ask you a funny question: Have you ever trusted any woman?

R-16: (Laughs shortly.) Well. . . . Oh, sure! A few. Well, no, I guess I never really felt sure. . . . (He appears and sounds so surprised by this that both counselor and Ralph burst out laughing.)

(Counselor noticed that the time for the session was a little more than over. Ralph followed her out of the room after she indicated the time was up.)

R-17: I know what you mean, but what do we do about it?

C-17: (Laughing.) I wonder if you are saying to me, "What are *you* going to do about it." This is going to be your responsibility. I'll do my best to be helpful, but the real job is yours.

R-18: (Very animated.) It's like what my optometrist told me this morning: I'd better get myself straightened out, and it's about time! It should have been done long ago.

C-18: I must say good-bye for now. Give my regards to Jane.

R-19: How did you know!

C-19: Tomorrow is Saturday, isn't it?

R-20: (Chuckling.) This week I won't see her until Sunday. But I'll give her your regards!

Discussion of the Third Interview with Ralph

This is a good interview because of the rapid movement toward more freedom of self-expression. Ralph becomes aware of the possibility of seeing his emotional problems. He begins to sense his repressed rage and discovers it is safe to discuss it. He begins to view his parents in a new light, and he is accepting the counselor's attitude: "You are free here to face more frankly your attitudes to your parents and to other authorities." This does not mean that the counselor is encouraging blind defiance towards authority, but the courage to perceive clearly the authority persons as real people rather than as symbols. "You are free here," does not mean the freedom of irresponsibility, but, rather, the freedom of individuality; this freedom is necessary to help him begin to enjoy responsibility.

Perhaps the Rorschach Test ought to have been administered by someone other than the counselor. Taking a test is a submissive experience, a dependency experience, unrelated to the treatment relationship and possibly a threat to the development of the relationship. When the counselor gives a test, she becomes the "testing authority," and Ralph is, for that period of time, submissive to her. However, from another point of view, it is helpful to the counselor to see how Ralph behaves during a test experience. It also gives her an opportunity to try to introduce some reconditioning, by making the testing experience as informal and as free of tension as possible.

SUMMARY OF THE RORSCHACH FINDINGS

Ralph's Rorschach responses revealed a very good intelligence which is functioning sluggishly and below capacity because of emotional disturbance. He is suffering from acute anxiety, and he experiences overwhelming fear when challenged to meet new situations. He seems to be quite immature and passive. His way of relating to authority is to be submissive.

He seems to sense his mother as implacable, unyielding and far away. He worships his father's authority, magnifying it and kneeling before it.

He seems to anticipate failure and to expect others to laugh at him because of his helplessness. There undoubtedly is a sexual problem because though he has a good capacity for sensual experiencing and a great hunger for closeness, he does not have the sense of personal authority to enable him to function on a self-accepting basis. His vitality has been damaged, and he feels trapped and unable to enjoy or express his basic impulses, his emotional and sensual self.

There is enough health in the record to make the prognosis favorable if this young man receives help in working through his emotional problems. One of his responses is a vivid description of his present stage of struggle. He says of the usual animals on Card VIII: "Then I noticed the animals . . . with one foot stuck in some substance, I don't know what. . . ." (Tell me more.) "Well, they are trying to get their leg free. They're just beginning the struggle. It's a rather large animal; it could be the size of a dog." (This is an interesting insight into his self-concept and his own unconscious measure of his vitality and aggressiveness. He thinks of a dog as a "big animal," whereas this particular configuration is often seen as a "bear," a "predatory panther," and other really large creatures—large in size and vitality.)

"This foot is in the air in search of more support, in order to pull this other one free."

Psychotherapy might well provide this support that Ralph needs in order to pull himself free from the forces that have trapped his energies. He is "just beginning the struggle," and needs help to struggle successfully.

This interview reveals some pertinent and helpful information about Ralph's mother. On the basis of this information, added to what we know of Ralph, we can hypothesize that she is a frightened, immature person, who needed her little son to be wonderful, perhaps because she was emotionally dependent on him. An immature mother may use her child as a mother, and obtain emotional sustenance from him without being able to give emotional sustenance. She is a baby leaning on a baby.

Ralph's refusal to read may stem partly from a refusal to answer her dependency needs. Perhaps the mother punished him so severely because of unconscious guilt over her unconscious emotional exploitation of her little son. She thus undermined his self-confidence and produced rage in him and made him helpless. He defeats her by not giving her the successful son she wants. He says, in effect, "I'll give myself to you, but not as you want me." He escapes her by his self-defeat.

Fourth Interview with Ralph

R- 1: I have a new problem: I was offered a job.
    (Looks brightly at counselor.)
C- 1: Oh, wonderful! What kind of job?
R- 2: It's working in a record shop, phonograph records.
    (His voice is apologetic.)
C- 2: That's fine. I love records. It must be fun to sell them to people.
R- 3: Yes, I enjoy it. You meet a lot of people, and all kinds of people, and I like that. But the problem is about when you'll be able to see me, because I'll be working days, and Saturdays. Can you see me in the evening? And could I come twice a week?
C- 3: I could see you at 6:15 Mondays and Wednesdays. Can you get here by then?
R- 4: Yes, that would be just fine. Are you sure it won't inconvenience you?

C- 4:   Not at all.

R- 5:   Fine. Thank you very much. Now I want to tell you about an experience I had this week that was not so good. I started out to my fiancée's home. Her father had a turkey farm as a hobby. He passed on last spring, and they've kept the turkeys up to now. But now Jane's mother has been finding it too much, so they wanted to get rid of the turkeys. So I thought I would be killing turkeys last Saturday. Before I left the house, I said to my mother, "Don't be surprised if I can get you some turkeys, but don't be disappointed if I can't get any. I'm not promising, so don't count on it." So I went up there, and I found that she had already killed the turkeys and had given them all away. A lot of people had been very nice to her after her husband died, so naturally she felt she wanted to give them something.

I came home, and my mother was probably tired after doing some housework, and she said, "Where are all those turkeys?" I told her, "I told you not to count on it." Well, she started talking about how selfish Mrs. ⸺ is, how unthoughtful she is, and all that. You see, Mother had invited Jane and her mother for a big dinner, so she said, "I can do that for them, but they can't do anything for me." You know, when she talked like that, I sort of saw hate in my heart very much at that moment. Because I love Jane and her mother very much. Another thing came up. Mom said she wanted my car this weekend. I took the car, and I deprived her of a chance to go to a party. I was very much upset by what she had said about Jane and Jane's mother, so I was glad to deprive her of the car.

C- 5:   Was there no other means of transportation to the party?

R- 6:   Oh, she's too good for a bus, or a train, or even to ever walk. She could get there all right, but she won't go unless she has the car. She's got the car today, but I'll have it tomorrow. Mom wouldn't walk half a block to the store because she wouldn't walk that far, and she wouldn't carry bundles. Dad's car goes to work with him every morning. My car was my mother's car before they gave it to me. She forgets now that it's mine.

It really did dig in deep, what she said. I felt hatred in my heart because Jane's mother was *not* being selfish; she's not like that.

I tell Mom she can have the car when I'm not using it, but there's always hard feelings if she can't have it. My sister—she's seventeen, the younger one—is planning to get her driver's license this week, and she had planned using one of the cars Saturday to go to the country. So now there are three people who want the car.

C- 6: I notice you say "the" car instead of "my" car.

R- 7: Yes, that's how it is. (Laughs.) I spoke to my sister and I said to her, "If I didn't use the car, I'd give it to you to use Saturday. You asked for it first, and I'd *rather* give it to you." Well, my sister will go with her friends, and I'll take the car, and Mom probably won't go to her party because she won't take a bus or train.

C- 7: I guess she doesn't want to go very badly.

R- 8: That's true. I never thought of that. She just made me feel that I was making it impossible for her to go because I was taking the car.

Another thing came up that I want to tell you about. A boy friend wanted me to help him paint his boat. So I did. Then his mother said she would give us each five dollars if we would paint the white fence around their yard. I told my mother about it later, and she said, "I wouldn't pay you to do it for me. In the first place, I wouldn't ask you to do it; in the second place, if I wanted you to do it, I wouldn't pay you for it. You don't pay me for washing your clothes. I wash your clothes and I feed you, and I take care of your room, and I don't charge *you.*"

You know, that made me feel so bad. That made me feel like she felt she was doing me a favor by taking care of me and my things. It shocked me to realize that she is even thinking the way she is. I felt I could just as well go out and be a boarder somewhere. I felt that she doesn't do these things for me because she wants to or because she loves me.

I feel that my family doesn't have the love for one another that they should. I feel uneasy and on edge when I'm sitting near them. After supper at night I do the dishes, then I go up to my own room and shut the door. I don't run out without telling them where I'm going. I'm friendly, I'm not mean.

Another thing: After dinner I'll walk around for a few minutes, smoking a cigarette and thinking about what I'm going to do next. Without waiting a minute, my father says, "Why don't you go *do* something." That always makes me angry. So I feel nervous about that. Last night my mother said it to me, so I said to her, "Now don't say that to me any more. I'm tired of hearing it." She right away changed what she meant. She said, "I didn't mean it that way. I meant, why don't you do something for me. Why don't you put up the curtains for me." So I did. And I did tear one of them, but it was an accident.

There's always some kind of trouble and hatred. Right now, my mother is having trouble with my father's parents. There's plenty of hatred there. Every now and then I go see my grandparents, and they tell me quite a story about how hard they worked for my dad. Grandpa said he worked nights to put Dad through college. Then I go home and tell that to Dad, and he says, "What! Who told you that! I worked my own way through college. That guy never did a thing for me." Well, that's confusing, and I don't know who is right.

About my own parents . . . they've always said that whatever they do for me they are *giving* to me, with no wish for returns.

(Thoughtful and silent.)

C- 8: What are you thinking?

R- 9: It has always been a business of being strict with me, to keep me on the straight and narrow road. For example, I was in high school, and it was winter, and we were not allowed to go out after dinner. One night I asked Mom if I could go out for a half hour to go sleigh riding. She stuck to her law; she said I could not go. I went upstairs and tried to study, but I couldn't study because I was thinking of all my friends out sleigh riding. It seems to me, that if she had let me go out for a half hour I'd have been satisfied, and then I could have studied.

Everytime she'd say, "No!" I'd lose my breath. . . . It would hit me in the heart.

I learned to hold my temper, probably too much. I'd hold it

in, and then when I got someplace alone I'd have to cry. Because everytime I'd hear her saying, "No!" I'd feel *hit*. One night I figured I'd ask her if I could go out after supper to shovel snow off the front walk. That way, I could at least wave to the kids going by. (Sits silently, head down.)

C- 9:　Was that granted?

R-10:　Oh, sure. That was work, so she let me do it. I feel that my relationship with my family isn't right. There is no love in our home. Are other families like that, or is it just my family?

C-10:　Every family has stresses and strains, but we'll learn about your particular family through talking about it. Generalizing isn't too helpful. Let's get to know you and know your folks.

R-11:　Yes, I can see that. I want so much to get married . . . to get away from the folks. I'd be much happier. I felt happier when I was away at school, just so I didn't have to be at home. When I was in high school, they told me they noticed I liked women a lot, so Dad said, "How would you like to go away to military school?" I said, "No!" But they made me go. My marks weren't any better there than at high school. Then, after the first year I met Jane. After meeting her, my grades went up. After dinner I'd walk her home, and in the mornings I would meet her. So I learned to like military school.

C-11:　(Laughs.) You learned to like Jane's military school!

R-12:　(Laughs heartily.) That's just about it. She's wonderful.

C-12:　Well, our time is about up.

R-13:　All week I was conscious of waiting to see you again, of wanting to talk to you.

C-13:　I wonder how you would like to write to me if you feel like talking to me between visits. Just scribble down what you are feeling, and put it in an envelope and mail it to me here. That's not an assignment, but just a suggestion of a way to relieve yourself of pressure.

R-14:　Yes, that would help. Because last week I was just bursting, and I didn't want to tell Jane about what my mother had said, and I wished I could talk to you. If I had written it to you, I probably could have let off steam.

Discussion of the Fourth Interview with Ralph

Ralph continues to face his real feelings towards his parents. The way he feels, as expressed for instance by his statement (in R-8), "I feel uneasy and on edge when near them," reminds the counselor of one of his Rorschach responses: He is "the little fish swimming between two seahorses. The little fish meets an obstacle and can't get through, and they laugh at him." He has not told us that they laugh at him, actually, but he so fears his father's criticism and his mother's strict attitude (as in R-9) that he feels weak and laughable in his own self-appraisal. He is "the poor little fish." Feeling "hit in the heart" when frustrated by his mother may mean being hit by his own repressed rage, which later comes through in tears and also in his self-destructive trend.

Ralph's memories and feelings build a more complete picture of family relationships. It is not yet time to stimulate him to understand his parents' behavior; he needs now just to pour out the feelings that he has repressed for so long. It is a good thing that he feels sufficiently safe with the counselor to be able to expose negative feelings towards his family without being overwhelmed by guilt.

With regard to the counselor's suggestion (C-13) that he may write to her if he feels under pressure: It is usually considered best to discourage the writing out of emotional problems; they must be saved to be *spoken* to the therapist, so that action and reaction can take place, and he can hear himself speaking of his feelings. However, because the counselor was seeing Ralph only twice weekly, the counselor considered the writing an opportunity for Ralph to drain off pressure. As it turned out, he never did write to her, nor did he ever make notes. Perhaps the suggestion was not without some good effect, however, in that it conveyed to Ralph the counselor's interest in his comfort during the time he was away from her.

Fifth Interview with Ralph

Ralph appeared happy and relaxed today. He swung around in the swivel chair at the beginning of the interview and gave the impression of being pleased with himself.

R- 1: This week went along very nicely. Right now I feel **all right.** I don't know what's wrong. (Laughs.)

I've been doing some careful thinking. Would a fear of the future enter into the kind of thing we've been talking about?

C- 1: What would you think about that?

R- 2: Yes, I do think so. I have a problem about the future. I feel I should be making some money. Tonight Mom said that the upkeep of an automobile is quite expensive.

I'm planning to be married, as you know. I don't know how because I have no definite prospects of earning money. The job I'll take on Friday is one I like very much, selling in this music store. I do quite well at that, that's why they always call me back. But they don't need me permanently, just for special occasions, like for Christmas. I suppose I could get a job at forty or fifty dollars a week, but that isn't enough. I'd like to be able to give Jane everything I possibly can. I think she is spoiled, and I'm sure *I* am. My mother said that someday soon I'm liable to knock my nose against a wall financially. I don't know what she thinks I *should* do, but she warns me like that. I'm more or less all mixed up about what I'd like to do. I've always had the aim of becoming an engineer. I have no idea about business. I'd like to know what I *could* do best. I have a friend who's in the same spot I'm in, not knowing what he wants to do. He has always planned to go into his father's business. He's in the same boat I'm in. He wants to learn the business from the bottom up, but his father feels he should go to college and then start at the top. But *he* feels he is wasting his time at college because he would rather be learning the trade. So he's all mixed up. Like me.

Now, I've always thought I'd be an engineer. But I'm fearful of the work involved. Friends brighter than I have failed at it. And I haven't a chance to find out if I would like it. I can't *try* being an engineer. I feel I *should* go back to college. I've always been told that a person without college. . . . Well, there *are* many people without college educations who are successful. But the question is, after college what will I do?

C- 2: You feel that if you go back to college now, you want to have a work goal planned out.

R- 3: Yes, it's time to figure out a goal to work for. If I could only find the best thing to do. Young fellas my age go out and buy a car, then they sell it, sometimes at more, sometimes at less.

I've never been able to do anything like that. I do have some money in a savings account. I've saved my allowances since childhood. My father has put it in the bank and I've been told not to touch it. If I took it out and invested it, I'd probably lose it all. (Quietly thoughtful.)

I'm worried, because I feel I want to give Jane everything, but I'm afraid I won't be able to.

C- 3: What sort of things do you enjoy doing just for the fun of it?

R- 4: Well, in college I always enjoyed the physical education department. I'd find more enjoyment in an hour in the gym than in a good movie or in many things. Come to think of it, a while ago our next-door neighbor said she always thought I'd turn out to be a physical education teacher, because I was always so crazy about things like that. Now I'm thinking about what I might be able to do in that line.

Say! (Sits forward in his chair, quite animated.) This really makes me think! I was speaking to a new man who came in for physical education up at home. He told me it was a regular four-year college course, not as much as with a B.S., though, because there was more physical education in it and less studying.

But that reminds me: I enjoy reading now a great deal more, and it's going along so much better. Somehow or other, nothing distracts my attention as it would have before. I've been doing a lot of reading this week and enjoying it. I was sitting at home reading, and suddenly I looked up and realized I'd been reading a long time without getting distracted. So I don't think I'd be so afraid of the college reading now. Especially, I wouldn't be so afraid of the work for physical education. (Quietly thoughtful.)

C- 4: What are you thinking?

R- 5: I was thinking about something that happened down at school. At the fraternity, one boy wondered how he could build himself up. I told him to come to the gym with me and we'd work out together. I was continuing my hobby of being in condition, and also helping him. I liked that. When I left college, he told me that he would miss me. I felt I had done something for somebody that they had really appreciated. (His voice is wistful as he says this.)

One day I was working out in the gym. I was lifting weights, and this other fella, a heavy-set fella, was watching me. I imagine he weighed close to two hundred pounds. He said, "Those weights don't look heavy." I was lifting one-hundred-fifty pounds. He kept laughing at how easy it was going to be for him. Then he grabbed them and almost fell over backwards. (Laughs heartily.) Gosh! So I showed him how to do it. I showed him the knack of it. The other fella standing there watching us came over to me and asked me what I was studying. I told him engineering, and he said I would be a good man in the field of physical education. That was his field, and he said it would be a good field for me. It's funny, it didn't penetrate much at the time, but it seems to be coming to my mind now. I used to go to the gym and forget everything else, and it sure felt good. But I never really thought about it as *work.*

C- 5: Perhaps you thought work was not supposed to be fun.

R- 6: That's right. But why shouldn't it be? You probably could do better at something you really enjoyed doing.

The more I think of it, the more pleased I am that I dropped out of college when I did. Because now this new idea really does excite me. It's quite an inspiration.

The fact that I now have something to tell Jane, that I have an idea about what I'd like to do. . . . I like that.

C- 6: You planned to go into engineering to please your parents; now you are grasping at this new idea just to have something to tell Jane?

R- 7: No! (Face very intense and eager.) This is really something I want to work at and find out more about. Anybody who wants to jump on my train can come along, and if they don't want to they don't have to . . . but I know where I'm going! Right now I'll find out all I can about physical education. Except that I'll be working now until after Christmas.

I still feel the problem about money, though. If a person had a lost uncle. . . . Say that I had a lost uncle, and he left me a considerable sum of money, and I went back to college, and I had nothing to worry about financially. . . . I'd do much better, wouldn't I? I worry too much about money.

C- 7: Tell me more about it.

R- 8: Well, Jane is spoiled, and I'm continuing to spoil her. She plans a trip this winter, to go South, but I'm afraid she'll have to go alone; I can't afford it. There are times when she doesn't want to spend money. But I think she is influenced by her college friends. They all go to Florida, so she wants to go, and all that. Last summer, being away from college, we did so much less and spent so much less. I remember, though, once when I wanted to spend money and she wouldn't let me. (Proudly.) We wanted to go into town, and it was terribly cold, and finally I wanted to take a taxi instead of waiting for the bus. She said, "You go alone, then, and I'll take the bus." So we waited and took the bus and saved the money. We just stood out on the cold highway until the bus came.

I think I have been spoiled a lot. I hear of other kids who had to go out and sell newspapers when they were young. I never did sell papers or get odd jobs. Am I irresponsible?

C- 8: I don't know. Are you?

R- 9: (Laughs.) I don't know. Am I? Sometimes I think maybe I am.

C- 9: We'll have to find out, won't we. Suppose we continue with that in our next session, since our time is running over. And if we think you are irresponsible, we will have to understand what we mean by that and what causes it.

R-10: I don't *want* to be irresponsible, but maybe I am.

C-10: If you are, that must mean your energies are flowing elsewhere rather than toward being responsible, so we have to see where your energies are going, or where they are tied up. Okay?

R-11: Yes. And I hope you have a nice Thanksgiving.

(Pleasant farewells, and the hour was terminated.)

Discussion of the Fifth Interview with Ralph

Ralph begins the session with a nice feeling of relaxation and relief from pressure. He shows initiative, introducing the idea of having done "some careful thinking." (R-1.) It reveals that Ralph is beginning to think in a new way, becoming accustomed to searching for self-knowledge, moving more expansively in this process and learning to relate insights one to another. (R-1 and R-2.)

The information contained in R-3 is a fine illustration of how money in the bank can give a person a feeling of financial and emotional poverty—if the process of putting the money in the bank is carried out as it was by Ralph's father. Here, in Ralph's description of the handling of his allowance, is an excellent picture of his confusion about his own identity: *"I've* saved my allowances since childhood. *My father* has put it in the bank and *I've been told* not to touch it." It is nominally *his* allowance, but actually and emotionally it is his father's money, his father's power. His father had no faith in Ralph's ability to take care of his own money; now Ralph has no faith in himself: "I'd probably lose it all." Also, there is undoubtedly a wish to lose it all, since it really has never been his anyhow.

The counselor's way of dealing with Ralph's question, "Am I irresponsible?" (R-8 through C-10) is important in terms of therapeutic technique. The temptation is to give reassurance, to say, "Oh, no, I'm sure you are not irresponsible!" However, this might not be the truth. The counselor sought clarification, and by so doing said in effect, "Let us look together for the truth of the matter, fearlessly." This attitude of not making a fuss about it one way or another, but of coolly finding out the facts is more reassuring than "reassurance." In fact, straight "reassurance" may stir up anxiety. For example, if the counselor had said, "Oh, no, you are not irresponsible, I'm sure!" or, "Don't worry, you couldn't help it," Ralph's reaction might well be as follows: "She feels that I am fragile, weak and frightened; she feels it is necessary to bolster my ego; that means I must be in pretty bad shape." (This might be consciously thought or unconsciously sensed.) Other reactions are also possible. He might feel, in effect: "She feels that irresponsibility is morally so bad that she tries to comfort me by telling me *it can't be* that I'm irresponsible. If she feels *that's* so bad, what would she feel about my other *worse* faults!" Then the communication between Ralph and the counselor would not be a good and useful and complete one because he would try to prevent the counselor from finding out what a disappointingly bad boy he really is, and would continue his fear of exposing his weaknesses. Thus, his rigid self-criticism, instead of being alleviated by "reassurance," would be reinforced, and the therapeutic process would not go forward.

The counselor works toward clarification, and clarification leads to strength and reassurance derived from within, by making the self-judgment more rational, more tolerant, more related to reality factors.

Sixth Interview with Ralph

R- 1: How are you today?

C- 1: I'm very well, thank you. How are you?

R- 2: I feel fine. (Settles himself comfortably in the armchair, ties his shoelace, and then proceeds as follows:)
Now, what have you found out about me?

C- 2: What have you found out about yourself?

R- 3: Well, I've changed my future again this week.
(Laughs, infectiously, causing counselor to laugh, too.)
Yessir, I think I've changed it again. I'm thinking that the first thing I should do is go back to college and finish my degree. I think a B.A. degree instead of a B.S. I met someone this week who told me about an interesting business plan. I'll tell you about it.

C- 3: Yes, please do.

R- 4: Well, after college, you go to this place in New York, where you work as a salesman in a department store, and they pay you two hundred dollars. You move from one department to another, selling all kinds of things, until you learn. After about a year—I think it takes a year—they guarantee you a job as an executive in a department store. Now, I was thinking. I like selling to people. And it's a very good future. Someday I can start a business like the one I'm working in now. You know, we have a variety of merchandise, and it's interesting. Along with the records department we have a section of gifts, toys, a little jewelry, men's ties, all that. . . . I like it very much, and I like people. I have no trouble selling people things. I must be all right because they have asked me every year to come back to help out at Christmas.
Well, my next step will be just to finish college. I think that line of work will be better than teaching. There isn't enough in teaching. It's nice, but I'd have a hard time.
I feel good, because I think I'm off to a good start.
I was speaking to a fella outside the store. He was starting out to be an athletic coach, a teacher. The more I thought about it, the more doubt I had about it. Not only financially, but, also, I'd be afraid I'd get too old too fast.

(Counselor probably looked surprised at this, because Ralph responded quickly in explanation:)

R- 5: Of course, others do it. We have a fella, an *old* fella, down at college. Of course, he can't do the work he used to be able to do, yet I don't see him leaving the school. I don't really know why I feel that way about it. I guess I feel I can make more in business than teaching. My boss I'm working for at home agrees with me and thinks it's a good idea. He's the manager, and he worked himself up to being manager. He said he'd like to see me in business, buying and selling goods. You don't have to go into just buying and selling; you can go into any branch of it you choose.

I was speaking to Jane about it. One of her girl friends has a boy friend graduating from Wisconsin. He's going to go into this. I can find out more about it through him. Jane can find out for me.

I've talked to more people lately who are interested in working in stores. Does everyone enjoy this kind of work, selling?

C- 5: I wonder why you ask that.

R- 6: Well, I know that every now and then I have to put a false smile on. Sometimes people want to listen to *all* your records and look at *all* your merchandise, when you're terribly busy. Of course, I haven't tried the wholesale side of business. That's quite a problem in itself. If you're working for a large outfit, it's different.

It would be nice to have a little store of my own. Maybe haberdashery instead of gifts and records. But I'd have to work for someone else first, and get to know the business thoroughly. This store I'm working at now, the owners are wealthy though young, and it's a very good business. The boss isn't good at selling. I'm better at selling than he is. I'm good at that. I have more patience, to show customers more things, than he has. Yet, you have to use a little psychology, too. If you show them too much, then they can't make up their minds.

Speaking of psychology. . . . When I was taking child psychology, I didn't find the reading difficult for that. I had a common-sense background on children, so that made it easier. After all, I knew something about children because I've *been* a child. It isn't like dissecting a frog, which is all new. The psychology teacher bothered me, though. He used all psychological terms in the course in general psychology, and I was not acquainted with those terms.

C- 6: How do you feel about going back to college studying?

R- 7: Now, that's a funny thing. I feel so different about it. I can't explain it, but I feel more confidence in myself. I feel that the problem was in concentration. Now I feel I could go right ahead and forget other things and read. Of course, I know I do have a tendency to worry. One fact I did worry about was that I didn't know what I was going to do. Right now my main idea is to get my college education completed. I was worrying about my marriage because I didn't know what I was going to be doing—I couldn't give any definite ideas. This time when I go back, I'll know right where I'm heading.

I think I *do* like to work with people. Of course, people are not as honest as you'd like them to be at times. For example, a person came into the store today, and I wasn't sure whether he was honest or dishonest. I don't recall whether he gave me three dollars or four dollars. I asked him how much money he gave me, and he said he gave me four dollars. The thing that made me suspicious was that he whispered something to his friend as they went out. He seemed to want to hurry, and now I'm not sure whether he was dishonest or not. Right away I wanted to put a dollar in the register to make it up. But I'll find out tomorrow. . . .

(Sits quietly, looking out the window.)

C- 7: What are you thinking?

R- 8: (Swings around to face counselor.) I'm thinking that *any* career will have its ups and downs. It's like that saying, "True love doesn't run smooth." Oh, I want to tell you about a talk I had with Jane. I said to Jane, "Do you expect a lot from me?" Saturday night we were up until two o'clock talking this thing over. We *have* been spending some money, and I'm thinking there's no need for spending money just because we feel like it. Jane said she wants her children to be able to have an education and to have nice things. That she wouldn't feel happy if we were scratching bottom for our food. What she is asking is not too much. There's nothing she would say or do to discourage me in any way. I asked her, "Would you be able to stick it out with me?" And, "Do you *love* me?" I said to her, "You're not marrying me for high financial standing? You weren't marrying a professional man? Would you marry me if I were a ditchdigger?"

She said, "There isn't a woman who is satisfied to scrape for enough money for food. I'll be honest with you: I would be unhappy, but I would stick with you through the thick and the thin."

You see, I was worried. Would she go back to mother, or would she stick it out with me? She wanted to know, did I think she was expecting too much, and I told her yes, that I had thought perhaps she was expecting too much. But then when she told me she wants her children to have a nice home and a good education, that's the same thing *I* want.

This weekend I spent only fifty cents, so I saw that she doesn't always have to spend money. My mother gets the feeling we go to the movies an awful lot, but we don't go more than once a week.

Jane said, "Do *you* think I spend too much money?" I realized I was wrong, and that it was my mother's idea, not *my* idea.

Then we were playing bridge. Jane knows bridge very well. Dad thinks he knows *his* game of bridge very well. Dad bawls Mother out all the time. Jane told me she couldn't possibly tell Dad what she thought was wrong with his game. And that's like me, too, because I couldn't tell him either. If I tried to tell Dad anything, he'd just continue thinking the way he does. Actually, this was the very first time I came right out and discussed things with Jane. I put all the cards on the table.

C- 8: That must have been a relief.

R- 9: Oh, it *was*! I should have done it long ago. Jane, though, was tearful because she thought I was accusing her. I explained that I wasn't accusing her. But suddenly I realized it was my mother's influence, not my own idea.

C- 9: I guess you are realizing that a man old enough to marry is old enough to think for himself.

R-10: That's right! Like last week . . . I told Mom I was taking my car to drive to the bridge. It's just a short trip, but she told me it was a lot of wear and tear on the car. Yet she'll take it just that distance to do her shopping. So I went ahead and used it. I figured it out that it would have cost me thirty cents without the car and a lot of time lost, so I figured it paid to use the car, and I used it. (Looks at counselor, waiting.)

C-10:   Good.

R-11:   Yes, just generally I feel more confident in myself. And I am gradually learning not to worry. And I enjoy reading more than when I first walked into this office. Also, I have a clearer conception of my future. Somehow, I feel freer. And I don't have to "give up" the way I used to feel. Now I know the world won't come to an end, and I guess I used to think it might have.

C-11:   That's good work, Ralph. Shall we stop here?

R-12:   Okay. (Then, while putting on his coat:) A lot of people worry about things that don't concern them. For example, people worry about France and Germany, and about war. I *think* about it, but I don't *worry* about it. If war does come, I'll *have* to think about it, so I'll think about it then. I'm not going to worry now about it. And about exams . . . I learned to say to myself after an exam, "You've taken the exam, you tried your best, now forget it."

Discussion of the Sixth Interview with Ralph

The flow of self-discovery continues. Ralph shows an increasing emergence of self-respect, with more courage to face situations that disturb him. He explores his relationship with his sweetheart, discussing with her problems that have been troubling him but which he had never before dared to talk about. He is exploring his interests, and he is becoming more flexible in his goals: "Any career will have its ups and downs."

However, one must not be too quick to see this as a firmly incorporated new attitude. When he says, "Any career will have its ups and downs," he has not really achieved this attitude, but at least he is aware of working towards it. The process of therapy is just beginning, and he has a long way to go to get rid of old established ways of feeling and to take on new ones. There is a burst of hopefulness and enthusiasm at the start because a new life beckons and there is a promise of freedom from old shackles. This has often been referred to as "the honeymoon" stage of psychotherapy, the period before the long hard task of patiently incorporating slowly earned gains, before the disappointments of inevitable "set-backs" and lapses into old patterns. This is the hopeful period before one learns how difficult it is to change. For example, one may recognize the need to give up perfectionism, and at the same time try to become *more perfect* through the psychotherapeutic process, rather than trying to establish reasonable, possible, practical, rational goals.

Why is Ralph so on guard against Jane's expecting too much from him? One may hypothesize that he is really projecting his own great hunger. He has not been given enough affection, and, therefore, cannot give to someone else out of abundance. He wants to give Jane a great deal, perhaps too much, reasonably and rationally speaking, because he measures her hunger by his own.

Seventh Interview with Ralph

Ralph walks in slowly, sits down in chair at desk, and puts his hand over his eyes.

C- 1: You seem dejected tonight.

R- 1: Yes, I had an experience last night I'd like to tell you about. (Long pause.) First, here's a receipt for you. I just paid my fees in the Guidance Laboratory.

C- 2: Thank you. You may keep the receipt. I'll make a note that you are paid up.

R- 2: (Settles down to tell counselor the following story:) Well, here's what happened. We have a stairway in our house, and it curves a little—that is, the railing curves—as it reaches the bottom. There's a sort of nook right there with a little table, and on the table there's a pretty little marble statue. It was a gift to Dad from one of his customers. Well, last night I was coming down the stairs and Dad was just approaching the stairs to start up. He had some boxes in his arms, and he didn't watch his elbow. He hit this statue and it fell with a crash. Then, instead of admitting he had run right into the thing with his elbow, he said it was my fault, because I crowded him coming down the stairs. Yet, I was several feet away from him when it happened, so how could I have been crowding him. That really got me angry. He was looking for an excuse, so he said it was my fault. I didn't say a word to him, but I thought to myself, "I hope *I* don't always have to find an excuse for *my* mistakes."

He had to have an excuse. I said to Mom, "Why didn't he just admit he didn't watch where he was going?"

C- 3: Why didn't you say it to him, rather than to your mother?

R- 3: *What?!* No, I couldn't say it to him. He wouldn't listen. It would just make him mad. But I didn't let it upset me.

C- 4: Why not?

R- 4: It was so stupid, I wouldn't let it bother me.

C- 5: Aren't you kidding yourself?

R- 5: What do you mean?

C- 6: Weren't you very upset?

R- 6: Yes, I suppose I was. I *was* angry. But I didn't see any need to do anything about it.

C- 7: Isn't it better to recognize that you are upset, rather than to try to convince yourself that you are not upset?

R- 7: Yes, I see what you mean. It's silly to pretend that I'm not angry when I really am. I suppose I feel it anyhow. You mean, I should get it out of my system.

C- 8: Yes. Relieve yourself of the strain of pretending to yourself.

R- 8: Well, I think that if he still held it against me today, I'd have to tell him how I felt about it. But today I know he is probably only mad about the statue and has forgotten me. Otherwise, I guess I'd want to tell him how I felt.

C- 9: If you carry secret resentments against him, you help build that wall between you that you told me about. If you thrash out your real feelings with him, you might build a closer relationship.

R- 9: But it's impossible to talk to Dad. When I told my sister that Dad broke the statue, she smiled and said, "Boy, I'm glad it wasn't me!" If it had been anyone but Dad, we'd never have heard the end of it.

One thing I have learned from the experience: that if I am wrong, I want to admit it.

I guess I felt he didn't really mean what he said, that he just had to say *something*. Because, at the movies last night, he was friendly and joking with me.

Dad is a funny person. This past week Dad and Mom had a quarrel. It was awful silly, really it was. And this time I'm sticking up for Mom. I really am. *This* time.

You see, Dad goes to meetings, and on other nights he goes to his motorcycle club. Mom sits up until he gets home, and then they go to bed. One night last week, my aunt did my mother's shopping for her, and she had groceries at her house for her. Mom said she was going to pick up the groceries, and she asked Dad if he would like to go along. He said no. She said she would also stop and see my older sister. That was all okay. Well, Mom went and picked up her groceries. Then she stopped and talked with my aunt for an hour. They are sisters, and they like to talk when they get started. That's natural. Well, when she got home, my dad was so mad, he just roared at her. "Where were you! What took you so long! Here I am sitting home, and you stay away all this time!" When Mom heard that, she really blew her stack. Boy, oh boy! She told Dad how he goes out fifty times more often than she does. And it's true. It's only a couple of years that Dad has given up a bridge club to spend a few evenings with his family. But then he is never home anyhow. He goes to a great many meetings. And some nights he has to work, so he's out every night in the week. Mom said, "I never ask you why you are out so long!" She was thinking how unfair and narrow-minded he is. Mom said, "Every time you do have a spare moment, you go off on your motorcycle instead of staying with me."

Well, what I've learned from that is that Jane and I will settle any argument we may have before the night is over, and not let it go for days at a time. Because Dad and Mom didn't make up until this morning, and even then Dad wouldn't back down but said the foolish fight was Mom's fault.

(Long pause.)

C-10: What are you thinking?

R-10: I'm thinking that really everything is going along pretty fine. Work at the store is slow, and I've had a lot of time to read. I'm reading *Sherlock Holmes,* and I'm reading three different newspapers and some magazines. Just to understand and enjoy the reading there at the store gives me satisfaction, because there are a great many distractions, yet I don't get distracted. I don't look up from my reading unless someone calls my name.

(Long silence.)

C-11: Tell me what you are thinking about.

R-11: About Dad and Mom.

C-12: You are making an effort to understand your parents.

R-12: (Enthusiastically.) Yes, I am! I'm watching them like I never did before, and I'm trying to understand them. I'm trying to understand their reactions.

Some cousins of mine were visiting us. They had their baby along. She's about eight months old, and awfully cute. We were playing together. I was on the floor and she was in her crib. She was playing with a toy dog, and she was getting temperamental. She was learning something about crying, that someone will give her a little more attention if she cries. No tears came; she just yelled. I went and offered to pick her up. She raised her arms and started smiling. She was very content when I brought her into the kitchen where the others were.

I was explaining to my father what the baby was doing, that crying was something she had learned as a way of getting attention. I guess I wanted to tell him something I knew from child psychology. I guess I felt he might recognize that I know *something*.

C-13: You need to prove to your father that you are a worthwhile person?

R-13: Oh, I do need that. I keep feeling I want to *tell* him, to *prove* something.

C-14: Why do you suppose you need that?

R-14: I don't know. I guess I never felt he considered me worthy. It must have started a long time ago. It has something to do with his wanting everything *perfect*. It's like the thing I told you about being afraid to work on model planes if he was in the room. I guess I'm doing the same thing with Jane, trying to prove to her that I'm a *man*! It's like my grades at college— wanting to be *sure* to pass all my courses. You know, it might just be something within *me*. Maybe *they* don't need it from me.

C-15:   You mean you are trying to prove yourself to yourself?

R-15:   Yes, because I remember that at college, in the beginning, I thought I would not be able to do college work. I worried that my family and Jane might think the same way I did.

I know now that I had the conception that college was much tougher than it really was. I *have* worked hard at college, and I expect to do better when I go back again. Now I feel I can concentrate much better. I can make a new start. This time I want to go with the idea of acquiring knowledge, not just to make marks or grades. It isn't the grade that really counts. For example, if a person is psychologically tied up on the day of the final exam, he may have done good work all semester and learned a lot, but not do well on the final.

I do feel different than when I first came here. Do you know, I feel a difference in the way my face feels. That sounds funny . . . but I do remember that my face always felt strained, as though the muscles were tense and tired. Now my face feels relaxed.

So far as Jane and I are concerned, it's definite that we are getting married this August. I told Mom, and she said, "Oh, dear, it'll be just when I start on my vacation."

I said, "Okay, Mom, if this wedding doesn't mean that much to you, that you can't postpone your vacation by two days, then don't come!"

Boy, I never used to talk like that! But the funny thing is that Mom has changed lately, too. Usually she flies off the handle, but now she backs down when I talk like that. I guess she knew I was really right about it.

But Dad would never back down, that I know. He stands on his dignity and he wouldn't admit he was wrong in a million years. After that fight with Mom, he wouldn't admit that he acted foolishly, but said that she was the one who was foolish. And he was the one who made the fuss because she stayed away for two hours.

C-16:   Why do you suppose he was so upset because she stayed away for two hours?

R-16:   I don't know, I'm sure. Mom feels he was just being narrow-minded and dictatorial. "Who does he think he is, to tell her she can't go out for two hours if she wants to."

C-17: Perhaps he is so dependent on her, he feels lost if she goes away for a little while. I don't know—I am only wondering what was beneath his behavior.

R-17: Maybe he needs a baby sitter! (Laughs.) I never thought of Dad that way. Yet, he certainly did act like a baby. I always thought of him acting so big and important.

C-18: Have you ever heard the old saying: "You don't need to be that big; you are not that small!"

R-18: I don't think I understand it. "You don't need to be that big; you are not that small . . . !"

C-19: Well, if a man feels like a baby, he has to pretend he's a general. Little boys play they are Superman. In a quarrel, the stronger person can admit he is wrong; the one who feels weak can't afford to admit guilt.

R-19: Oh, I get it! (Leans forward, eyes blazing.) I think you've got something there! That's like how he couldn't admit he knocked the statue off the stand. He just could not admit it was his fault. Dad *always* has to blame someone else. I have yet to hear him take the blame for anything he does wrong. But, you know, Mom was always afraid of Dad, so I had to be afraid of him, too. If *she* was afraid of him, golly, what could *I* do?

C-20: So you could not get strength from either of them.

R-20: No. That accounts, I guess, for why I was always afraid. It seems to me I just never stopped feeling afraid. Always afraid to try to do things, because I knew I couldn't do them the way Dad wanted me to do them.

C-21: He wanted you to be perfect?

R-21: Oh, *yes*! (His voice is tearful.) He never took into consideration that he was a grown man and I was a child. *He* could be perfect if he wanted to, but he should not have expected me to be perfect. All I ever felt was failure, failure, failure. (Wipes his eyes.)

C-22: Did you get the feeling it would be easier not to try a thing at all rather than risk failure?

R-22: (Heatedly.) That's exactly it! I always knew I would not be able to do a thing perfect enough to please him. That's why, I guess, I would hide my model planes if he came into the room. I knew he would criticize.

C-23: That's a tough spot to be in, isn't it.

R-23: You said it is! Why can't Dad be perfect himself, but leave me alone?

C-24: Do you think he gets strength or comfort from his perfectionism? Think about the incident of his knocking over the statue last night.

R-24: Why, last night he was *scared to death* when that happened. I wish you had seen his face. No kidding. He was so scared, he just could not admit he had done an awkward thing. He *had* to blame it on me.

C-25: Apparently he feels he cannot afford to make mistakes.

R-25: I see what you mean! So he isn't perfect either! He *was* scared last night. That must mean he's as scared of failure as I am. My gosh! I always thought of Dad as being way up on a pedestal (reaches up)—with a big thick wall between us. We all have always been afraid of him. There was only one time in my life that I ever defied him, but that was not done directly, either. (Chuckles reminiscently.) I did it through my sister. Though I never understood until now just what it was I was doing. My elder sister wanted to get married, but she was afraid to tell my parents. She was afraid to tell even Mother, not just Dad. She was nineteen, and the boy was very, very nice, and there was really no reason for her not to marry him. Yet, she had to feel afraid. I understood how she felt. She came and told me about it, and I got her all steamed up to go right in there and tell them about it! (He throws one leg over the arm of the chair and laughs uproariously.) Boy, did I work on her! I did all I could to give her the nerve to go tell them. You see, I was wishing I could have nerve enough to talk to them myself, but I did it through her. That's terrible, isn't it?

C-26: What's terrible?

R-26: That children should have to be afraid of their parents. Boy, I never want my children to be afraid to come to me. It's funny . . . they were always *telling* us to come to them with our troubles. (Mimics his parents, using a sanctimonious voice.) Yet they scared us to death so that we would never dare to go to them with anything at all. The three of us, us kids, we would talk to one another. If there had been only *one* of us! (Looks heavenward and throws up his hands.) That would have been the end!

C-27: You kids were buddies.

R-27: Yes, we never went to our parents, only to each other. You know, I'm learning an awful lot from my parents' mistakes.
(The hour was drawing to a close, and counselor began gathering her things together.)

R-28: (Hitting desk with his fist.) When I think of my father way up there on his pedestal!

C-28: Perhaps, in the long run, you will be a source of strength to him.

R-29: (Incredulous.) You mean *he* needs *me*?

C-29: I don't know. Let's wait and see.

R-30: Well, that would really be something . . . ! But that's not as important to me as making a life of my own, and getting away from my family altogether. That's why I feel that getting married is the answer for me.

C-30: Better understand your present relationships. You don't want to relate to Jane in the same way you are related to your parents. To really make a new start, you want new understanding.

R-31: Maybe that's why I keep saying that I hope I don't make the same mistakes my parents made.
(On the way out of the office, Ralph turns to counselor in great earnestness.) Gosh, this way of thinking is something so new to me. It's such a wonderful thing.

Discussion of the Seventh Interview with Ralph

In this interview, Ralph was helped to obtain some understanding of his father's behavior and attitudes. Perhaps the greatest value in this, for Ralph, is that it strengthens and gives more reality to his "new way of looking at things." He sees that the counselor's attitude to him is not a special dispensation, given through her "goodness"; it is a real force, an idea, a tool which he, too, can use. He can use it in thinking about his father as well as about himself. He reacts with joy to this discovery, and he ends the session with the statement, "Gosh, this way of thinking is so new to me. It's such a wonderful thing."

Eighth Interview with Ralph

R- 1: How are you today?

C- 1: Very well, thank you. How are you?

R- 2: (Smiles and stretches as he sits in usual chair.) I'm feelin' good, but I'm tired! The Christmas rush is going pretty strong. I had a very nice day yesterday. I enjoyed myself with Jane very much. The weather was poor, but the spirit was high. I got up to her place about ten o'clock in the morning. I went to bed reasonably early the night before, and asked Dad to wake me at seven. At five to eight Dad rushes into my room and says, "I forgot to wake you up. Get up."

Jane was waiting for me when I got there. We didn't do too much in the morning. We saw a movie, and after the movie I had a headache and pain in my left eye. I felt a heavy head coming on for two days. I've been working long and hard at the store and then staying up late reading. It was glary, driving in the rain, but I managed all right.

Gee. . . . (Laughs.) We were sitting in the car, having such a good time. We were laughing, and Jane was rubbing my head. It was nice. She said she didn't want to leave me last night. (Blushes and chuckles.)

Everything went all right since last Wednesday. I received fifty-six dollars for my week's pay. It wasn't bad. (Thoughtful.)

I saw the fight over television. Did you hear the fight?

C- 2: No, I didn't.

R- 3: You're not interested in fights.

C- 3: Yes, I like to listen to them, but I happened to have a meeting that night.

R- 4: Television is better than being there. I guess Madison Square Garden is feeling it in the ticket office. They are going to discontinue it after the first of the year.

I spoke to Jane about that business plan I told you about. She didn't have any further information, so I guess I'll go over there after Christmas and see whomever I have to see about it. I'm still interested in it. (Thoughtful.)

C- 4: What are you thinking?

R- 5: Something happened at the store today that was rather odd. We received a box of ties, and one corner of the box was torn open, and a couple of dozen ties were pulled out. Luckily, they were insured, so we filed a complaint at the post office. I don't understand people who can do things like that.

(Thoughtful silence.)

C- 5: Tell me about it.

R- 6: (Looks up with big smile.) You mean, tell you what I'm thinking?

C- 6: Yes.

R- 7: I was thinking about things at home. Home is cheering up. Maybe it's because I'm having a different outlook. Maybe it's all in me.

My automobile is down getting fixed. Now I'll be anxious to get it all in shape.

About my reading: I *have* been able to concentrate more. I should be sure before I go back to school that my reading has improved. Is there any way we can check up on it?

C- 7: What would you suggest?

R- 8: Some sort of test, or something?

C- 8: Perhaps you are ready to try a reading test. Would you like that?

R- 9: Yes, I would. I'd like to see what's what.

C- 9: All right. We can do that next time you come here.

R-10: Fine.

. . . I spoke to Jim, the manager at the store, and told him my friend needs a job at the store. I said I'd like to see him get the job. He's going to start next Wednesday. He'll work the two weeks before Christmas. I hope he turns out all right. I feel responsible.

(Thoughtful.)

You know, I'm looking at the world through rose colored glasses. (Swings leg over arm of chair.) So I have nothing to talk about. I feel now I could be as responsible as the next one. I have built up more self-confidence since I've come here.

The other night we were playing bridge, and Jane said something to her brother about not playing cards right, and he just said, "All right, Jane," as though to say, "Keep quiet." After a while, *I* played the wrong card, and she corrected me. But I listened to her, because I wanted to learn. Later, Mom said, "She'll do that more than once. She'll tell you what to do." I said, "That's okay. I want her to tell me if I'm wrong." Jane does know a lot about that particular thing. I told Jane when we were alone, though, "I didn't like that tone of voice you used. You can talk to me in a more pleasant tone." She said she was sorry, that she didn't mean to do that.

(Ralph swings around in chair and notices picture on the wall.) What picture is that?

C-10: I don't know. Isn't it some famous building?

R-11: It looks so much like a building I was working to put up last summer, the ———— Building. (Looks at counselor eagerly and proudly.) I didn't tell you about it! I helped build a building! (Throws head back and laughs heartily.) Boy, oh boy! It was one hundred and sixty-five up, and I was climbing around on it. Would you like to hear about it? (With much enthusiasm.)

C-11: Yes, I would.

R-12: (Settles down to tell a story which, very obviously, holds a great deal of meaning for him.)

Well, last summer I decided I needed a good paying job. I heard about someone's saying his son had worked on construction, on a building project, so one day Jane brought back that idea to me, and so I went over to a place where construction was going on. It was the first part of July. I went over and asked for a job. He asked if I could climb. I said, "Sure." You see, I was thinking of how I always climbed trees when I was a kid. (Laughs uproariously.) That wasn't what they meant by "climbing," see? Well, he said to come in on Monday.

Well, I finally got there, in my army shoes and fatigues, with a lunch box. I looked around to see how to get to where we were supposed to go. A fella there said, "Look, there's the ladder." Geez! There was a tiny little ladder. I was scared to death, so I started right up. I wasn't on to how it was done, so the first thing I did was hit my head on a steel girder. There were girders about a foot wide we had to walk on. The sun glittering on the steel made me dizzy. But in about three days I was walking around on the girders like the rest of the boys. I determined I'd master that. And after a few days, instead of using the little ladder, I would slide down the girders like the old-timers did. The first day I was there, I dropped a tool, and the boss said, "That's okay. But remember, if you drop anything, don't try to follow it down." It was okay if there was no one below to get hit.

(Ralph describes the work in detail, drawing diagrams to make it more explicit.)

One thing you learn on a job like that: you learn that you are much stronger than you ever thought you were. One man did get killed, but he was fooling around and slipped off. You can't fool around up there.

C-12:   You must have learned that you have tremendous courage.

R-13:   Well, I used to be plenty scared. One day I was walking on a girder that had rivet heads, and my ankle twisted, and I fell. But, lucky for me, I fell straight ahead, onto the girder. My heart stopped for a moment, then it went a mile a minute.

C-13:   Wow!

R-14:   (Laughs.) Yeah, that was a close shave.

I worked there four weeks. I told them when I left that they were under-paying, and that they would have to pay me more if I ever did that kind of work again.

C-14:   You know, you tell a story very well. You made the whole experience so vivid to me, I felt I was living through it with you.

R-15:   (Pleased.) Well, golly, it was a plenty vivid experience!

C-15:   *The New Yorker* magazine might like to print that story. I'm sure many readers would be interested in learning all that you've just told me.

R-16:   Do you think so?

C-16:   Yes, I do. You could try, if it interests you.

R-17:   Gosh, I'm no writer.

Well, I had a good time on that job, but I decided I wouldn't want that kind of work as a career. Those people have no higher ambitions. They are not interested in using their heads. Now, I'm enjoying the work I'm doing. I think I've found myself, pretty much. Once this week it was thrown up to me about engineering. Dad said he's so busy, he turns down jobs. Mom says, "See what you could be going into?" I said, "Yes, I understand fully, but I'm not going into engineering."

Dad said that recently he met an engineer who had become a liquor salesman. There, he had gone that far—he had a degree and everything, and then gave it up. I'd rather give it up right now. I just decided it's not for me. And if I were in my dad's office, it would be my dad that people want to see, not me. As he said himself, "They don't want an apprentice; they want me."

If I were in Dad's office, I'd be afraid of his correcting me all the time.

C-17: You mean, it would be the story of the model planes all over again.

R-18: Yes, exactly! It's always the same. I wouldn't be able to work at all if I were working near him.

C-18: Had you considered a job away from your father's office?

R-19: Yes, I've given thought to that, but still I don't think I want engineering. I don't think I ever really wanted it.

(The hour was drawing to a close.)

R-20: (Putting on his coat.) I had occasion to help my kid sister the other night. You know, Joan, the younger one. I used psychology and tried to get my mother to use psychology. Joan is in a high school play, and she was still out rehearsing at 10:30 the other night. Mom was getting all excited because she wasn't home yet. I said to Mom, "Now, look: When Joan comes home, don't right away ask her why she stayed out so late. Don't spoil her evening. Ask her, 'How was the play?'" But I wasn't in the room when Joan got home, so I don't know if Mom did that or not.

C-20: But it was good of you to want to help your sister. And you had the right idea.

R-21: I use psychology in the store, too, all the time. A little girl came in with her mother to buy a tie for her father for Christmas. The mother liked a blue one, and the little girl liked a different one. So, I used psychology. I took away both ties, and I brought out a different box that had another tie of the same kind that the mother liked. I said to the little girl, "How do you like *this* one?" Oh, that was fine! She liked that one fine! (Laughs joyously.) She never recognized it as the same tie her mother liked. The mother looked at me with such a surprised look. Everybody was satisfied.

C-21: You're a good psychologist.

R-22: Things *are* different at home, too, and I know it's all because I have a new perspective.

Discussion of the Eighth Interview with Ralph

It is interesting that Ralph has less fear of physical danger than of the danger to his self-esteem presented by his father's critical attitude. He is able to climb and walk upon the girders of a tall building, but he is afraid to be with his father or to contemplate sharing an office with him. This is a stark illustration of how critical attitudes can produce fear.

There are evidences of some movement in Ralph towards an easing up of his self-criticism and a little more freedom of self-assertion. For example, he does not sit stiffly and quietly in his chair; he falls into the swivel chair with a relaxed abandon, throws one leg over an arm of the chair, and swings gently around while talking. In this interview he took the opportunity to look around the office and enjoy the pictures on the walls. He is also a bit more courageous in his relationship with Jane. He spoke his protest when she used a disrespectful tone of voice in talking to him. He is apparently less frightened by the reading challenge, for he asks for a reading test. He is aware that perhaps his own changing outlook accounts for what seems to him to be a more cheerful atmosphere at home.

His identification with the counselor is expressed in his "use of psychology." (R-20.) The counselor encourages his "new way of thinking" by giving him credit for being a good psychologist. She accepts gladly his attempts to employ "her" techniques. She welcomes his growth and he is thus encouraged to grow more. In this relationship, submissiveness is not required of him; on the contrary, self-assertion is admired. This does not mean, however, that he can slip off like a cloak his old submissive way of relating. His submissiveness is expressed in his relationship to the counselor by his being "such a good patient"—he keeps reporting that things are so much better, thus complimenting the counselor and also trying to be what he feels she wants him to be. It will become clear to the reader, going through the interviews, that Ralph's path is not a smooth one. He has many set-backs, and it will be seen that these set-backs often follow right on the heels of a declaration that "everything is better."

There is some question in the counselor's mind as to whether it was therapeutically sound for her to suggest that Ralph write for *The New Yorker* the interesting story he told her. It may have had some value in terms of showing appreciation for his ability to tell a story; on the other hand, it sets a standard for him, puts a responsibility on him that does not really belong to this situation. Fortunately, he is able to say "No," at once, instead of saying he will try to do it for her, as he might have been impelled to do were he being more submissive to her than he is.

Ninth Interview with Ralph

R- 1: I haven't been so good today. Everything was on edge at work. I think I should snap out of it and not feel that way. I have felt nervous and tense, and I didn't want to say too much to anybody. I've had a headache all day. Do I have to take that reading test tonight?

C- 1: Not if you prefer not to.

R- 2: I was afraid all day you'd make me take it tonight.

C- 2: I wonder why you thought I would force it upon you.

R- 3: I don't know. I should have known you wouldn't do that. But I have a headache, and I don't think it would be such a good idea to take it tonight. Do you?

C- 3: I think that's good sense. We can easily postpone it.

R- 4: This has been a tough day. Sometimes I say things I don't mean. So I just stayed away from everybody as best I could. It was a feeling within myself. So I just stopped talking.
Last night Dad brought my car back. There's a lot wrong with it. Last night I drove it a little bit. The battery is going lower and lower. It wouldn't start. I finally found that the ignition wire was out. So I told Dad to take it down tomorrow and have it fixed. But I don't know—I don't think that could have been anything to upset me today.

C- 4: Did you have any anxiety about taking a reading test tonight?

R- 5: I thought about it a great deal, and I wondered what it would be like.

C- 5: What does taking a reading test mean to you at this point?

R- 6: It might mean finding out how well I'm doing. Except that I have nothing to compare with. I don't particularly like it because I still think my reading is awfully slow. I do read more than I did. I read at home as much as I can. Of course, it's after nine o'clock when I come home, and I'm tired. I wonder if this job is doing me any good. Of course, it's better than sitting around. You actually feel better for doing something, even though you get awfully tired. Well, I stay up at night to read, and then I write my letter to Jane.

I've had moods like this before. Sometimes, like at school, when I felt like this, I could not be near anyone for a while. I'd go take a walk, and then really feel like a different person when I got back. I snap myself out of it by telling myself it's silly. I don't know why today. . . .

C- 6: When did it start?

R- 7: It was just this afternoon, but I don't know why.

C- 7: What happened at the store today?

R- 8: My friend started work there today. I was trying to help him get the knack of things. But that didn't bother me. I always approach customers very nicely. One thing that did make me irritable this morning was that I had just fixed a nice rack of ties, and some woman came in and started pulling and messing the thing all up. It's quite a job getting the ties fixed. I had them all hanging straight, and they really looked nice. I liked the way I had them all arranged; then this woman doesn't give a darn, but starts pulling them.

C- 8: The customers don't appreciate your handiwork?

R- 9: No! (Considerable feeling.) They don't care! Geez, whenever a woman reaches for a tie, I rush to go for it first, so I can put it back where it belongs. So, that was one incident this morning that aided my tenseness.

And I had some disturbance a couple of nights ago—a bad dream of some sort. I had a sense that it was disturbing, but I don't remember what it was.

Do you think that incident about the ties would be enough to put me into this mood?

C- 9: I don't know. I wonder if it doesn't upset you to get so little appreciation of your efforts to keep things neat and in order. Perhaps you have no sense of fulfillment because no one cares whether or not the ties are in order?

R-10: Yes, it upsets me very much. (Voice is almost tearful.) Gosh, one of the fellows said, "Some people feel you're just a slave. That the customer is always right." He said he feels he's as good as anybody he waits on. And it's true, some of the customers do treat you like a servant. You might feel you're doing well financially, that you are helping the store by selling a lot, yet there is nothing of your ability showing.

Everything in the store is very neat and nice. I make it a job when I have to straighten out the ties. I should make it pleasurable, instead of making such a job out of it. I suppose if I changed my attitude, I might hear someone say how neat the store looks, and it might be partly because of the way the ties look. But I don't know. (Puts head down on hands.)

C-10: What does the tie-rack experience make you think of in terms of your life at home?

R-11: What do you mean?

C-11: Is anybody particularly neat at your home?

R-12: *Oh!* (Groans and waves his arm.) *Exceptionally* neat! Brother! Let me tell you about it. (Sits up straight in his chair, and talks with enthusiasm.)

My home has been standing nineteen years. It is decorated every few years. It does not look as though anybody lives in it or ever has lived in it. In the living-room, the sofa has a cushion stuffed with duck down, and it is so very soft. And there are other comfortable chairs in that room. But if anybody is at the house and sits on that sofa, Mom rushes forward to plump up the cushion and make it look as though nobody sat on it. If anybody sits on those chairs, if Mom doesn't fix them as soon as the person stands up, then she'll be sure to have them all straightened out mighty *soon*. She has to make it all look as though nobody ever sat on them.

Jane got a great kick out of that. At her home, they have a fire in their fireplace all winter, and the place looks as though somebody lives there. At our house, you never can ask to have a fire in the fireplace. It just isn't allowed. At Jane's we maybe can have a newspaper on the floor, and the couch looks used and sat on. You can tell people live there.

Mom and Dad brought me up to believe that: "Everything has its place, and everything should be in its place." That's an old saying of my Dad's. I wasn't allowed to put a school banner over my bed in my room, because I might get a hole in the wall from the tack!

Oh, I could tell you so many things! (Strong feeling.)

I'm afraid to bring friends into the house—even into the kitchen. After all, they might bump the woodwork! (Mimicking his mother.) Mom says, "The cellar is good enough." Well, the cellar *is* very nice, for a party—though I've only had one party in my life. But the rest of the house is Mom's showroom. She'd die if any little thing went wrong.

Why, I'll show you something! In the breakfast nook, one of the chairs is close to the radiator, and she was so afraid it might bump the radiator cover and chip it a little bit that she covered the back of the chair with rubber!

If Mom wants me to bring in the storm windows, and I'm carrying them into the house, she follows me around shouting, "Don't chip the woodwork!"

I feel funny about bringing a person into the house. They might chip the woodwork! It's "don't" this, and "don't" that. "Don't sit on the bed!"—especially if there's a spread on it. And, if you *are* caught on the bed, better be sitting on the middle, not on the edge, else the mattress will be lower on one side than on the other!

At Jane's, I just sit on the floor and do what I want.

C-12: Did you ever want to mess up your mother's house?

R-13: (Shouting, smiling, gesturing.) By golly, I've often thought how I'd love to chip all the darn woodwork she loves so much! Just go through the house and chip every bit of it!

C-13: Did you also want to mess up the rack of ties?

R-14: I *do*! When a woman messes up the tie rack a little bit, instead of fixing that little place, I walk up to the rack and mess it *all* up. I just knock off every tie on it, and start all over.

I'll tell you: I think I've got the same thing, too, that my mother has, come to think of it. For example, after I polish my car, people had better open the door by the handle, and not get fingermarks on the door! (Laughs.)

Do you think I worry about things too much?

C-14: You tell me.

R-15: Yeah, I think I do. Jane says I worry too much.

C-15: Tell me more.

R-16: Well, I want to have a thousand dollars in the bank before I will feel secure. Not for myself, but for Jane. But she doesn't see it that way.

C-16:   Apparently you do not feel that security lies within yourself.

R-17:   But it isn't for me, it's for Jane.

C-17:   What do you think Jane would prefer to have from you: one thousand dollars in the bank, or your feeling secure within yourself and with your own abilities.

R-18:   (Laughs.) Yeah, it's true; it isn't anything she wants from me. But I feel I owe that to her. I don't want to let her down.

C-18:   Let's go back a moment to what we just were talking about: your mother's need for a perfectly clean and orderly home, and your need, too, for perfect order. In that home, that very clean and perfect place, what was the attitude toward sexuality?

R-19:   Nobody ever talked about it! Dad did mention something to me one day about a wet dream. I must have been fourteen or a little younger. He asked me if I knew what was meant by a wet dream. I believe I gave him a wrong answer. But I don't know whether he straightened me out or not.

C-19:   Did he talk to you about masturbation?

R-20:   No, I don't think he ever gave me any information at all. Masturbation is one thing I never did.

C-20:   Why was that?

R-21:   I don't know—I just never did. Someone once said to me that if I never did that, it meant I was undersexed. At school I once mentioned that I never masturbated, and they did not believe me. I told them I'd try it. So I did try it that very night, but I couldn't make it work. The next morning, when I went to urinate, I was thoroughly sore.

I did one thing when I was very much younger that Mom has mentioned to me. When I'd be napping, she would catch me holding it.

C-21:   Did she use the word "catch"?

R-22:   Yes, I think so. That's how I remember her telling me about it.

C-22:   So, holding your penis while you slept must have seemed a wicked thing to do, if you thought of being "caught" at it.

R-23:   Yes, I see what you mean. Yes, I think that is probably true.

C-23:   How does Jane feel about sex? Does she think it is wicked?

R-24:   Well, Jane and I have heated sessions. Sometimes when we are alone together, and our bodies are very close, and each one knows what the other one is thinking. . . . She said she would, if I wanted to. But it's a mutual feeling that we wait until the wedding. Many times when I've been with Jane, I've had to get up and walk around. Because many times, after kissing a girl, I'd get all wet. I guess I want to wait, because it would be a different feeling with Jane.

You know, I just noticed—my headache went away. I had one all day. Until a year or two ago, I never took an aspirin. My family's religion was Christian Science, did I tell you? They turned to it the year I was born. And we have no medicine in the house, ever. At one time I never used to miss Sunday School. It was always interesting. I very seldom went to the church part. I think it's hard for anyone to be a Master Christian Scientist. Mother can't understand the full meaning of it. I don't know why she goes. I can't see what she gets out of church. (The hour was drawing to a close, and Ralph prepared to leave.)

R-25: (Putting on coat.) You know, there is something in other religions that you don't get in Christian Science. I once visited a Baptist Church, and I really got a *feeling* (presses hand to his stomach)—something I had missed.

I wish Dad had taken me out into the woods more, on hiking trips and picnics, to enjoy nature and get to know the world. We never did anything *for fun*! Everything had to have a serious purpose. If I ever have sons, we'll go out together into the country and the woods. Just me and my son, or sons. Jane can be in on other things, but a boy and his dad should get to know each other better and do things together just for the fun of it.

Discussion of the Ninth Interview with Ralph

This was an exciting interview, and the things that happened in it seem to be self-explanatory. Perhaps just one or two points may be elucidated or at least given further thought.

In the beginning, when Ralph says, "I wonder if this job is doing me any good," he may be expressing unconscious doubts as to whether this therapy is doing him any good. He has not felt well all day, and this is discouraging to him. One possible hypothesis is that the prospect of coming to the counselor for a reading test may have interfered with the treatment relationship: Ralph has had the feeling that "this new way of thinking" would lead him out into freedom and fun, self-realization, the capacity to do things and to enjoy life. When the sessions were devoted to expression of feelings and the finding of insights, Ralph felt that his inner world was expanding. As soon as the counselor became a testing authority, she seemed to become the same force in his life as his mother, his father, his teachers, his girl friend to some extent and his own excessive demands on himself. That is, the counselor, by proposing to give him a test, becomes identified with the forces in himself which make him feel tested by every life situation. He is therefore bound to feel hopeless, trapped, enraged, confused, because it seems he is back where he started and is fated to stay there. The material that emerges in the interview gives a clearer picture than ever of just how hemmed-in he has been by absolutism and perfectionism.

What does Ralph really mean when he says, at the end of the interview (R-25), that he wishes he and his father had done more things together for the fun of it? One may ask whether he is really saying, "I wish Dad had been able to save me from Mother's slavery to order and cleanliness. I wish he had helped me to get free of all of that, so that I could have found myself and become a real man." Then he says that Jane will have to stay out of it when *he* takes *his* sons out. In other words, it is as though all women are like his mother: they teach submissiveness, slavery to order, slavery to cleanliness, fear of sexuality, fear of self-assertion. He will do for his son what he feels his father failed to do for him: make the world safe for masculinity.

Why does Ralph, in instance after instance, assert that he will do things differently, that he will not behave the way his parents did, that he will be a better father, a more understanding parent? It is as though his hunger for a stronger, kinder father will one day be supplied to him by his own fatherhood. In other words, he will get a good father by being one.

Tenth Interview with Ralph

(Ralph seems to be cheerful tonight.)

R- 1: Oh, boy, we're busy at the store now. I'm feeling good. I bought some nice Christmas gifts for Jane. I got her some of her favorite perfume and a silver bracelet she's been wanting.

C- 1: Those are thoughtful gifts.

R- 2: Do you think so? (Smiles.) I hope she likes them. I'd like to take that reading test tonight.

C- 2:   All right. I have it right here.
        (Counselor administered the Nelson-Denny Reading Test,
        Form B. Ralph was very slow, and counselor feared the experi-
        ence might be a discouraging one.)
C- 3:   (At end of test period.) That's a very dull test, isn't it?
R- 3:   Yes, it's very dull.
C- 4:   Would you like to fill out the hour with another test that is
        more interesting?
R- 4:   Yes, I would.
        (Counselor gave Ralph Dr. Strang's informal reading test,
        using the *Reader's Digest* article, "What Are We Afraid Of?"
        Counselor was certain Ralph could do better with this one and
        thus avoid leaving him in a mood of discouragement. Also,
        the spirit of the article is optimistic. Ralph read it in seven-
        teen minutes, which is slow, and then answered the questions.)
C- 5:   What did you think of that test?
R- 5:   That was much more interesting. I think I did pretty well on
        that one. (He appears to be more cheerful now.)
        (The time was beginning to run over the usual hour. Coun-
        selor and Ralph closed the session with the plan to discuss both
        tests next time.)

Discussion of the Tenth Interview with Ralph

The counselor had decided after the ninth interview that she would
not give Ralph any tests, and thus avoid being in the position of testing authority. However, Ralph asked so cheerfully for a reading test
this session that the counselor complied, thinking that perhaps the dis-
advantages of giving the test might be outweighed by the opportunity
of weaving the test experience and performance into the material of
the counseling work.

Eleventh Interview with Ralph

R- 1:   Well, how did I do?
C- 1:   Tenth-grade level. Now we can work up from there.
R- 2:   (Laughs.) That's a nice way to put it. But I think I am reading
        better than I used to. I believe I was tired that night. I also
        could hear your watch ticking.
        (Counselor and Ralph went over test in detail. For example:)

C- 2: You got this right and this right and this right. Now let's study what you did here, on number four.

R- 3: Well, I'll tell you. I used the process of elimination with the ones I didn't know. But that seemed to be a very slow method.

C- 3: Yes, you are very deliberate and thoughtful about it, instead of going directly to the one that looks most likely. You sort of chew on every word.

R- 4: That's a good description. Once I get onto a word I can't seem to move off it. I can't just swallow it; I keep chewing. I don't know what I expect to find.

For example, here is this word I got wrong: "arrogant." I've heard that word used so many times. "A very arrogant soul." But it just wouldn't come to me what it meant exactly.

Here I got the word "guise" right. But I must have been guessing, because now I don't know what it means.

C- 4: Guess again.

R- 5: "Appearance?"

C- 5: That's correct.

R- 6: (Very pleased.) I got it from *dis*guise.

C- 6: You don't trust your feeling about words. You spent a long time on the vocabulary, and you got much of it right, but you couldn't get enough done because you kept doubting yourself.

R- 7: I always like to be sure that I'm right.

C- 7: Your perfectionism gets in your way.

R- 8: I guess that's right. I think I make more mistakes that way.

Here's a funny one. I know it now; why didn't I know it when I took the test? For "spontaneous" I put "fierce." I can see now it should have been "unconsidered." I can see it means something not considered. I wonder why I chose "fierce."

C- 8: Maybe it makes you feel *fierce* and *angry* to be afraid to be spontaneous!

R- 9: It's strange what the mind does. I do get sore and feel ruffled up inside while I'm pondering and pondering. Now, isn't that the strangest thing!

Now look, I had this next one right, and now I'm not sure what it is. To "infuse" is to "instill." I guess I knew that to *dis*till means to take out, so I just knew *in*still must mean to put in. In other words, when I thought I was just guessing, something in me really knew.

C- 9: Yes, you need to have more faith in that "something in you."

R-10: How do I go about getting it?

C-10: Tell me what you think in answer to that question.

R-11: I should think I'd have to find out why it's missing in me. Other people seem to have it.

C-11: With time and effort you'll work it out.

R-12: I feel more hopeful—as though I'm on the edge of finding out new things. I never felt this way before. . . . Come on, now, let's not stop. I want to see how I handled the paragraphs. (Counselor and Ralph spent remainder of session going over the paragraph section of the test. He showed the same hesitancy here in trusting his own judgment.)

Discussion of the Eleventh Interview with Ralph

This interview helps to clarify the ways in which Ralph's reading difficulties grow out of his personality patterns. The counselor had observed Ralph carefully while he was taking the test, and now could add her observations to his. (For example, C-3 and R-4.)

The comments he wrote after reading the magazine article are worth examining. He repeated several variations of the theme that "people are lazy." He said, "People just don't want to work," and, "There is plenty of work to be had if a person wanted it," and, "The American people are getting lazy." These ideas were not expressed or implied by the author of the article. If we regard the reading and discussion of the article as a projective technique, his responses to it tell a good deal about himself. They show, for one thing, how preoccupied he is with his own problems, so that he reads them into the article and cannot lend himself to what the author is trying to say. His comments also reveal how much he castigates himself with the meaningless and fruitless stereotype, "lazy." He is caught in the mire of self-contempt and needs help to extricate himself.

Twelfth Interview with Ralph

Ralph spent the better part of this session describing, in minute detail, an automobile accident he had had during Christmas vacation.

R- 1: We hit this snow-drift, and the car turned right over. Jane didn't want to get out of the car; she seemed to be dazed. I had to get tough with her. I said, "Get right out of that car!" And she did.

The car was lying upside-down across the middle of the road. I don't know how we escaped getting killed. We weren't even hurt! But then a big truck was coming down the road, and I walked up the road, waving, to stop it. It was dark, and the driver stopped just before he got to me. He was shaken. He said, "Boy, I don't know how I happened to see you." You see, I didn't have any lights, or flash-light, or anything.

Jane was in a tight spot, because she didn't know which side of the road to stand on. There were deep snowbanks on both sides. She figured the truck might swerve into one of the snow-banks if it hit our car, or if it saw our car too late to put on the brakes. She was afraid it might drive into the side she was standing on.

Thank heavens that driver saw me.

C- 1: Well, you were lucky, weren't you.

R- 2: Gosh, we sure were.

C- 2: There's something I'd like to ask you.

R- 3: What's that?

C- 3: Since you knew there had been a snowstorm, why were you out?

R- 4: (Defensively.) The roads were clear, really they were. Except for this one big drift of snow that covered the road unexpect-edly. We were going up to do some skiing.

C- 4: Doesn't it seem to you that you were asking for trouble, to take your car out on the highways after a heavy snow? Just to go skiing?

R- 5: I guess it was. I didn't see it that way at the time, though. I'll tell you something, now that you mention it.
(Sits quietly, face flushed.)

C- 5: What is it?

R- 6: I'd never be able to say this to anyone else . . . but . . . when that car turned over, I felt a moment of great happiness. It was almost as if I was glad we were having an accident. Maybe I wanted to wreck the car, so that Dad would have a good sized repair bill. Or . . . it was just as if this were a way of showing him I could do something, that I could wreck the car! That sounds terrible, doesn't it.

C- 6: Terrible or not, it's better to get at the truth of the matter. You know the old saying, "Know the truth, and the truth shall make you free."

R- 7: (Smiles with relief.) You always make me feel better. Don't you ever get mad?

C- 7: You do enough scolding of yourself; you don't need me to do any whipping. There's too much of it already.

R- 8: But to be glad of an accident! Just to show my father I could do it! That's spiteful, isn't it. To want to wreck the car. I didn't do it deliberately, but I was secretly glad it happened. (Sits quietly.)

C- 8: What are you thinking?

R- 9: In a few weeks I'm supposed to be going back to college. To anyone else, I would say I'm glad at the idea. To you, I have to admit how I *really* feel. I don't feel I'm ready to go back.

C- 9: Tell me about it.

R-10: Well, I feel that what I'm doing here, with you, is more important. That I'm just getting to know myself, for the first time in my life, and that's more important than going back to college now. It's wrong to stop here, right in the middle. That's how I *really* feel. But. . . .

C-10: But what?

R-11: I can say all that to you, because you understand, but I could never make Jane or my folks understand.

C-11: I wonder whose life you are trying to plan constructively. . . . Your mother's? Your father's? Jane's? Who is going to college?

R-12: (Laughs.) Okay, okay! That's just the kick in the pants I needed. I guess I can count on you to give it to me. That's exactly the thing that's wrong with me, isn't it, that I can't decide anything for myself. If I could do that, then I *would* be ready to go back to college. If I go only to please everybody else, against my own best judgment, then I'm *not* ready to go back.

C-12: Sir, that was well said!

(Ralph left the interview with an air of vim and vigor.)

Discussion of the Twelfth Interview with Ralph

Why did Ralph experience "a moment of happiness" when his car turned over? He said, "I could show Dad I could do something." The automobile accident and his reaction to it carry out dramatically our hypothesis that, at present, Ralph's only available path to self-assertion is a self-destructive one. This is a more vivid, more sharply defined example of the pattern than the self-defeat expressed by his school failure, but it is essentially the same underlying pattern. Accompanying this negative self-assertion is an expression of revenge ("I'll give Dad a good-sized repair bill!") against the figure of authority whom he considers responsible for his inability to assert himself in more positive ways. He feels guilty about this negative way of life, and when he confesses to the counselor his wish for vengeance, he is surprised that she can listen to it without becoming angry.

After getting this off his chest, he is able to arrive at a strong decision: "It is more important to know myself than to go back to college." In R-12 he recognizes his inability to make plans for himself based on his own real wishes; he understands how much he lives in terms of trying to win approval.

This interview is a vivid picture of how the repression of one's own desires in the effort to win approval leads to the accumulation of rage, the wish for revenge and the use of self-destruction to hurt others, as well as to punish one's self for feeling enraged and destructive.

Thirteenth Interview with Ralph

Ralph was pale today. He appeared to be shaken and depressed. His voice at the beginning of the interview was scarcely audible. He seemed close to tears.

R- 1: Well, everything's gone wrong. I broke the news to Jane, that I'm not ready to go back to college. It started quite a discussion. She had her heart set on my going back. She said she would not marry me unless I went back. She suggested we break the engagement.

I tried to explain to her what we were doing here, and she could not understand what my difficulties were. I couldn't make her understand what the situation was. She said she would give me one month to get ready to go to college.

You know, these are things that make you want to throw in the sponge. You should have seen me driving home. . . . I guess I was hoping to kill myself.

She said I *promised* to go back in February, for *her*. I love

Jane. Gee, this has upset me something awful. I told her, "I wish you could speak to Mrs. Ephron. She could tell you much more about me than I could."

I don't know what to do. She figures that the longer I stay out of school, the harder it would be for me to go back. She feels this is a year wasted.

C- 1: How do *you* feel?

R- 2: You *know* how I feel. I feel I should not go back until September.

Jane said, "What about your friends, your family?" I told her I would see what I could do about preparing to go back in time. She thinks you think I'm emotionally unbalanced. She said that a person getting married should be emotionally balanced and have a sense of responsibility—or something like that. I told her I'm just getting to know myself. She claims I can do it. She says, "You can do it. Just go ahead and work." She is a very intelligent girl, and she studied psychology, but she just doesn't understand this. I can feel, but not explain it clearly to her. I told her . . . things that have happened to me as far back as I can remember . . . things that are in my mind that I have to bring out in order to face them.

I told Jane . . . I can't sit down, as at a lecture, and pick out the important parts, and put down only what's necessary. . . . I always tried to put down every word.

C- 2: That's the same thing operating, isn't it? You lack confidence in your own judgment, so you find it difficult to let yourself select what you consider to be important.

R- 3: That's it exactly. Jane put me on the fence. She doesn't understand all this. Now I have a very important decision to make . . . whether to go back to school now or later.

You know, there was one thing she said that bothered me something terrible. She said, "What about my brother and my mother, and all my friends?" That turned my stomach. You should have seen me driving home! If I did what she wanted me to do, if I went back to school now and if I didn't make the grade, she wouldn't like me.

C- 3: You are shifting authority from yourself to others.

R- 4: That's right. I guess if I do it because Jane says I should, I won't like her. I didn't love my mother for exactly the same reasons. So now if Jane bosses me like my mother always did, I won't like it.

C- 4: That's right. You've always been on trial, somehow. You remember how much you've talked about needing to prove yourself. Now you have to prove yourself to Jane. That is probably the thing that is making you feel so depressed. You need to be loved for your own sake, and not be on trial.

R- 5: (Quite stirred.) That's it. It makes me feel so hopeless. I feel now she didn't mean what she said when she told me she would stick to me "through the thick and the thin." She wants to leave me if I don't go back to school right when she wants me to. Postponing school for six months isn't much "thick or thin," is it. (Gets up and walks around.)

I wish I hadn't promised her that I would go back. Because I didn't really mean it. I didn't have the nerve to say to her, "Look, Jane, I have to do what I think best. Either you do respect my judgment, or you don't."

C- 5: You are eager to rise to your manly height.

R- 6: I felt like a worm, not like a man, when I promised her because I was afraid not to. That was cowardly. I know that.

I keep thinking how it turned my stomach when she began worrying about what her mother would think, and what her brother would think. All my life I've tried to please my family, and I'm just trying to stop doing that so much . . . and now she is worrying more about what her family thinks than what I think, or how I feel.

I don't want to lose Jane. I love her. But I know it's no good this way. It turns my stomach. It isn't right.

I think I'll write her a letter. I'll tell her she has to understand this thing, and respect my judgment. Do you think that's a good idea?

C- 6: Do you really need to ask me that?

R- 7: You're right! (Very excited now.) If I ask myself, I *know* the right answer! There will be many more important decisions coming up all through life, and if I let Jane always make the decisions for me, against my feeling, there won't be love between us. If she is always going to scare me by saying, "Do what I want, or else I don't want you."

C- 7: You are getting clearer on all this, aren't you?

R- 8:   Yes, I see what I have to do. There's really no choice. I'll do it by writing to her.

(By this time, Ralph had lost his pallor, his voice was strong and his manner was more enlivened. He still seemed tired and shaken when he left, but his cheeks were pink and his voice had dropped its depressive note.)

R- 9:   Wish me luck, Mrs. Ephron. I'm going to try to be a man, for a change.

Discussion of Interviews Thirteen, Fourteen, and Fifteen

These three interviews tell an exciting story. The significant material in them emerges so clearly that any comment seems superfluous.

Fourteenth Interview with Ralph

(Some sessions back, while walking to the elevator with counselor, Ralph had asked to be given a Bellevue-Wechsler Test. It had subsequently been scheduled for this evening. However, Ralph asked that the time today be devoted to interview, and the counselor, of course, agreed to this.)

R- 1:   Well, I wrote a letter to her, but got no answer yet. After I wrote it, I felt good. I wondered why I felt so *good*. (Stretches luxuriously in his chair and smiles.)

I said in this letter, "I hope you'll give back the promise I gave you last Sunday, about going back to school in February. I should have told you right then and there that I wasn't going back. I have decided strongly that I am *not* going back." I also said that I was sorry, but I thought it best.

I feel that if this is going to make such a difference to Jane, now is the time to find out.

I talked to my sister today . . . the older one. I was talking to her about this situation with Jane, and she said the exact same things you said. She said, "It's about time you started thinking about yourself."

Knowing Jane—*you* don't know Jane, but she does—she said that every time Jane came down to the house, she had to be *doing* something, that she can't just sit and read a magazine or book. My sister said to me, "Your father has money, but you won't get any of it when you're starting out. I didn't."

Now that she is married, she's doing with a lot less than she had before she was married. Yet they are happy. And I don't think Jane could do it. She's the same way at her own house. She can't stay home, she has to go to the movies. And of course her mother always comes along. Jane's never done any cooking, any planning or any cleaning up afterwards, but she'll drive sixty-five miles to go to a show.

Ah-h-h-h (stretching) . . . I do feel good!

C- 1: I suppose you feel you've established your self-respect.

R- 2: Yes, no matter what the answer to my letter is, I'm *so* glad I wrote it. I felt different the minute afterwards.

You know, I've always adored my sister, and now more than ever. She said she has nothing against Jane, but that it's best to find things out now rather than later.

You know, this sounds funny but I might be even a little disappointed now if Jane does make up with me. Maybe, if I really admitted how I really feel, as I wouldn't to anybody else, I'd say that I would really like to be free, and go and come as I please, and do as I want, and not have to be worried about how Jane likes it. I do want the feeling of being free.

C- 2: You never felt that *you* had *rights*. I suppose if you achieve that feeling, you won't need to run away from your family or from other relationships in order to feel free.

R- 3: Say, that's quite an idea. It hits me, you know? It really hits! Because it's so true that I never considered I had *any rights* whatsoever! For example, I was never able to talk back to Mom. If I tried to talk, I'd get this: (Throws his right arm up before his face, as though warding off a blow.) I mean, I'd do this, because I'd get an awful look, and she'd threaten to hit me. My hands finally would make a joke of it. What an awful look she'd give me! (He imitates, making a vicious, terribly angry face. Counselor is reminded of Ralph's response to Card I of the Rorschach, "an evil face.")

I guess I've always wanted my mother's love because I knew I wasn't getting it.

A boy I know was talking about how he had been brought up in an orphanage, and never had the things he needed. I was thinking to myself that I wasn't much better off, that I would rather just once have a pat on the back and a nice, "Hello," from my father than the money he gives me.

Gosh, it would please me an awful lot to give my children the love I never got.

I keep remembering my mother saying, "Don't talk back! Don't speak back to me!"

You know, when I was writing that letter to Jane . . . ordinarily I'd have to go to my room and be all by myself to write a letter like that. This time I sat down right in the living room and wrote it.

My first accomplishment is to prove myself to myself. The rest will follow. I feel wonderful, as though I had seen the light. (Laughs joyously.) Now I even feel different about going up to ———— for an interview. I feel much more secure. It's a different feeling. I want to find out about that plan—get all the facts. I feel confident about it.

I just remembered something. Up at school we had a Golden Gloves tournament. They matched me with a fella twenty pounds heavier than I was, and he looked much bigger. Before going into the ring, I had a feeling of fear. I felt it was unfair. So, instead of being on the aggressive, I was on the defensive all the way. All the time we were fighting, he'd be hitting me, but not hurting me. I knew I could have taken him. After the fight, the referee said to me, "What on earth was holding you back!" So now I see it's just one more incident of the same thing: never having faith in myself, and always holding back.

C- 3: Yes, and I suppose you do the same thing with reading. You can't let your eyes be aggressive and reach out and take in the reading material.

R- 4: (Very excited.) It's so interesting! Just to think! Just think, a few weeks ago you could have said that to me and I wouldn't have known what you were talking about; now I know just exactly what you mean by that.

(During the walk to the elevator, Ralph said he'd been having more headaches. When counselor asked if now he would agree to seeing an eye doctor, Ralph said he would do so.)

Fifteenth Interview with Ralph

Ralph is smiling from ear to ear as he comes into the room.

R- 1: Well, I feel *good!* I never thought it possible to feel *this* good. I brought two letters with me, from Jane. I want to read them to you. This first one here she wrote to me before she got that letter I wrote to her. Listen:

(Ralph reads the letter to counselor. It is filled with detailed instructions about what to do and say at his forthcoming interview with an executive at the place of business he hopes eventually to enter.)

R- 2: Do you know what I said to myself after I read this letter? I said to myself, "Wouldn't it be awful if, after memorizing all the instructions in this letter, I should be sitting at the interview, and I should suddenly forget part of what I had memorized." I would have to say to the man, "Excuse me, while I take out Jane's letter and find out what I'm supposed to say next."

It burned me up. Why should she feel that she knows what I should say and do at an interview—at *my* interview! In the past, I'd take that from her and be grateful, because I was glad to be a boy, I didn't have to be a man. Now I realize I have as good a head of my own as I need. I know exactly what I want to say at that interview, and I even disagree with some of her instructions.

Well, I have more to tell you. This is really good. (Savoring the moment.) I feel like a new person, I'm telling you. The night she got *my* letter—you know, the one telling her I was not going back to school just now—she telephoned me. Boy, oh boy, what a phone call! What a different situation. For once, *she* backed down, not me. She denied saying she wanted to break the engagement. She tried to deny everything she said to me. She was frightened.

It was quite different from the way our phone calls usually are. Usually, I pick up the phone and say, "Yes, dear," and wait timidly to see if she is going to be nice to me, or what. This time I did the talking instead of the waiting. Instead of being pushed to the wall, I pushed her. I was aggressive.

But the thing that really gets me—you were so right—she not only is taking all this from me, but she seems to show more respect for me!

C- 2: If you are very masculine, she will have to be more feminine, and that will be a good thing for both of you.

R- 3: That's right. I just thought of a cartoon I saw, of a man who is like what I used to be, and like a man shouldn't be, and like I don't want to be. It shows this man in a doctor's office, and he is calling up his wife and asking her permission to have an operation. He says, "Dear, may I have an appendectomy?" (Ralph and counselor laugh in companionable appreciation.) Well, that's just about the way I was.

Now I want to read you the second letter, the one Jane wrote to me after the phone call.

(Ralph reads aloud a long, earnest, affectionate letter, a letter that does not have the business-manager tone of the other letter. In this one, Jane assures Ralph of her love and tells him never to be afraid to tell her anything; that she felt hurt because he made a promise to her only because he was afraid to say what he really wanted.)

R- 4: Isn't this letter altogether different from the other one? Now I have to wait and see if she really means this, or if she is just backing down now because she got frightened. You know, she might just be pretending, sort of, until this blows over. But from now on, I'm going to be the aggressive one, and never be the way I was before.

C- 4: Good.

R- 5: I experienced the same thing when I went to ———— for my interview. I'm a different person. Formerly, I'd have gone there feeling scared and . . . somehow . . . I don't know how to describe it . . . but sort of apologetic, as though I didn't belong there and he was only tolerating me. But this time I walked in straight and sturdy, looked Mr. ———— right in the eye, offered him my hand, sat down and told him my plans. He recommended a business course. He said, "Expand your education, then come back, and I'm sure there will be a place here for you, and advancement."

He said a nice thing. He said he liked my appearance and

my manner, and he thought I would be successful. Well, the only way I can explain it is that it didn't feel like a man and a boy; it felt like two men talking. It felt good. That's what I want to be able to do even more.

C- 5: That's a very grand story.

R- 6: Isn't it, though? I told you, I feel like I'd seen the light! (Laughs joyously.)

Oh, I want to tell you about my sister and her husband. They both said they've been seeing a big change in me, and they said, "It's about time." My sister's husband said he had been itching to tell me, for a long time, that I was letting Jane push me around all over the place. But he didn't tell me because he knew I wouldn't take it from him.

Say, you know, that's the funny thing about this. This is the kind of thing that has to come from within you. When I hear my own voice saying things, I stop and listen and think it over. If he had said the same things to me, I'd want to punch him in the nose.

They both said they had nothing against Jane, but that they were sick of seeing me jump around to follow out her every word and whim. My mother has told me the same thing, but I'd never listen to her, either. It had to come from out of myself. It's a very strange thing.

(As Ralph and counselor were leaving the office, Ralph grinned at counselor and asked, "How'm I doin'?" Counselor replied, "You are a very rewarding person to work with." Ralph was pleased. He said, "I'm beginning to see what I've missed all my life, and I can't tell you what a good feeling that is.")

Sixteenth Interview with Ralph

(This interview followed a two-week vacation period. Ralph brings a big grocery bag and places it on the desk in front of counselor.)

C- 1: What may this be?

R- 1: I brought you a present! Paper-shell pecans right from California. Dad and Mom brought them back from their trip. I thought you might like some. It's so much better than what you get in the stores.

C- 2: You could not have brought me a more welcome gift. Thank you ever so much.

R- 2: You are most welcome. Say, I've been raring to see you. I missed you. Tell me, how have you been?

C- 3: I had the flu, but otherwise I had a pleasant time.

R- 3: Oh, sure, you must have had a pleasant time, with the flu! (Laughs.)
I'm sorry to hear you were ill. That was a tough break.

C- 4: Well, I'm all right now. And how are you?

R- 4: Well, nothing much happened to me. Let me see. The week-end before last, we went to a party, and I had too much to drink. I don't like to do that. The next morning we went to see a movie in the morning, when the prices are cheaper. (Chuckles.) We saw "Mutiny on the Bounty." Have you seen it?

C- 5: No.

R- 5: It was pretty good. Well, then we went over to the Queen Mary, to see some girls off who were going to Europe. We drove all the way through the storm. Couldn't see much further than the car itself.

C- 6: Did you *have* to go out in the storm?

R- 6: (Laughs.) Well, gee, the snow just suddenly came up. It hadn't snowed too much before we set out at 4:30.
And last night I almost had an accident. But it isn't always my fault!

C- 7: If you had a son who was always having narrow escapes, what would you think?

R- 7: I'd think he was crazy.

C- 8: (Smiles.) Well?

R- 8: (Grins.) Aw, gee. . . .

C- 9: No fooling. Why do you want to flirt with death?

R- 9: It makes life more fun, don't you think so?

C-10: If you are asking my opinion, I'd say, "No." Why do you think it makes life more fun?

R-10: I don't know. You might say the same thing about my working on that building.

C-11: Yes, that's true.

R-11: Well, the only way you're really safe is to stay in bed! (Laughs.)

C-12: Seriously, Ralph. . . . I wonder if you don't have a sense of emptiness. You perhaps feel you are not important, not very interesting, without much to talk about. So, you have to create drama, a phony kind of drama, to make yourself feel important. Do you think there is anything to that idea?

R-12: You mean, I have close shaves, like last night, in order to feel that I have interesting things to tell you?

C-13: Yes, exactly. There's something in that, isn't there?

R-13: Yeah. I guess I do feel that I'm not particularly interesting. But I'll tell you, I *have* been feeling good. I've been feeling good right along lately. I went down to ———— to see my friends down there. I stayed with one of my fraternity brothers, and I just got back last night. I miss Jane, of course. She's back at school. She wrote me about her marks—one C, two B pluses, two B's. It's just wonderful, because for quite a while she was on probation. . . . I feel good about it.

C-14: Not jealous even a little bit?

R-14: No, really I'm not. Because now I feel I'm going to do just the same as that when I get back to school.
What else shall we talk about? Mom and Dad said it was very rainy in California. Of course, it was a rest for Mom, and she enjoyed it, but they could have had much nicer weather.
Let's see, what else can I tell you.
They were all sorry to hear I wasn't coming back in February, but I got the general feeling that they were really concerned, and when I told them what I was doing, I felt I'd be back in September, raring to go.
It was funny—they were kidding me about Columbia's basketball team. (Discusses basketball at some length.)

C-15: Well, Ralph, what problems are bothering you?

R-15: None. I'm going to look for a job tomorrow.

C-16: Do you realize you still haven't been examined by an eye doctor?

R-16: Oh, that! (Laughs.)

C-17: No fooling. It is something that I feel should be done. For all we know, you may have an eye condition that is interfering with your progress in life! Will you go?

R-17: You don't think my doctor is enough?

C-18: No, I don't. You may have a new mysterious eye condition they've just discovered, and your doctor would not have the knowledge or equipment to discover it if you had it. You said a long time ago that you *would* have your eyes examined.

R-18: Okay, okay, you win. It's against my principles, but I'll do it. (Amiably.)

(Counselor gave Ralph an eye doctor's address and telephone number.)

C-19: Will you call him tomorrow?

R-19: Yes, I will. I really will.

C-20: That's good. By the way, perhaps I ought to tell you that the Friday evening class is beginning the new semester. Do you think it would be a good idea to see how much you could get out of it this time?

R-20: No, I'd rather work with you.

C-21: Oh, I did not mean that you would go to the class *instead* of coming to me; I thought of it as something extra. The teacher is so expert at teaching all the reading and studying techniques. You would simply be getting some additional help.

R-21: Well, I have to see about a job first, and I might not be able to get away on Fridays.

C-22: It's up to you, of course.

R-22: Well, I'll see. But I don't think I want to.

Say, I bought a nice new suit. I really needed it. Almost forgot to tell you about it. I was going to wear it here tonight, to show it to you, but the weather was so bad. Gee, it's really good-looking. I couldn't pass it by. I saw it, I took it in my hands, and the fellow in the store said, "I won't sell it to you." I said, "I know—if I like it, I'll buy it, you won't have to sell me." I told him to take off the ticket, and I put the suit right on. He said, "I can tell you've been a salesman at one time or another." It needed very little done to it to make it fit right. I'll wear it here some day, so you can see it.

C-23: Good.

R-23: You know, I've been reading more lately. No longer than an hour at a time, but I read rapidly, and I found it interesting. Before, I never used to care about it.

C-24: That's encouraging, but we still have to find out why your eyes won't take more than an hour of reading at a time.

R-24: Well, I'll call this doctor tomorrow.

C-25: Okay. I guess our time is about up. Thank you again for the present.

R-25: You are very welcome. I hope you will enjoy eating them. But I'm sure you will, they're really wonderful.

Discussion of the Sixteenth Interview with Ralph

This is a very poor interview, from the standpoint of therapeutic technique. The counselor made numerous digressions, intruded repeatedly throughout the hour, not permitting his free associations to develop their own direction and momentum, and, in fact, nagged Ralph—what with solemn reminders about his not having gone to an eye doctor, insisting that he call the doctor the next day, suggesting he join the Friday class, and so forth. Perhaps she was suffering after-effects of the flu, which is not an excuse but a possible partial explanation of non-characteristic behavior. However, this bad example should be encouraging to neophyte counselors. It shows how many mistakes one can make without doing permanent damage.

It was therapeutically defensible to challenge Ralph about his neglect of his eyes and his self-destructive trend expressed in his driving, but it was not done well and Ralph did not pick up and work on the problem of his needing to bring exciting stories to the counselor, like bringing gifts in order to be accepted. He feels uninteresting without dramatic events to relate, as though he is so bored with himself that he feels the counselor will be bored with him. He is bored because he is not being his real self; life can become exciting for him if and when he loses his fears of expressing his own real feelings.

Seventeenth Interview with Ralph

Ralph comes to the appointment today wearing dark glasses.

R- 1: Gee, what a day! I'm so tired. I saw the doctor, and so far as I know there's nothing wrong with the eyes, other than what was pointed out to me by my optometrist—astigmatism and far-sightedness.

C- 1: Well, that's good to know, isn't it?

R- 2: Yes, it is. But I have another appointment for Saturday morning. Here it is . . . I can't read it. (Hands counselor a slip of paper on which is written an appointment for an examination for aniseikonia.) What does it say?

C- 2: This is very interesting. They want to do a special examination to find out if you have an eye condition they've discovered only recently. They are doing research in it now. It was the thing I spoke of the other day.

R- 3: Now isn't that strange! You spoke of it, and here they apparently think I might have it.

C- 3: Maybe you don't, but it will be mighty interesting to find out.

R- 4: My gosh, it sure will! Can you tell me anything about it?

C- 4: I don't know much about it, except that it causes terrific strain because each eye sees a different image at the same time. They don't cooperate.

R- 5: Well, I might well have it, judging from the amount of strain I have when I read.

Well, I received a job, to start tomorrow. I'm going to work for an art shop in town, just to earn some money. I'm replacing one of the regular salesmen who's taking a winter vacation. It'll run for six weeks, including the time they'll need extra help for inventory. The hours are funny, though. The hours are from nine to six, or six-thirty. That has to be changed. On Mondays and Wednesdays I'll have to get off at five, to get here.

I'm really not feeling too well, because I can't see. It gives me a stomach ache. Other than that, I'm fine and have no complaints. . . . I'm very, very tired.

What else can you tell me about the mysterious eye condition I might have?

C- 5: I don't know anything more about it. I'm sorry. I wish I did.

R- 6: That's okay. Maybe I'll be able to tell you about it after I take the tests.

C- 6: That would be nice. I hope you'll do that.

R- 7: All right, that's a promise. I will tell you all about it.
(Sits quietly.)
You know, I imagine this could be like a sickness, like drinking alcohol, this condition I've had. I've been thinking about myself. I just hope I keep in the new track and don't have a relapse. There may be certain things I'm still not used to . . . I've acted one way so long. Excuse me a minute. (Takes out nail file and cleans finger-nails.)
It's not that the past is attractive to me. It's just that changing

from twenty-one years of doing things one way to doing them a new way may be a little difficult. Is that correct?

C- 7: Your thinking is very sound.

R- 8: Thank you. I won't ask you what to do about it because I imagine that the only thing I *can* do is keep trying. Right?

C- 8: Right.

R- 9: Things at home are fine these days. Dad still acts his old way. When he came back from California, it was, "Hello, Son," and that's all.

"Did you have a nice time?"

"Yup."

"Catch any fish?"

"A few."

So, I said to myself, "The heck with that! I'm not going to pull teeth." I gave him plenty of lead questions, and I felt cheerful and excited, but there was no response from him. So I gave it up.

R-10: Here, will you have some hershey with me?
(Offers counselor a candy bar.)

C-10: Thank you, I'd love it.

R-11: I was scolded for having that blow-out. Dad asked if I checked the tires after the car turned over that time. I said yes, that I checked them for alignment. He said, "But don't you know that when a car turns over, there is awful pressure on a tire?" I said, "I didn't think of that." He said, "It's time you learned to use your head." I said, "Dad, I don't claim to know everything." Also, I said, "If you knew this, why didn't you tell me to check the tires?" And Mom said the same thing to him.

After Dad left the room, I said to Mom, "That's the trouble: Dad thinks I know everything he does, and that if I don't, I should." But if she started an argument with him, he wouldn't understand anyhow.

Gee, it was wonderful when my sister and her husband and I were at our house, and Dad and Mom were away in California. We were really *living* in that house for once. I was happier when Dad and Mom were away.

Will you have more hershey? (Counselor shakes her head.) Are you sure?

C-11: I love the stuff, but I have to watch my weight.

R-12: Now, don't you worry about watching your weight. You're just right. Now have some more of my candy.

C-12: Well, now, if you put it that way, how can I refuse?

R-13: That's right! (Very pleased and gracious.) Say, I'd like to tell you about a dream. Would you like to hear about a dream?

C-13: Ummmmm.

R-14: Well, I just happened to remember a nightmare. I thought of it the other day. It was a nightmare I used to have over and over again when I was much younger. All the dream consists of was a shed, a dark little house. I was chasing this person. I don't know who the person is. But once he got in that house I was frightened. And I never went into the house. I remember that dream because it kept recurring. I can't even tell you how long ago it is that I had that dream for the last time. . . . I hear the person in that house, but I'm afraid to go in there, and I don't know what the fear is.
(Removes his dark glasses and looks around the room.) Say, are there some people who can't see any better than I can see now? Everything is hazy.
(His pupils are still very dilated. He puts his glasses on again.) I think I told you that I received one letter from Jane, about her grades?

C-14: Yes, I remember.

R-15: She says ——— is an awfully difficult college. For a long time she was on probation. She claims she is studying hard there. But she always has a funny feeling of feeling terrible after an exam. She says what will she do if she doesn't pass. But I always know whether I've passed or failed an exam, don't you?

C-15: Yes, I think I usually have some idea of how well or how poorly I've done.

R-16: Well, that's how I feel.
I keep thinking about Dad, for some reason. Sometimes when Dad was just walking with me on the seashore, I'd feel so good. I'd want him to be like that all the time.
Dad's never been a *stingy* man, but I always hated to go to him for money. He gave it always, but I hated to ask. Many times I would go without things I needed, because I didn't want to ask.
Another thing: when Dad talks to you, he pounds on the desk,

or on the arm of his chair, with a pencil. (Demonstrates how his father punctuates every word with his pounding.)

I feel like saying, "Stop lecturing, and just *talk!*" It's always the thump, thump, thump with his hand on his chair-arm, or his fist, or his finger, or a pencil on the table or on the desk. It almost puts you to sleep, honest!

I don't recall all I told Dad the night he bawled me out about the tire. I more or less told him a little of what I was feeling. I told him I haven't lived fifty years, and that my common sense wasn't the same as his.

I ignore his authority much more than I used to. I go to my room and listen to the radio or read. I just stay away from them as much as possible.

It makes me so mad . . . Dad never talks. It's just "Yup." And the other day I was talking to him and he didn't turn around to face and talk to me. He stood with his back to me, at the kitchen sink, and I had to talk to his back. I felt like grabbing his shoulders and turning him around.

Well, I've given up talking to him. It's like talking to a wall. You know, I always said that there was a wall between us; but I guess he is the wall.

Another thing that bothers me about our house is the way we never have company. I guess Mom feels it's too much work or something. If I want to bring a friend home just for a sandwich at noon, Mom says, "Why don't you let him go home to eat!"

You know, we were never spanked, and my punishment came from Dad through Mother. She would always say to me, "If you don't do such-and-such, I'll catch it from Dad."

C-16: You mean, that *she* would "catch it"—or you?

R-17: No, that *she* would. That Dad would punish *her* if we didn't do something right.

C-17: How did that make you feel?

R-18: It made me feel like an awful heel if you caused your mother to get punished! I guess it was really worse than direct punishment would have been.

C-18: Yes, I should think so. But your Dad never spanked you?

R-19: No, never. Say, I can't see my watch, but it feels late.

C-19: Yes, it is time to stop. We'll go on next time.

R-20: Next time, I'll be able to see where I'm going.

C-20: Well, take care of yourself.

R-21: Oh, I can see my way around, really. It's just that I can't see to read.

C-21: Good-bye, then, until next time.

R-22: Good-night. See you Monday. Have a nice weekend.

C-22: Thank you. You, too.

R-23: Thanks. I'll try.

Discussion of the Seventeenth Interview with Ralph

It becomes more and more clear that Ralph has a great need to measure up to the demands of his father. Otherwise, he feels like a failure and becomes defensive. It is not easy to distinguish now between what the father actually demands of him and what Ralph now *feels* is demanded of him.

There is something quiet and sober in this hour. Ralph evaluates what he has achieved thus far, and states his fears of what difficulties may lie ahead.

Eighteenth Interview with Ralph

R- 1: I'm sorry I wasn't able to get here Monday. Jane's mother was sick, and I could not get away.

I got lost on the subway tonight. I ended up at 116th Street and Lenox Avenue. How did that happen, do you know?

C- 1: No, I'm sorry. Subways defeat me. Once I rode from 96th Street to Riverdale, and I went on reading, because I thought Riverdale was the final destination and that the train would stop there. But the train went into reverse and went back to 96th Street, so I found myself at the starting point when I looked up from my book expecting to see my destination.

R- 2: (Laughs.) Boy, what a funny feeling that must have given you!

C- 2: Yes, I had a strange moment.

R- 3: So did I, tonight, when I found myself over on Lenox Avenue. Say, before I forget, could you tell me how much money I owe? (Counselor looked it up and told him.)

R- 4: That's fine, thank you. I'll pay it a week from today. Could I make up the hour that I missed Monday?

C- 4: Yes, if you like. Can you come in Friday afternoon?

R- 5: Oh, that would be grand. Thank you very much. What time?

C- 5: I'll be here at four for a class, so I could see you at three. Can you make it?

R- 6: Yes, I sure can. I'll be here at three. Well, I think I'll tell you about the job I took and gave up. I didn't like it. Are you interested?

C- 6: I am interested in anything you are interested in telling me.

R- 7: All right. Well, I was getting desperate for a job.

C- 7: Why *desperate*?

R- 8: I felt I needed to do something. Just to be doing something. Well, the job as it was originally described to me was that I was to deliver things and do some sweeping and dusting, for twenty-five dollars a week. On the first day he had me carry out ashes, clean the floor, and dust and rearrange all the art objects and ornaments in a big glass showcase. I didn't even start on deliveries until 3:30. So I didn't finish until 6:30. And *then* he asked me to sweep the floor *again*.

C- 8: Wow!

R- 9: Yes, exactly. That's just how I felt. He kept asking me to do all these things in addition to our original bargain. So the next morning I told him I wasn't satisfied. He said, "Then why did you take the job?" I said, "I'll give anything a try, but for twenty-five dollars a week I don't want that kind of job."
I came home and said to Dad, "I quit my job." And Dad said, to my surprise, "That's the wisest thing you've done. If you start on a job like that, you have no time to look for a better one. Next time you'll know better."
So, it was an interesting episode, wasn't it?

C- 9: Yes, it was.

R-10: He was some guy, wasn't he? I mean, the man who owned the art shop.

C-10: He was an exploiter.

R-11: Yes, terrible. For instance, I asked another fellow there how often those cases got dusted, and he said about every month or so, but I think that if I had stayed I'd been doing it every week. But I'll tell you (smiles beamingly at counselor) . . . after I did it, it was *good,* it really sparkled. Now I'm tellin' you, I really made it look very neat.

C-11: I am sure you did.

R-12: Yup, I sure did. I liked doing that part. Balancing the vases, a big one on this side, then a big one on that side, then the smaller ones, then the ornaments. (He draws pictures in the air.)

C-12: Have you given thought to finding other outlets for that capacity in yourself?

R-13: I guess I should. I'll have to give that some thought.

R-14: The man and wife who own the shop couldn't even get along with each other. Say, I never heard two people curse at each other as much as they did. My goodness! It was something awful. It really was.

You know, I've been thinking, I might have that . . . what do you call it? Ann . . . an . . . something?

C-14: Aniseikonia?

R-15: Yes! That's it. I think I might have it for this reason: *I'm* more relaxed, and I am feeling much better generally, but when I tried reading this week, my eyes got terribly tired. And they shouldn't, because I am feeling so much better generally. I feel that I'm *living* a life instead of *leading* one.

C-15: That's a clever way of putting it.

R-16: (Grins.) You like that?

C-16: I sure do. Don't you?

R-17: Yes, it expresses what I mean.

R-18: Say . . . (reaching for a wallet in his pocket, and extracting a newspaper clipping) I felt awful bad that I missed this salesman's job that I *should* have gotten.

(He expresses considerable chagrin.)

C-18: Why do you feel so "awful bad" if you miss an opportunity?

R-19: That's what Dad said. He said, "There's a place for everybody in this world, and you'll find your place, so don't worry."

Say, in about six months now I'll be getting married. Isn't that great? I can't wait.

You remember my telling you about Jane's not feeling well? I went to see her, and after I'd been there a few hours, she seemed to recover completely. She had had a stuffy head, but it just all cleared up.

(Chuckles.)

Her mother was in bed with a sore throat, and couldn't talk very well.

Oh, I wish you could have been there! (Laughing robustly at something that occurred to him.) I helped Jane sew some curtains for her mother's bedroom. She wanted to put wide ruffling on them, and with the amount of material she had to work from, I could see it was a geometric problem. She just started cuttin'. I said, "Hey, wait a minute!" She said to let her alone, that she knew exactly how to do it. (Ralph gives a very funny detailed account of the cutting and sewing of the curtains. Jane spoiled two curtains by cutting them too short, and Ralph helped her repair the damage by working out an extra ruffle.) Jane couldn't see how it was done. I tell you, (laughing) I just had to hide the scissors when I saw how she was cutting. Gee, we had so much fun.

Oh, wait, that isn't all! Then the sewing machine broke. Then we had an argument. It started with the ruffling. She told me I didn't know how to do it. I felt that was okay, since I'm a man and she's a woman. But I had already done half of it when she said I didn't know how. I let her do the other half.

But then the bobbin thread broke, and she didn't know how to get it into the machine again. But she insisted that she knew how to do it. So finally I just went into the other room. After a while she came in and said, "Fix the bobbin!" I said to her, "You have an air of knowing how to do everything, so you go in there and fix the bobbin."

She didn't know what I was talkin' about, so I gave her some examples. Once, up at school, she had asked me to fix a little bookcase. It needed a new piece of lumber to replace one that had split. She wanted me to just do a patch-up job, but I knew that old piece of wood was shot and wouldn't hold. I said I would take the bookcase home and fix it right with new wood and repaint the whole thing. She said, "Oh, then I'll do it!"

So now I said to her, "Now look, if I tried to fix that bobbin, you'd start telling me how to do it." She began to cry and said, "Would it be better if I don't talk to you at all?" I said, "Yes, sometimes."

So she went in the other room, but a little later, as I was listening to the radio, she came over to me and said, "Will you please fix the bobbin?" I said, "Yes, would you like to come watch me?" (Very dignified.) She did, and I fixed it, and I showed her how to thread it properly, not the way she'd been doin' it. So, from then on it was very nice.

She is somewhat like my father; she has a hard time admitting her mistakes. It's hard to tell her her mistakes. When I told her what she was doing, she sat sulking. That kind of thing used to make me nervous, but no more. I've gotten over feeling nervous!

Before I started coming to see you, Jane used to often make me nervous by the way she talked to me. It made my stomach feel awful inside. Like the time she said she wouldn't play cards with me. Aw, gee, what that did to me! But this time I said to her, "You come here and sit down and don't be a know-it-all." I said to myself, "Was that me talking?" (Laughs.) "Nice going," I said to myself.

(Stretches luxuriously and beams at the ceiling, then turns and smiles at the counselor.)

Aw, this is so much nicer. Honest, I'm really grateful for all that's happened the past few months. I'm so glad it all happened before we were married. Now I know she's going *my* way. If she doesn't want to go *my* way, the heck with it, she can go *her* way.

You see, I love Jane, but I know the love wouldn't last long if I let her push me around. Now she *tells* me that I mean a great deal to her. I know she misses me when we aren't together. And I do feel I mean more to her.

And now I'm not as desperate for getting a job as I am for getting a *good* job. I'm too good for that. You know, in the past I'd not have been able to quit that job. I'd have thought it was my fault, somehow or another. Also, I'd have thought, "What would the family say if I'm not working."

You know, he even wanted me to work on Sundays. I said, "Oh, no, not on Sundays."

(The hour was up, and counselor made the usual gesture of beginning to gather her things.)

R-20:   Well, live and learn. (Gets up and puts on his coat.) So you think I did right in quitting?

C-20:   Yes, I do. But do you really need me to tell you that?

R-21:   Okay, okay! (Grinning.) Then I'll see you Friday?

C-21:   Yessir. Friday at three.

Discussion of the Eighteenth Interview with Ralph

Ralph is pleased by his own increasing assertiveness. His self-affirmation is growing and has more meaning for him. His behavior with Jane is not just angry defiance, but is based on real understanding: "The love wouldn't last long if I let her push me around."

The first positive statement about his father (since the first interview) occurs during this session. It is impossible to know whether the father has so rarely been encouraging, or whether Ralph's defensiveness has made him unaware of possible warm gestures from the father. His growing self-confidence would free him to hear encouragement to which he may have been deaf previously.

Nineteenth Interview with Ralph

R- 1: (Settles back in chair and proceeds to tease:) Now tell me everything.

C- 1: Well, I could tell you a dream I had. Very interesting.

R- 2: Well, before that, what would you like us to talk about?

C- 2: Anything you would like to talk about.

R- 3: Mom left today to get her hair done. She won't drive in icy weather or foggy weather. So I'm just wondering where my car is at this moment. The roads are one sheet of ice at home. I was thinking of bringing the car tomorrow when I have my eyes examined.

C- 3: Is it all right to drive after you have your eyes dilated?

R- 4: I don't know. But I do want to go upstate. I took the trip this fall. I never saw anything so beautiful. Gosh, the trees, and the sun. But tomorrow it may not be so pretty, huh?

C- 4: No, probably not.

(Ralph is quietly thoughtful.)

C- 5: (After several minutes.) So . . . you have no more problems.

R- 5: No, I haven't. Everything's fine. I haven't found a job yet, but I'll wait until I find one that suits me.

And my headaches still come back if I read. When I read, my head feels heavy, uncomfortable, though it isn't a sharp pain.

C- 6: Please be sure to tell all that to your eye examiner tomorrow, won't you?

R- 6: Yes. It's a woman, a Miss ————. (Takes out his appointment card and looks at it.) Oh, the appointment is ten o'clock, not ten-thirty. It's a good thing I looked at this.

This woman says it's a very interesting examination. It's the newest thing, and it must be interesting. I do hope I'll be able to see well enough to drive afterwards. Well, even with eye drops, I'll be able to drive. I couldn't read, but if I could walk through the city, I'm sure I could drive.

(Silence.)

C- 7: What are you thinking?

R- 7: I'm trying to think of something to tell you. I'm not worrying about anything now. I'll just let the future come.

I was reading all this afternoon, and it left me with the feeling of having a heavy head. When I get up in the morning, my head is clear, and I imagine it would stay clear if I didn't start in reading. So I am anxious to get my eyes examined.

(Silence.)

C- 8: You have no problems now, with the exception of the eye condition we suspect. So . . . you feel you do not need me any more.

R- 8: No, I still need you.

C- 9: What for?

R- 9: Well, even though everything is going smoothly and in many ways I feel like a completely different person from the one who first walked through that door, I'd like to continue with you for awhile until I feel really secure in this new feeling I have. In the meantime, maybe we could practice things, like outlining, for example. I feel that now I have the patience to concentrate on study habits that used to upset me before.

C-10: Want to start right now?

R-10: (In a burst of enthusiasm.) Sure!

C-11: There are a number of books on my desk. Would you like to select one that interests you, and read to me?

(Ralph selected a book on nature study. He read a paragraph and then commented as follows.)

R-11: I used to read by letters, letter by letter, and I never skipped a single letter in a word. Now I'm at least reading by words. Maybe eventually I'll graduate to phrases.

C-12: Right!

(Ralph continued reading. Whenever his reading was particularly choppy and word-by-word in cadence, counselor interrupted and made comments on the story, to stimulate Ralph to focus on the meaning of what he was reading, and to show him she was listening for story-comprehension, for pleasure and with interest rather than critically. After two such interruptions, the reading became smooth and expressive; he had made the shift to emphasis on comprehension. He commented:)

R-12: It's much better just now, isn't it? I feel I'm doing better as I go along. I'm enjoying it.

(The rest of the hour was devoted to reading aloud and discussing the material in the nature-study book. Counselor took turns with Ralph, reading aloud. Ralph showed considerable knowledge about trees, animals, birds, flowers and plants. He reminisced about pine groves he had walked through and about various phenomena he had observed in nature.)

R-13: (At end of the hour.) I felt today that I read better than I ever did before. Did you get that impression?

C-13: Your phrasing was good and your reading became expressive as you concentrated on the meaning of what you were reading.

Discussion of the Nineteenth Interview with Ralph

Ralph's relationship with the counselor becomes increasingly freer, and he generally shows more self-reliance. The purpose of C-8 is to stimulate Ralph to formulate his present problems. Ralph expresses the wish to do some work with "study habits"; he says that he now has the patience for it. This interview marks the introduction of work on reading and study habits.

Twentieth Interview with Ralph

R- 1: Well, I've got it!

C- 1: What?

R- 2: Aniseikonia!

C- 2: So you *do* have it!

R- 3: Yes, I *do*! I told Mom about it. I said I've probably had it all my life. Mom said nobody ever found it before.

I suffered miserably after that examination. It wasn't a very extensive examination. There was a lot of lining-up of my eyes. I'll try to explain it to you the best I can. (Draws a diagram for the counselor.) First of all, we started with this chart. This is how I saw it every time. I couldn't get those arrows to point at each other together. (Ralph tells counselor in precise detail, and with drawings, all about the examination.)

C- 3: You have a remarkable memory.

R- 4: Well, I made a special effort to remember it all, because I thought it would interest you.

C- 4: Thank you. That was very thoughtful.

R- 5: It's okay. . . . They gave me a prescription to take to this address. If the snap-on lens corrects my vision, I'll have it made right into the glasses I have now. I'll rent the snap-on lens to try it out for a month. If the strain is not relieved, it still may not be the correct lens.

After the examination, I drove up to see Jane. I had such a headache. I never had one like it before. My head was just about ready to break open. I asked Jane to put up with me if I acted irritable. But as soon as Jane knew I had a headache, she gave me two aspirin, but it didn't help. And I felt nauseated. That's an indication to me that we are finding out more and more what's bothering me. Mom said to me, "Do you suppose we have really found out what is wrong, and we can 'go to town' now?" I feel it's possible.

After I had a nice night's sleep, I woke up Sunday feeling like a million dollars. Aspirin didn't do any good, so it must have been more than a normal headache. But in the morning I felt good. I tried to be as pleasant as I possibly could. It seems to help if you act pleasant. Before, most anything could make me irritable and excited. Now I try to make the best of everything. And I really had a lovely week-end. I went shopping with Jane. You know, it wasn't a doctor who gave me the test. It was a lady. I asked her if bright light would bother me with this condition. Not bright light when my eyes are rested, but if my eyes are a bit tired. She said, "It's just because your eyes *are* tired that the light hurts them."

I feel I could feel so much better if my eyes had less strain. Both my eyes don't see the same images. I asked her if it was definite, the diagnosis. She said it is absolutely definite and outstanding, and she gave her report to the doctor, and he saw it right away, and he had the final say on it. I have to go back to him in a month to see if the new lens has helped me. I don't know if it is correctable or not. I'll have to find out.

R- 6: Here, you aren't eating any candy. (Ralph had brought a box of Valentine candy which both counselor and Ralph ate during the interview.)

C- 6: Thank you. It's good.

R- 7: (Nods.) The headache I had was similar to the ones I usually have, only much sharper. I felt it an awful lot.

C- 7: I'm sorry you had all that discomfort.

R- 8: Well, it was worth it to find out a thing as important as this is. Well, now we'll have to see if the glasses will correct it.

Let me tell you what we did. There wasn't much doing, so I said to Jane, "Let's go window shopping." So we went through all the department stores, and we looked at furniture, and had day dreams about our house. I told her if there was anything she wanted for her birthday, to please tell me about it. She saw a coffee table and said, "I'd like that!" I said, "You will get that, but now let's get something for your birthday."

Finally we went to a jewelry counter. She said she would like to have an electric clock. They brought out a very nice one. It was lovely. So that will be my present to Jane for her birthday. I like doing it that way.

She is really trying hard to save money, too, and she is doing well, too. The money I spend is in going up to see her over week-ends. I'd rather not spend money during the week, because I have more enjoyment when I am with her—which is a natural reaction.

I hope the eye thing does wonders, because I'm ready for it. (Laughs.)

R- 9: By the way, I wanted to tell you. . . . After the eye test, the top half of my eyes felt awful dark, sort of blacked out. Strange. (Thoughtful.)

Well, I can't wait to see what those glasses will do.

The weather is thawing out nicely. Only, when you are driving, you keep going through puddles. But my car isn't built too low, so, through all that water, it only gained power. The moisture mixed with the gasoline makes it more powerful.

C- 9: You have so many interesting bits of information.

R-10: It's nice to be that way, but I'd be pleased to be an authority on one thing. That's what I'll do. I'll settle down to business administration and learn the whole thing and become an expert.

I've been wondering whether I want to go back to ———— College or not. I don't know how good their business instruction is. It's not a bad school. It's rated pretty high.

I've been hearing about other colleges, from various people. There's ———— College, where you get two months for Christmas, but you have to work during those two months. They get you a job and you have to work. You bring back a written report, plus your employer's report.

Gosh, I thought all colleges were like ————. And I felt I was a failure, and that all colleges would deal with me the way they did. I thought I was just one of those who simply could not get through college.

I think I'll write away for catalogs from a few other colleges, and then I'll know better what I want to do.

C-10: Good.

R-11: Do you know anything about ———— College?

C-11: Everything I have heard about that school has been excellent. I think you'd do well to follow your plan to explore a little. Why not write for their catalog, too?

R-12: Yes, I intended to. So you like that school?

C-12: Yes, very much. . . . Let's stop here, shall we? Our time is about up.

R-13: Okay.

Discussion of the Twentieth Interview with Ralph

The discovery that Ralph has aniseikonia is a big relief to him, since it removes some of the self-accusation. The counselor feels relieved, too, that Ralph's eyes are receiving responsible medical attention.

The counselor wrote to the physician for information about "aniseikonia," asking specifically whether it was regarded as having psychogenic origins. The physician's reply follows:

Dear Mrs. Ephron:

Aniseikonia is a term applied to a measurable asymmetry of the size or shape of the retinal images formed in the two eyes. When corrected with especially ground lenses, symptoms referable to the condition are often relieved. It is true that this condition is found in many eyes and does not always produce ocular symptoms. We frequently have the impression that there is a psychic factor.

Sincerely,

Twenty-first Interview with Ralph

R- 1: Well, tonight I feel just fair. I have a toothache. It aches something awful. It felt so bad, I didn't feel like coming here tonight, actually. I guess I have to have the wisdom teeth out, a couple of them.
(Silence.)

C- 1: What are you thinking?

R- 2: I'm thinking how this tooth hurts all the way down my neck. Next Saturday is Jane's birthday. I've been polishing that clock once in a while. It's really nice.

The eyeglass man said he would get the glasses done in a week at the longest, and that was last Wednesday.

I had a little discussion with Dad last night. He can't understand. He says, "I know you are not reading all day long, and when you are not reading, that's wasted time." He was referring to a job.

I said, "If I get a job, it's going to take an awful lot of my time. Then I come home tired and cannot get as much out of my reading as I should." He's as bad as Jane in trying to understand what I'm doing here. I even told him that it's possible that I won't go back to ———. (His college.) I said that there are certain things that that college doesn't give me that other schools might.

I told him I'm looking for a job, but I won't take any old job. I want to get something really worthy. They are laying people off now instead of hiring them. I said to my Dad, "What are you so upset about?" I never did talk to him like that before. And he took it from me, because he saw I was right.

I think that the next time I look for a job it will be a part-time job. I want to be able to get here on time. I don't want to take a full-time job and then have to say I'm sorry, I can't stay this night or that night.

As far as the money angle goes, that's not what I'm going to work for. I'm mainly working for experience.

Dad said last night, "Everybody has a place, and that place is the right place. Here is your goal, and here is your working toward that goal. If you are floundering around out there, how are you going to get there?" I said, "How do you know I'm 'out there'? You can't point out the line for me, because that might not be the right one for me."

You see, he picks out one straight line for me, and he assumes I'm floundering because I'm not on *his* line. Yay, yay! (Shouts exuberantly.) I really felt like telling him to mind his own business, but I'm living at home, at no cost, and I feel I have to be nice to him.

I received a letter from Jane today. It was awfully nice. She was thinking about how things would be after we are married. She has a job connection out there in ———. It would be so nice, she said, if she could get a job and be there with me. That made me feel good, because if I go out to ———, to school there, maybe she would get a job there and be right with me. I wrote to them for a catalog and an application.

Dad talked to our optometrist about my aniseikonia. Dad said he doesn't know anything about it. I said, "It's true it's something new, but if the people at the Medical Center say a thing, it's true." I think Dad must have had the feeling that if our optometrist doesn't know, nobody knows.

C- 2: While we are on the subject of your physical well-being, tell me again when you had your last complete medical check-up.

R- 3: That was three years ago, when I went into the Army. But, as you understand, I would never go for a medical, except for insurance. The Army doctors did a thorough examination. I was okay.

This week I've been careful not to read for too long at a time. If I read for an hour, as I told you when I first came here, I'd get breathless. I'd be puffing like a steam engine.

Dad said to me, "Look at Helen Keller. She didn't even need her eyes to become a student." I had told Dad I wasn't using my eyes as an "excuse" . . . and that was his answer.

I don't know. . . . Dad always gave me the feeling I wasn't a go-getter. I always knew he would give me anything I wanted. And, also, Dad taught me if ever I wasn't sure of anything, to fall back on him. I'm not going to teach *my* son that. Also,

Dad always told me, "You've got to push, you've got to fight, you've got to go after what you want." It seemed to have the opposite effect on me. I can't quite figure that one out. (Puzzles over it.)

C- 3: Perhaps you felt that if he had had any real assurance you could make the grade, he would not feel it necessary to do so much urging. It was as if he were saying, "You've got to fight, I'm afraid you can't."

R- 4: Exactly! That's it! That's just the feeling it gave me. It made me feel hopeless, instead of encouraging me. Gee, I hope I'll be a good parent!

C- 4: You're on the way to being one.

R- 5: I hope so. (Earnestly.) I don't want to make those awful mistakes.

Today I went into a travel bureau to get some ideas for a honeymoon. Friday, Jane and I will look over some pamphlets and decide what we might do. I'd love to go to Mexico, but we can't afford it. Jane would like to go to England, but I think that's even *more* expensive.

Gee, my tooth feels better. How do you account for that! Today my Dad told me to go see a dentist. He's getting so inconsistent. He always used to say, "There's no intelligence in matter. Forget the pain." Mom sprained her wrist, and he told her to forget it. When he sprained his ankle, he had to limp. Well, whatever did it, my toothache is gone.

Discussion of the Twenty-first, Twenty-second, Twenty-third, and Twenty-fourth Interviews with Ralph

These interviews seem to be clearly self-explanatory. In the twenty-third interview, the counselor perhaps ought to have referred Ralph to sources of information about colleges throughout the country.

Twenty-second Interview with Ralph

R- 1: Well, what do you think of them? (His new glasses.)

C- 1: They are very handsome, indeed. They really do you credit.

R- 2: Thank you. I like them myself. Why weren't you here Monday? (Teasingly.)

C- 2: It was a legal holiday. I'm sure I must have mentioned it. Did I forget to tell you?

R- 3:   Well, I'll tell you the truth. I came up at noon to see if this place was open. I was in New York anyhow. I asked at the information desk, and he said there was no school. The door downstairs here was locked. Then I came back to New York Tuesday to get my glasses.

C- 3:   Please forgive me for forgetting to tell you about the holiday. Apparently I did forget it.

R- 4:   That's okay. Really it is. Don't give it another thought. Anyhow, listen, I want to tell you something: I was reading today with these glasses for four hours, and it was surprising how comfortable my eyes did feel. It was wonderful. That's more than I'm used to at any time. I feel fine.

I went and asked the person who made the glasses, "Will these correct the condition?" He said, "No, you've had it all your life, and you will always have it." I felt that was the answer. Gee, I wonder if it's more difficult to detect it in children. . . . But I sure read for a long time today.

C- 4:   How was your concentration?

R- 5:   Very good. I was reading this little blue book (67). It has very good, true things in it. Like this article on "How to Develop Reading Interests." Did you read this one?

C- 5:   Yes, but I'd enjoy hearing it again.

(Ralph reads aloud. The cadence of phrasing is uneven, sometimes choppy, but it improves markedly as he goes along.)

R- 6:   Sometimes when I try taking in more than one word at a time, I get the wrong word. But, where there's a will there's a way! (Ralph continues reading aloud.)

At the end there, I tried to go too fast, so that makes me go too slow. Let's see now, I think I can answer the questions easily. (He is referring to the comprehension-check questions at the end of the article.)

(Ralph went over the questions and answered them all correctly and adequately. Apparently the word-substitutions in his oral reading had not interfered with his comprehension. He had said, "attack" instead of "attract," "we are" instead of "are we," and "socially" instead of "sociability.")

R- 7:   You know, at school I used to just sit and read and read and not know what I was reading. So, what I did just now was good, wasn't it?

C- 7: Yes, *very* good.

R- 8: I took time to put my book down, take my glasses off, and just think about what I had read. Seems that I remembered it that way. I remembered what you once told me, that Dr. Strang said she sees people in the library reading, but she never sees them just thinking about what they have read. Shall I outline the article now?

C- 8: If you like. What will be your purpose in doing so?

R- 9: Well, I've heard you say it helps to become aware of the structure of what we read, and outlining the main ideas should give me the structure.

C- 9: Yes, and then the important details will cluster around the main ideas to which they belong. It's useful for remembering what you read.

(The rest of the hour was spent in practice in outlining, drawing schematic pictures of paragraphs, discussing the purposes and methods of skimming, and so forth. Ralph's manner was calm and earnest.)

Twenty-third Interview with Ralph

R- 1: Well, March is here. Did it come in like a lion or a lamb?

C- 1: A little of each, I think.

R- 2: Say, did you ever hear from my college?

C- 2: Oh, yes.

R- 3: What did they say?

C- 3: Well, they said they found you friendly and pleasant, and that you caused no trouble. They said that somehow you had missed the psychological tests they usually give.

R- 4: What do they mean! They just didn't give any! You know, I wrote to ———— College, and they are going to send me a catalog. They've already sent me an application blank.
Well, I liked the work we did here last time. I think I ought to do some more. I was thinking . . . when you say I shouldn't pronounce every word, well . . . I feel I won't know the word unless I pronounce it.

C- 4: Let's try something today. I'll give you thirty seconds to skim this article. See how much you get out of it in that time. It will hardly give you time to do any "pronouncing."

R- 5: Okay.

(Ralph reads an article in the blue book while counselor times him. After thirty seconds he is able to give the main idea succinctly and a few of the major details. He laughs with pleasure.)

R- 6: This is like a game. Who would have thought I could get so much in *thirty seconds!*

C- 6: Now, suppose you re-read the whole article, and I'll time you. We'll keep a record of your speed and the accuracy of your comprehension, and we'll be able to watch your progress and discuss it as we do more of these exercises.

(Ralph reads the article, at a speed of approximately 240 words per minute, then answers the questions correctly.)

R- 7: I just noticed something: The first time I read this, a long time ago, I marked, "Reading fast is the most important thing." Now I see that comprehension is the most important thing of all.

(The remainder of the hour was spent in reading, silently and aloud. Near the end of the session, Ralph set aside the book in order to speak about something on his mind.)

R- 8: Should I go to ――――― College? Jane might get a good job there, so perhaps I ought to go there. Don't you think so?

C- 8: To me the important question is, why don't you make your own decision?

R- 9: Yeah, it's the same old thing, isn't it? I ought to be making up my own mind about things.

C- 9: I know I have said to you that I like ――――― College, but that does not mean you have to apologize to me if you want to go elsewhere—does it?

R-10: No. I know what you mean. It's the same old thing. I can see it now so clearly when you point it out to me that way.

C-10: Well, I guess we have to stop here; we've used up all our time. We'll continue in our next, shall we?

R-11: Okay.

Twenty-fourth Interview with Ralph

Ralph looks unusually well tonight. He has good color, his eyes sparkle, and his expression is brightly alert.

R- 1:   (Teasingly.) I was going to stay downstairs and listen to a lecture, but I thought you would be waiting for me. . . . Do you mind if I take off my tie?

C- 1:   No, not at all.

R- 2:   (Removes tie, folds it and puts it away in a pocket.) Say, don't your feet get cold in those shoes?

C- 2:   No. When the weather gets very cold, I wear boots.

R- 3:   (Shakes his head wonderingly.)
Say, I saw television last night. Court of Public Opinion. They held a regular court. Last night they discussed Palestine, and the various issues. They had a war correspondent who covered Palestine and the Far East all through the war. And someone who taught Turkish. It was very interesting. I enjoyed that. And, of course, they are dealing with problems that are world-known. Then they take a vote. Next week is a very interesting subject, too; I think it has to do with the Marshall Plan. It will be interesting to find out more about it.
Well, I received my new license this morning. The car was officially turned over to me. The car formerly was in Dad's name. A fifty-dollar bill for insurance goes with it. But, if I want the car, I have to pay for that, too.
(Thoughtful.)

C- 3:   What is it?

R- 4:   As I left the house today, I had the vague feeling that something was wrong. I hope not, but I had the same feeling the day my dog died. I was away from home, but I had the feeling something was wrong.
Gee, that was my favorite dog. (Takes out wallet and shows counselor picture of his dog.) Nobody missed him like I did. He was so good to me. He used to play with me. He played with me and with nobody else.
Time passes so fast. It's hard to remember exactly when it was. I guess it was in high school. He wouldn't listen to anybody but me. I don't know why. The thing I liked was that it was a dog with lots of life! Gosh, I've dreamed of Buddy coming back—so I must have missed him an awful lot.
Some dogs you just can't do things with. My friend has a boxer. He jumps up and puts his front paws on your shoulders. And

he pesters and licks you and tries to sit in your lap. And his big tongue! He makes me miserable. *My* dog would *appreciate* being petted, but he wouldn't fret and pester you.

I used to let him run, but he'd come back when I called. My family would put a chain choker on him, but I would take his collar off and he'd walk right next to me. I never had to leash him. Wasn't that something?

C- 4: He loved you.

R- 5: Yes, I guess that must have been it. Once my mother threw a dust-cloth at me, and Buddy flew at her and held her wrist. And whenever Jane kissed me or fooled with me, the dog would get serious about it. Maybe he got jealous. (Thoughtful.)

C- 5: What are you thinking?

R- 6: Nothing much. Just remembering Buddy. I guess he was pretty important in my life. He gave me something no one else gave me. I could always be sure of him. It makes me feel good to think of him, but it makes me sad, too. I guess I really miss him. Did you ever have a dog?

C- 6: Yes, I have a wonderful dog, a cocker spaniel named "Suzy." She has silky black and white fur, and I think she's quite magnificent. I know how you feel about Buddy.

R- 7: It's funny how much you can get to love your dog. Isn't that true?

C- 7: Yes, indeed. I'm convinced Suzy has the biggest intellect and greatest heart of any dog that ever was!

R- 8: Do you have a picture of her with you?

C- 8: Yes. (Counselor takes snapshot from her wallet to show to Ralph.)

R- 9: She *is* beautiful! No wonder you rave about her. . . . It's so hard to realize that a dog like Buddy can die. The thing I loved so much about him was that he was a dog with lots of life!

C- 9: I suppose Buddy had the qualities of spontaneity and fearlessness that you wanted for yourself?

R-10: Yes! I loved that in him so much! I guess it was what I wanted to be but was afraid to be. It's funny that I'm thinking about him so much today, too, because I was thinking on the way up here about what we talked about last time. Do you remember? Near the end of the hour?

C-10:   About your need to please everyone, including me?

R-11:   Yes. It was wonderful the way you put it. I couldn't get it out of my head. You said if I didn't want to go to ———— College, I didn't need to apologize to you for it. It seems that all my life I have felt I had to apologize for whatever *I* wanted to do. It's made me angry to think about it, but it also gives me a new feeling of freedom. I can see how hard it is to fight this old thing in me, yet I feel I'm really on the way to doing it.

I didn't have to worry about pleasing Buddy; he loved me all the time. He was a good influence in my life, wasn't he?

C-11:   It seems so.

R-12:   And so are you. It's wonderful the way you never slip up on anything. Saying what you said last week was so plain and natural, and yet it meant so much.

C-12:   Thank you. You must take some credit for yourself, too, for making such good use of a challenge.

R-13:   (Laughs pleasantly.) Okay, okay. That's enough of complimenting each other for one day. Let's get to work now! I think we should talk about my vocabulary today. I've been noticing how I look words up in the dictionary and then forget them and have to look them up again.

I've got a fickle memory, anyhow. Most of the things I remember are being scolded, like for coming in with muddy shoes. Also, another time I came home wet. Mostly punishment is what I remember. Maybe that's why I don't want to remember anything, because all I can remember is unpleasant things. (Grins.) Say, I'm right on the beam today, don't you think?

C-13:   Yes, you look alert and you sound alert.

R-14:   Well, if life begins to feel more pleasant, maybe I'll feel it's worthwhile remembering things, and my memory should improve. In the meantime, can you teach me any tricks to help me remember words?

C-14:   Let me ask you: do you enjoy doing things with your hands? Making things, painting, fixing things?

R-15:   Yes, I always have. Don't you remember I told you about making model planes? And I enjoyed working on that building.

C-15:   Well, let's experiment with the kinesthetic method, the Fernald Method, as it is called.

(The counselor taught Ralph the Fernald Method (19), which consists of seeing the word, hearing it, saying it in syllables while tracing it with the forefinger, then writing and saying it while the original copy is out of sight. If unable to write it accurately, the individual does not look at the word and write it, but goes through the process of tracing and saying the word until it is learned. Then he again tries to write it. The newly learned words are arranged in alphabetical order on cards in a filing system.)

Twenty-fifth Interview with Ralph

Ralph was wearing a bright red shirt today and looked very well and cheerful.

R- 1: Well, Mrs. Ephron, I had a terrific week-end. I worked on theses.

(Counselor looks at Ralph questioningly.)

R- 2: I dictated to Jane while she typed. It was great.

Say, I want to tell you . . . last night I was reading, and I suddenly rubbed my eye. It itched and began to puff up.

C- 2: What was it?

R- 3: I don't know. I had it once before, and that was when I was painting the kitchen. It happened then to *both* eyes. Last night it happened to my *left* eye. A little rubbing seems to set it off. Both eyes get so swollen, I can hardly see. I think it is some sort of irritation. They get all blood-shot, all red.

C- 3: What did the doctor say?

R- 4: I didn't get a doctor.

C- 4: Why don't you show it to a doctor?

R- 5: No, because it happens so infrequently.

C- 5: I really wish you would.

R- 6: Well, last time it might have been the paint when I was painting the kitchen. But this time I wasn't near any paint.

(Reaches for a brief-case and takes out a bulletin from ———— College, and leafs through it.)

There's a lot of information here. I myself would think this school would be great fun. There is so much material here, I could spend quite a while going through it. Both B.A. and B.S. degrees are given. I just received this today.

C- 6: And you are trying to make up your mind?

R- 7: Well, there are other plans entering into it. If Jane has difficulty finding a job in —————— (the locale of his former college), we'll go out and look around in ——————. And it might be possible. She wants to teach high school English, and she's all out for *helping* the kids.

By the way, did I ever get an intelligence test?

C- 7: No, why?

R- 8: Those tests I've had so far don't tell what my I.Q. is, do they?

C- 8: I can get some idea of it from the Rorschach, but it is not as exact as the Bellevue-Wechsler would be.

R- 9: When I go back to school, I'd like to be able to say that my I.Q. is such-and-such.

C- 9: All right. I'll have someone give you a Bellevue-Wechsler if you like.

R-10: Why don't *you* give it to me?

C-10: I think it would be better to get an expert, someone with experience in giving and interpreting them. I'm experienced in Rorschach work but not the other. You might as well have the advantage of being tested by an expert.

R-11: Okay, that's fine. (Leans back in chair with a rather luxuriously relaxed air.) Shall we practice some reading now?

C-11: There is a chapter in this book I think you might like to read. (Ralph kept swinging about in his swivel chair while reading to himself.)

C-12: Tell me something: How are you reading, with interest? Or are you somewhat lackadaisical?

R-12: No, I really am interested, because I always liked lion stories.

C-13: You feel it is worth doing?

R-13: Yes, I like this. Why do you ask?

C-14: I shouldn't like you to do something you did not feel was worthwhile, just because I suggested it.

R-14: I see what you mean. You want me to assert myself with you, too.

C-15: That's right. And I want you to assert yourself with the reading material, too. In other words, do you feel you are making an active attack on that printed page?

R-15: Gee, I see what you mean, all right. Yes, when you are really interested, you do that. You go after it. Well, now, I'll tell you.

(Humorously and teasingly.) I *want* to do this. Because I have no problems on my mind just now, I'm feeling good and I feel like reading. I've been doing the stuff in that blue book, too, and it's really good stuff.

(Counselor and Ralph both read silently for about ten minutes. Then Ralph removed his glasses and rubbed his eyes. His eyes looked red and tired.)

C-16: Do you think you might call the doctor and go in to see about your eyes?

R-16: Well, I think it's because I've been working them pretty hard. (He is quiet for several minutes.)

C-17: What are you thinking about?

R-17: Jane received word from someone at school to have her eyes examined. Her eyes seem to be giving her trouble, too. So I'll make an appointment for her one of these days. But we have so much to do and so little time to do it. . . . I'm glad Jane doesn't have her mother's attitudes. For example, her mother believes in disciplining by creating fear in the child's mind. Jane doesn't agree with her mother but doesn't tell her.

(Ralph discusses at some length Jane's work, attitudes and interests. He respects her ability to put a good deal of time and effort into her work. He also feels she has a sincere interest in young people.)

I found out today that our honeymoon will have to be shortened because prices have gone up. I'm working through a travel bureau, and, from what I understand, where we are going is very nice. We'll go for two weeks to ———.

C-18: It's wonderful there. I know it well.

R-18: Really?

C-19: Yes, you'll love it.

R-19: Now I'm looking forward to it more than ever. Jane and I expected to enjoy it, but now it seems even better than it did. We worked so hard yesterday on our thesis. I say "our" because *I* worked so hard on it. I feel I contributed.

That's another way I've changed, by the way. The last time I dictated, she couldn't stand it because I gave her one word at a time. But this time I did it by phrases, and it went along so smoothly.

I was comfortable, and I could tell by the speed of her typing where she was, and I was one phrase ahead of her. It made me feel good, because last time I wasn't able to read that way. She even commented on how much better it was this time. Gosh, it made me feel good.

Well, I am sleepy. Tonight I'll go home, eat my supper, and go to bed.

Today I was sitting in my room reading, and I happened to look out, and I noticed a big truck getting stuck in the mud. So the steam shovel just came behind it, lifted it and shoved it right out. It was funny to see. And interesting the way a man can swing that big arm around and push boulders around as if they were nothing. And the *power* that has, to pick up a truck! And the truck was full of dirt, too. They're excavating for a new house.

I get up at eight o'clock every morning, at the latest, just so I'll have enough time in the morning to get some good reading done.

(The session was drawing to a close, and Ralph arose to put on his coat.)

R-20: Jane has to write a story for her English course, and I'm going to help her with it.

(Cheerful farewells.)

Discussion of the Twenty-fifth Interview with Ralph

Ralph still wants an intelligence test. He wants to prove that his dropping out of school was not for lack of intelligence. His need to show his I.Q. mirrors his lack of faith in his ability to prove his intelligence by his behavior. It also reflects a cultural attitude in the schools, attaching great importance to the I.Q., whereas it is only one part of the total equipment of qualities which an individual brings to life situations.

The counselor was pleased to hear Ralph make the statement, "You want me to assert myself with you, too."

Twenty-sixth Interview with Ralph

R- 1: How are you today, Mrs. Ephron?

C- 1: Very well, thank you. How are you?

R- 2: I'm feeling fine. Well, yesterday I did quite a lot of concentrated reading, and today I didn't do much. I followed up a lead on a job, but it wasn't for me.

(Lighting his pipe.)

My eye itches, and I just rub it. But the itching becomes greater, and, the more I rub, the more I want to rub, until it becomes swollen. I don't think it's serious. I'm not going to worry about it.

This morning I told Mom I was going out to look for a job, I might not be home for lunch. I said I'd call her if I got a job. When I got home, Mom said, "Why didn't you call?" You could see her throat and lip tightening, and the eyes. . . . It was a tense feeling that she had, like the tense feeling I used to have talking to Dad.

She *said* it was no inconvenience that I didn't have the car home, but she was so tense that it *must* have been an inconvenience. She doesn't like to go by bus, and she took a taxi. I told Mom that nothing definite was told to me. I said, "I didn't have any idea you wanted to go anywhere. Why didn't you tell me?"

The thing is, it didn't bother me at all. It *used* to, that kind of thing. It would upset me for hours. But this time I knew it wasn't any fault of mine, that she didn't make her wishes clear, so I felt very calm about the whole thing.

You see, what she really meant was, "If you're not coming home by noon, call me." But I thought she wanted me to call her only to tell her if I had a job. I felt it was a big improvement in me that I could settle it in my own mind right away and not feel miserable or guilty or upset.

C- 2: Yes, that's very good.

R- 3: Whenever I hear myself tell you things, it makes them clearer to me. Now I'm getting so I can tell them to you when you aren't there, and it gets clear. Pretty soon I'll just be able to tell them to myself, and won't need to imagine that you're there, or try to imagine what you would say.

(Silence.)

C- 3: What are you thinking?

R- 4: I feel good. I haven't anything more I need to talk about. I brought along my blue book.

(The remainder of the session was devoted to reading exercises in the blue book, first skimming them and then trying rapid reading. He found that he could get a great deal out of a thousand-word article by skimming it in sixty seconds. He was very happy about this new sense of mastery, this proof of his ability to read rapidly and remember what he had read.)

R- 5: Another thing: I noticed while I was skimming that I wasn't pronouncing the words, that I was just taking them in with my eyes, and I understood them anyhow.

Discussion of the Twenty-sixth Interview with Ralph

In this interview there is an important indication that Ralph's attitude toward himself is becoming more rational, more adult, less anxious and defiant and self-defeating. He says, "Now I'm getting so I can tell thoughts to you when you aren't there, and it gets clear." (R-3.) This is a nice description of his growing self-affirmation.

It is interesting to see how he checks with the counselor his own new attitudes, his unaccustomed spontaneities, his own sense of what is real and what is better. If he gets her acceptance, he feels free to establish his point of view as a new strength of his own. When he says, "I feel good," he perhaps is really saying, "I'm beginning to be myself; I don't have to feel haunted or threatened. I can let my self-propulsive energies guide me freely, for I can trust my own feelings. This makes me feel joyous and eager."

Twenty-seventh Interview with Ralph

(As Ralph and counselor were settling down for the interview, counselor told him she had arranged for someone to give him a Bellevue-Wechsler Intelligence Test on Wednesday, and to be prepared to stay a little longer if necessary.)

R- 1: Did you have a nice week-end?

C- 1: Yes, very pleasant, thank you. Did you?

R- 2: I had a wonderful week-end. We went to a house-party up at school. Dancing, tennis, plenty of good food. . . . It was strenuous, but a lot of fun. It stretched every muscle I've got. I left there at eleven last night. Got home at three. Had a flat tire.

Say, did I show you my new hat? (Shows it to counselor. Counselor admires it.)

Well, I got up at ten today, and had a hard time getting up. I've been reading all day. I've been reading *Sherlock Holmes* lately. The stories are short and very interesting. I've been trying not to be so self-conscious about my reading. I think I'm reading well.

Something quite nice happened to me today. Mom came to me and said Dad has invited me out to dinner with him tomorrow night to a men's club. So, that will be nice.

Did I tell you about my tire?

C- 2: I don't seem to remember anything about a tire. . . .

R- 3: Well, I looked under my car and saw this bulge on it. On the side wall of the tire was a big cut. I said to Mom, "I sure hope you don't expect me to pay for the new tire!" She said, "It's your car now, so it's your responsibility." I said that would be true if I were the only one using the car, but as long as five people are using this car, it's not my full responsibility. I think the cost should be divided five ways. If they don't, there'll be trouble. Don't you think that's fair?

C- 3: Do you really need my sanction here?

R- 4: No, even if you disagreed with me on this, I'd still feel right about it. Though I'd prefer to feel that you see it the way I do.

C- 4: It sounds quite fair that if five people share the use of the car, the responsibility is thereby shared five ways.

R- 5: Of course. Well, I don't think there'll be any trouble. (Silence.)

C- 5: What are you thinking?

R- 6: I'm thinking that Dad's finally noticed I'd like to go out with him once in a while.

I know there'll be one man there who likes me awfully well. They have been friends of the family a long time, and they have no family. He'll be there, so I know I'll enjoy myself.

I've been thinking it over, and I spoke to Jane about it, and I'll talk it over with my folks soon. I want to ask what they are going to give us for a wedding present. I'll say, if they ask what we want, that we want money to use for our honeymoon, or part of it.

I told Mom I'll refuse to pay for the tire fully. She said, "Don't tell me, tell your Dad." I said, "I never can talk to him. He's like a clam, and always too busy to talk to me." So eventually I'll have to tell him about the wall between us, and that he isn't helping matters much.

When he comes home late, I go down to talk to him, but he has his paper in front of him, and I can't get any response from him. After a while I just get disgusted. I feel he doesn't want me around when he doesn't want to talk to me. I know I'll have to talk to him about it, but it doesn't do any good.

I'd love nothing better than to be able to sit with Dad and talk with him. I had some nice talks with my brother-in-law while Dad was in California. But with Dad—he sits on one side of the room, and I on the other, and we never talk to each other. He wouldn't put the paper down. He'd probably just say, "I'm reading a book. Why don't you pick one up yourself." He doesn't give time to anybody for talking. Unless you say, "Dad, I've got something important to say to you, will you listen to me?" But I don't want to make an appointment with him— that's no good.

Well, that's enough about that for now. Let's practice some more skimming and rapid reading. I brought my book.

(Remainder of hour was spent in reading practice.)

Discussion of the Twenty-seventh, Twenty-eighth, and Twenty-ninth Interviews

The material of these three interviews seems too obvious to require any elaboration. Ralph and his father are growing a little closer and are beginning to do things together.

Twenty-eighth Interview with Ralph

(Counselor had planned a two-hour session with Ralph, so that a Bellevue-Wechsler could be administered after a brief interview.)

R- 1: It's so beautiful today, I decided to get closer to heaven. I've been up flying. I was up with my friend, Bob, but I was doing the flying.

C- 1: Oh, do you know how to fly a plane?

R- 2: No, but I did it today! I'll learn to fly in the next war, I guess. You know, Truman announced there'll be compulsory military training and a draft. (Quite cheerful.)

C- 2: How do you feel about it?

R- 3: I feel I won't come back from *this* war. It'll be an easy war. Just go up in a plane and press buttons. (Gestures pressing buttons.)
I didn't hear much of Truman's speech. I didn't really *care* to hear it. Of course, I don't think Russia will want to fight. But Truman did say, "Put up or shut up." (Ralph says all this in a light, bantering tone.)

C- 3: You seem to take it lightly.

R- 4: Well, I know there is nothing I can do about it. In the last war, I lost interest reading about it, but when I was invited to join the Armed Services, then I began to get interested. They should let the greedy higher-ups get into a boxing ring and fight it out.

C- 4: Yes! That's right!

R- 5: Oh, say! I heard the most wonderful speech last night, at Dad's club. It was really wonderful. That man went through an awful lot. He was a steam-fitter, and a minister, and now he's a professor of social psychology. Gosh, the way he put his points over! He did it through telling stories. It was grand. The only trouble was that we laughed so much we didn't let him talk. It was altogether a good day yesterday. In the morning Dad took me along with his motorcycle club. The one he borrowed for me to use was a beaut. We rode out to ———, had lunch, and rode back. I found it exciting.
(Miss ——— arrived to administer the Bellevue-Wechsler. Counselor introduced Ralph to her, then went into the other room.)

Twenty-ninth Interview with Ralph

Ralph arrived a half-hour early today. He is looking well.

R- 1: Did you have a good vacation?

C- 1: Yes, thank you. Did you?

R- 2: I had a wonderful vacation. Of course, I didn't do much that was different from any other time. I read a lot, worked a lot. The only difference was that I didn't come over here.

(Takes a small package from his pocket.)

I thought you might like to see this.

(Counselor unwraps the little package. Inside is Jane's wedding ring.)

C- 2: This is very beautiful, Ralph. Jane will love it.

R- 3: Oh, she does. She helped pick it out. She's crazy about it. She wants to start wearing it now, can you imagine that! (Laughs.)

C- 3: This is a great moment in a man's life, isn't it.

R- 4: It certainly is. It's great. (Carefully puts the ring away.) If ever she wants a plain band, too, for wearing when she isn't all dressed up, we can get that, too.

Did you get a report yet from Miss ————?

(Referring to the girl who had given Ralph the Bellevue-Wechsler the week before Easter.)

C- 4: No, it's been vacation. She's been away.

R- 5: Well, it was very interesting. Some things about it surprised me. For example, when she'd ask me to do something in fifty-eight seconds, and I'd do it in five seconds. She said speed helps, but that I could take my time and do it very slowly if I wished.

I had a very lovely week-end. I had an enjoyable dinner on Easter Sunday. Everything seems to be going along nicely. I can't say that I have any problems.

Last night I stayed over at Jane's mother's house. I slept very well and felt quite at ease. I worked on the garden there this morning, and I came home at noon. About three o'clock I started out to come here.

Do you like my new shoes? I got them dusty this morning. (Brushes them off.) You know, I never had such comfortable shoes. Do you remember when I bought them?

C- 5: The day you had drops in your eyes and couldn't see what you were buying.

R- 6: That's right! But they turned out to be the most comfortable shoes I ever had. I've worn them only three days, and they feel like I've worn them all my life.

I didn't do any reading yesterday or today. My eyes feel good. The glasses seem to be very effective. I'm going tomorrow morning to have my eyes tested and checked again, and then I'll take these glasses down and have them made permanent.

One day last week my eyes did get tired, but that's natural, isn't it?

C- 6: I don't really know. Better tell your eye people about it.

R- 7: But, look, don't *your* eyes ever get tired?

C- 7: Well, I guess I'm never aware of my eyes' becoming tired; I might just feel generally tired at the end of the day.

R- 8: That's it. I did feel tired all over that day. Do you like this tie?

C- 8: Terrific.

R- 9: I felt like getting all dressed up. I had a nice bath, and I felt so clean, I thought I might as well *look* clean.

C- 9: Is that your new suit you were telling me about?

R-10: Yes, do you like it?

C-10: Very much. The color is right for you.

R-11: Thank you.
Were you out last Sunday night?

C-11: Out?

R-12: Yes, I was wondering if you noticed the fog we had.

C-12: No.

R-13: Well, I was out driving in the worst fog I've ever seen. I had to drive with just small lights on, else I wouldn't have been able to see at all. (He explains the principle of fog lights.) It was so warm out, yet there was ice and snow on the roads. The fog was really terrific.
(Silence.)
Every week-end Jane and I do something toward the wedding. Next Saturday we are going to look for her wedding gown. It's going to be a formal wedding. I don't know if I'll like being warmly dressed in August. (Laughs.) I don't know yet what I'll be wearing, tails or cutaway, or something like that.
Gosh, I'm hungry. I had crackers and milk before I left, but I should have had more.
(Silence.)

C-13: What are you thinking?

R-14: I'm thinking I'd like to eat a big steak, but soon I'll go home and eat a nice Virginia ham we are having tonight.
Would you like me to read something to you? Though I don't feel up to it.

C-14: Whatever you say.

R-15: Okay. (Takes out Dr. Strang's blue book of exercises.) Which one are we on, do you know?

C-15: No, I don't know.

R-16: Oh, here we are. It's number five.
(Ralph did the usual skimming and rapid reading.)
You know, I have learned to skip words. Is that all right?

C-16: Tell me what you think about it. I want to hear your observations.

R-17: Well, I find I don't miss as much as I used to think I would. I've got so I pick out words that look important, and the rest sort of just rolls in with the important ones. You don't have to look at all of them.

C-17: That's excellent.

R-18: Do most people read that way?

C-18: I don't know, but I just thought of an experience you might be interested in hearing. I once had the privilege of studying Victorian Literature under Howard Mumford Jones, and he used to assign many books per week, every single week. Finally, all the students began to feel frantic, because they could not keep up with his assignments. One day one of the students found courage to complain about the impossibly long reading lists. Jones said that undoubtedly none of us had ever learned how to read properly. And he picked up a book and began turning pages, running his eye up and down each page quick as lightning. He told us that he had expected us to do a great deal of skipping, and to just get the general idea, style and flavor of each book he assigned. It was a course designed to cover the whole period of Victorian Literature; had it been an intensive course in just Dickens or Thackeray, he'd have expected more critical, more creative reading. The point I'm trying to make is that Jones was trying to tell that class to suit their method of reading to the purpose of the course. We all had been reading too carefully and thoroughly.

R-19: That's just it. It makes you feel guilty if you skip a single word. Sometimes I would find myself thinking as I was reading, "I'm sure I missed a word up near the top of the page; I'd better go back and find it, to make sure."

C-19: Yes, I know exactly what you mean.

R-20: It's such a relief to find that it just isn't necessary. (Picks up a book.)

C-20: Want to read a little of that for dessert?

R-21: Okay. This time I'll read to you. Here is an article about tropical plants and animals. Are you interested?

C-21: It sounds fascinating.

R-22: All right. Here we go.
(Ralph reads the article fluently. Then Ralph and the counselor have an animated discussion about movies that magnify insect and plant life.)

R-23: (As the session was ending, and he was preparing to leave:) Say! I forgot to tell you about Dean Jones, down at school. I went down there last week. Do you remember how he never called me in or anything when I was on probation? Well, last week he greeted me very warmly, I wish you could have seen it. He said he was so glad that I was working with Dr. Strang, and that as soon as he learned I was connected with Dr. Strang, he knew I would be okay, because he says she is such a grand person.
And he told me he had called in a boy who was also a slow reader, like I was, and he told this boy all about what I had done to get help, and he recommended that he do the same as I had done. Well, the boy went home and talked it over with his father, but his father said it was all silly and foolish, and he wouldn't let him do it. Isn't that a pity?

C-23: It's a crime.

R-24: Yes, it sure is! Now that poor boy is probably worried sick that he'll flunk out or something. So, Dean Jones says that when I come back there, he is going to want to call me in from time to time to work with him.

C-24: Wonderful!

R-25: (With tremendous excitement.) Isn't it, though? He wants me to tell those kids how I profited by the kind of help I got here, and that they should do the same. And they will sooner listen to me, because they know I've been through it! Gosh, the whole thing makes me feel so good. Isn't it great?

C-25: Yes, it's terrific. And I wonder if you couldn't gather together a little group and teach them your new reading techniques.

R-26: Oh, gosh, no . . . ! I wouldn't know how.

C-26: I think you could. You could probably give a helping hand to that boy. Wouldn't you like to?

R-27: Well, the trouble is that there is more to it than just the things I could teach them. I couldn't do what you did with me; I wouldn't know how. I wouldn't know how to bring things out the way you did.

C-27: Well, I was thinking that you might just give the reading tips you've learned, like suiting your style of reading to the kind of material you are dealing with and your purpose in reading it; you know. And, with being friendly and interested in the boy, your help might go a long way.

R-28: I feel that the best I can do would be just to explain the kind of help I got, and talk them into coming for help just the way I did. They just don't know. Gosh, when I was there, I was all alone. Nobody knew what was going on at all. Now, the Dean at least called this boy into his office to talk things over, which he never did before.

C-28: You know, this is mighty exciting.

R-29: Isn't it, though? Gosh, I was so excited . . . ! I'd like to ask you a favor.

C-29: Go ahead.

R-30: Well, when I get to see my intelligence mark, from that test I took—I'm sure it's going to be good—I'd like you to send it to him before I go back there.

C-30: I'll be glad to send it. In fact, I've intended to send him a whole report about you when you go back, giving whatever information will help them to help you. We can map it out together, so you will be in on it.

R-31: Gee, that's grand. Thanks a lot.

He asked me how I felt about taking courses again. I said I wasn't afraid at all, that there was such a big difference in me, I was ready to just sail into those courses!

I told him all about my aniseikonia, and he got quite excited about it. He said that all children should be tested for it in grade school.

C-31: He's right.

R-32: He certainly is. Oh, it's late. I'm sorry, I'm keeping you so late. So I'll go home now and eat Virginia ham.

C-32: Eat up good! Good-bye, Ralph. See you Wednesday.
R-33: Good-bye. Take care of yourself.

Thirtieth Interview with Ralph

Ralph, ruddy and looking as though he has been outdoors all day, greets counselor with a big smile.

R- 1: How are you?
C- 1: I'm very well, thank you, and I'm pleased to tell you that the test you took before Easter proves what I knew all the time. (Teasingly.)
R- 2: What? (Smiling.)
C- 2: You have superior intelligence.
R- 3: Oh, are you kidding me?
C- 3: No, I'm serious.
R- 4: Did you get the report from her?
C- 4: No, all I have is the one message, that you fall in the group called "superior."
R- 5: What number is that? Don't they have a number? Is it 140, or something like that?
C- 5: All I know is what I've told you. I'll probably get the report next week.
R- 6: Well, that's sure good news. I had a feeling I was doing all right, though, because I was enjoying it so much.
Here, you must have a cigarette with me. You know, I don't smoke all the way coming over here, so that I can enjoy a cigarette with you. Isn't that nice?
C- 6: Yes, it is nice. I appreciate the sentiment.
R- 7: Gosh, wasn't this a wonderful day? I was out today with Dad. Every now and then he warms up and becomes a human being, and that feels so nice. He and I were scattering some lime on the lawn. He called up for topsoil, and they didn't deliver it today, so tomorrow I'll have the job of putting it on the lawn. And we washed the car and simonized it. Gee, it sure looked good.
We worked together all day today, and it was nice, you know?
C- 7: Yes.
R- 8: Well, I checked on my glasses. They checked and rechecked, and everything was fine, so I took them down to 45th Street

where they have the glasses made, and they will make the adjustment permanent. But it will take five or six weeks!

C- 8: Oh, my goodness, that's practically the rest of this semester!

R- 9: (Taking glasses out of his pocket.) But they are making a completely new pair, and I have these to use in the meantime.

C- 9: Oh, you fooled me. You made me think you would be without glasses.

R-10: I'm sorry. (Laughs.) So! You say I'm smart. Well, I'll be walking around thinking that I *am* smart.

C-10: I hope so. It would seem a pity to be smart and not enjoy it.

R-11: Yes, I agree with you. Well, got the stop watch out? Would you like to take a test?

C-11: Yes, if you like.

R-12: Okay, I'll get out the watch and give you the test.

C-12: (Laughing.) Oh, oh, so that's it!

R-13: Well, you promised. You said, "Yes," when I asked, "Would you like to take a test?" But I'll let it go this time. Here is the watch. *I'll* take the test.

Say, I tried to get some information (very serious) . . . and, so far as the sun-flower is concerned, which we were discussing last time. . . . (Ralph and counselor burst into laughter at this serious introduction to the subject of the sun-flower.) As I was saying, facing east is their original position. Look, like this: (He demonstrates with a book.) They follow the sun this way, bending over backwards, and then they just naturally want to return to their original position.

C-13: That is interesting, isn't it?

R-14: Yes, it is. What was the other thing we didn't know about?

C-14: Wasn't it about water-lilies? Whether or not they do submerge at night, as the book said?

R-15: Oh, that's right! Well, I forgot that. I'll have to look it up for next time, if possible. . . . Well, I'm ready. (Counselor gave Ralph sixty seconds to skim the sixth article in the blue book. He finished skimming just as the sixty seconds were up, and he said, "Isn't the time up?" Then he revealed an adequate grasp of the essential points of this article, gleaned by skimming.)

R-16: Say, wasn't that good?

C-16: It was *very* good.

R-17: (He is very alert and bright-eyed.) I tell you! I'm learning that more and more—of how much a person can get out of his reading if he just *goes at it*. I used to think you had to read every word, but you don't have to read every word. You can do a lot of skipping and yet know what it's all about. (Eyes sparkling, big smile.) Gee, that makes me feel good, you know?

C-17: Yes, it's a wonderful discovery. It's so much more fun, too, when you attack a book vigorously instead of just trudging laboriously through it.

R-18: I find I can skip all around, and it doesn't really seem to matter.

C-18: What you are saying reminds me of some advice given by Lafcadio Hearn. He was a writer and was lecturing to some students learning to write fiction. He said it was best to start writing the part of the story that seemed most vivid and exciting at the moment, and let the rest of the story build up around that beginning.

R-19: Yes, I can see that. Then it wouldn't be so boring. You could start work on something that was really interesting.

C-19: That's right. He also gave an example of a Japanese artist drawing a horse. He said it didn't matter what part of the horse the artist started to draw first, that it certainly wasn't necessary to start at the nose and finish at the tail; he could do just as well if he started with one hoof, or the middle of the back, depending on what appealed to him at the moment.

R-20: Of course! Gee, that's really right, isn't it. Yet, you'd never think that way. I guess we are trained to start at a beginning and be very systematic.

C-20: Yes, that's just it. Now think of how much more interesting a book can become if you tackle it with that kind of freedom. For example, suppose you have a new textbook; let's say, a history book. Why not look anywhere you wanted to in the book—end, middle, beginning, all over—and get a feeling of what the thing is all about. Then, you could read a little of whatever appealed to you as you leafed through it. By the time you wanted to do a study job on it, you'd have some feeling of mastery over this book—that it had not intimidated you, but that you sailed right in and got acquainted.

R-21: Gee, I like that idea. Oh, but what would happen if you were studying a book in child development, where they start with the infant and go on up? Wouldn't you have to read in that order?

C-21: Does it really matter? I wonder. Do we need a mechanical sequence, or can not an active mind put material into proper sequence. Suppose you read first about the behavior of an adolescent, and secondly about an infant, your mind at once arranges the two in correct sequence. Isn't that true? Or what would you say?

R-22: I was thinking it's the same with all kinds of material. Your mind has to be sorting things out all the time. It's no different with reading.

C-22: Yes, that's a good observation.

R-23: It's like you said: you have to constantly *select* what's important when you're reading. So, you have to put things in the right place, too.

C-23: It always comes back to the question of self-confidence, doesn't it? A willingness to take risks, to decide for yourself what seems to be important and to be creative in your thinking about the material—not attempting rote memory.

R-24: This is an exciting way to think. I like it.

C-24: I like to think of things in the image of a mosaic, rather than in A-Z sequence. It gives you a better feeling for a rich pattern of thought, rather than a thin line. Here's a big area, not static, though. . . . You keep filling in, shifting around, reorganizing. . . . Do you know what I mean?

R-25: Yes, I do. (Sits back, thinking.) You know, when I used to read history, I used to try to remember every single separate fact as I went along. (Knits his brows.) I would say, "*This* is a fact, I must remember it. *This* is a fact, *this* is a fact, I'd better not forget it." And it was terrible! It occurred to me just this minute that it would have been so much easier to just look for the central ideas, and then all the facts would just naturally fall into place. (He becomes eager and animated as he thinks about this.)

C-25: It's like trying to hold onto two hundred loose beads; if you had them in a pattern, it would be easier.

R-26: Exactly! (Draws a circle in the air.) There it is, all there, instead of so many separate things to remember.
(Sits thinking.)

R-27: Well, now we've got that settled, shall we proceed with the study exercise . . . ? We'd better, it's getting late.
(Ralph read the exercise at the rate of 287 words per minute, a gain of 87 words per minute over last week. Then he answered the questions thoughtfully, critically, correctly and creatively, discussing the reasons for his choices.)

R-28: That was pretty good, wasn't it?

C-28: It was excellent.[2]

R-29: I'm really anxious to get back to school, you know?

C-29: Mmmm.

R-30: The Dean was so nice to me when I was there. While I was in his office, some faculty members came in, and he took the time to introduce me to each one and to explain what I had been doing this year. It was nice.

C-30: How far is your college from New York?

R-31: It takes me about three hours to drive it.

C-31: I wonder if you would like to come see me from time to time next year.

R-32: Oh, I would! You mean, on a regular basis?

C-32: We can make it definite—say, once a month, or once in three weeks. Something like that. Just to keep in touch and talk over how things go for you.

R-33: That would be grand. I didn't know you'd be here next year. I'd like very much to plan it that way.
You know, I realize I am certainly a different person from what I was. I understand now what a discouraging sort of person my mother is. For example, this morning she was shaking her head and saying, "You're a brave boy to get married now." She meant, because of the high cost of living. She doesn't see how we're going to do it. But it goes in one ear and out the other. I feel there's a way to do things you want to do, so I'm not scared. But I can't convert Mom to have confidence now. I can't change her now. I see so clearly how helpless she is, always was. She can't do a thing without Dad's help, without at

2 The counselor means "excellent progress," and "excellent discussion of the questions." The rate of speed is still not very rapid for this kind of material.

least asking him first. Poor Dad. You know, I feel sorry for him now. It must be very hard on him.

Mom is always saying, "What will happen to me when Father dies."

C-33: Oh, oh!

R-34: What?

C-34: That just slipped out. I couldn't help wondering what *you* would do under those circumstances.

R-35: Well, I would try to help her all I could, because she is so helpless. But I don't believe in having in-laws living with you. You know what they say, that you can't have two families living peacefully under one roof. You know, she doesn't do *a thing* without asking Dad, and she taught the same thing to me, so I was always afraid to do things. Now I know there are better things, and I'm grabbing onto them gradually. I'm realizing there are better ways of doing things in life than the way she taught me. She was always so terribly discouraging.

Say, did I tell you? Next Saturday I'm going shopping with Jane. We are going to pick out her wedding dress. It seems that it is all right for me to see her wedding dress, but I'm not allowed to see *her* on the day of the wedding, whether she is in her wedding dress or not.

We are having quite a time arranging things. I thought I'd have a tough time deciding who to choose for best man. My fraternity brothers are all good friends, and I didn't want to have to make a choice. Finally I solved it by having my brother-in-law, my sister's husband. He's older than Jane's brother, so it seemed only right.

Say, did I tell you I bought my mother an orchid for Easter?

C-35: No—how nice!

R-36: Didn't I tell you? Well, I'll tell you. This year Mother bought little gifts for everybody. She got me a tie, and she bought Jane a scarf, and a little something for everybody. Dad never thinks of giving Mom flowers, so I thought I would give her an orchid this year. I went in the day before and ordered a gardenia for Jane and a beautiful orchid for Mom.

The next day, as we sat down to dinner, I leaned over and put the orchid in Mom's lap. Gee, you should've seen her. It really made her happy. A little later, she asked me, "Who thought of it?" I said, "I did. I thought you'd like it." She said, "It means an awful lot to me." I said, "Well, gee whiz, Mom, I love you." She blushed and laughed. I said, "I'm not kidding, Mom, I *do* love you." We were all at dinner, and it was all so nice.

C-36: That's a very beautiful story.

R-37: Yes, it was lovely. . . . Say, I'm keeping you overtime.

C-37: We'll stop here, then. We have fourteen more sessions this semester, approximately, did you know?

(Ralph was putting away his blue book.)

Isn't it funny—we accidentally planned things well, because you have fourteen more exercises in the blue book, so we can do one each session and finish the book.

R-38: How did I manage to get up to 287 words per minute! I don't want you to think I was practicing these at home! I save them for here.

C-38: Any extra practice you get is all to the good, so why *not* practice them at home?

R-39: But I want you to know that I don't!

C-39: I believe you, I believe you! But the point is this: Why do you regard this as a test situation? This little book is for study and practice, and the more you use it, the better.

R-40: Oh, I see what you mean. I was thinking of it more or less like tests.

C-40: I guess our schools do that to us. They tend to turn exercises into tests, so you are accustomed to that approach. But we'll talk about it again, shall we?

R-41: You're right, it's late. Take care of yourself and have a nice week-end.

C-41: Thank you. You, too, have a nice week-end. Good-bye.

Discussion of the Thirtieth Interview with Ralph

There are some pleasant developments in this interview. The counselor is pleased for Ralph's sake that the Bellevue-Wechsler report placed him in the superior group;[3] he seems to need so badly this objective reassurance about his intelligence. However, so long as he

---

[3] Ralph's score placed him in the eighty-sixth percentile, which means he is thirty-six percentile units above average. In other words, an objective test of his intelligence places him in the upper fourteen percent of the population.

needs this reassurance, the counselor's work with him is far from finished. She would like him to know how bright he is without the evidence of the intelligence test. The counselor, therefore, tries to pave the way for continuing the therapy, inviting him to return the following fall.

He has a more mature attitude toward his mother now. He sees her more clearly as she really is, and, having aired out his feelings about her, he can now afford to feel his positive emotions welling up in him, without the fear of being enslaved by her. If he can achieve freedom from her subtle controllingness, he does not need to escape her through subtle defiance. He can express his objections directly, and thus feel free to express his love directly. His guilt toward her is alleviated, since he no longer harbors secret repressed resentments; he has released these repressed bad feelings and "has room" for the good feelings to come in. Thus, he realizes his love for his mother and wants to express it. This is a wonderful, even thrilling, example of how a more accepting attitude towards one's self leads the way to love of others.

Thirty-first Interview with Ralph

R- 1: Well, Jane got her dress. I wasn't allowed to go along.

I've been up at Jane's, working on the garden. Gee, you can do a lot of work on a small place, if you want it to look nice. Every Monday I'm out on my feet. I keep going so much on week-ends.

Everything is shaping up very nicely. I have to write down to school and find out if two friends down there can come up and be ushers at the wedding.

I have no problems now, but a couple of nights I had a tough time sleeping. I felt disturbed. Consciously, I felt I had nothing to be nervous about, but in my sleep I was tossing all over. Last week, that was. . . . I was a bit late tonight, but the bus was late. I haven't as yet received any word about an apartment at school, but I've asked my fraternity brothers to keep an eye out for an apartment. The government will pay for my school, and Jane will be working, so that takes care of the money angle. We made out a tentative budget, and an awful lot of things won't cost as much as we had down. We even had an allowance for an automobile, and money for furniture, and entertainment, and kitchen utensils.

I was going to ask Dad and Mom to help pay for the honeymoon. They said they were going to give us *nothing*. Mom said, "After you get married and are ready to set up house, you will get five hundred dollars from us for furniture."

This wedding is going to be bigger than I thought. Jane wants everything according to Hoyle. There's going to be a bachelor's dinner and a bride's dinner. Then comes Saturday. Tell me, what am I supposed to do all day Saturday! (Counselor and Ralph laugh at note of mock desperation in his voice.)

R- 2: Oh, it's going to be a lot of fun and a good time. I'm going into this with my eyes wide open. Before, I used to wonder what I would do at a wedding. Now I think I'll just have a good time. I'm not nervous at all about it.

C- 2: Have you any ideas why you were restless the other night?

R- 3: No. Maybe it's natural to feel restless before taking such an important step. All the excitement of it. Because I don't feel worried. I'm satisfied that I'm doing the thing I want to do. (Silence.)

C- 3: What else do you want to tell me?

R- 4: I can't think of anything else. Do we have time to work on reading tonight?

C- 4: Oh, yes. What would you like to do?

R- 5: Well, first I would like to discuss with you an idea I read, that one should have a definite interest and aim when reading something. And I don't agree with that. Many times you read something and you don't know what you are reading about until you read deep into the material. I may not have a definite purpose in mind, other than broadening my knowledge.

C- 5: Tell me more.

R- 6: Well, it just occurred to me that in a way that *is* a definite purpose; I would be trying to broaden my knowledge about *something*. The thing I'm reading would have a title of some kind, which wouldn't leave me in the dark about what it is I'm going to read.

C- 6: I wonder why you are concerned about this particular problem at this particular time.

R- 7: What do you mean?

C- 7: Let me repeat to you two statements you have made this hour: "I'm going into this with my eyes wide open," and, "Many times you don't know what you are reading about until you get deep into the material."

R- 8: I get it! I want to know ahead of time. I want a guarantee that my marriage will work out okay, just like I want to know what I'm reading before I start even to read it. It's like what you said about my Dad, that he can't afford to make mistakes, and I'm like that, too. I have to know ahead of time that everything is going to work out exactly right, so he won't be able to say, "I told you so."

You'd expect a person to feel like that before an important step like marriage, but isn't it strange and remarkable how it is with my reading. My mind wanders off to worrying about whether I'm reading right, whether I have the proper purpose, whether I'm going to remember enough of it, whether I'm reading the way I'm *supposed* to read. So I get in my own way. I see this very clearly today. Isn't it funny how you can see a thing and then keep forgetting it, and then it comes up again in another way. (Ralph is quite excited; he gets up and walks around.)

It's terrific the way you caught onto it today, and then made me see it. I shouldn't be so afraid to make mistakes, and then I could enjoy whatever I do. Take reading: I'm not afraid I'll make mistakes when I read a Sherlock Holmes story, so I read fast and well, and I enjoy it, and I remember it.

C- 8: It holds no threat.

R- 9: That's right. It holds no threat. But if it's something I *have* to read, then it's different. (Sits down again.)

C- 9: Is finishing your education something you choose to do, or something you have to do?

R-10: No, I *want* it. So, since, as you say, I'm *choosing* to do it, it's no different from choosing to read *Sherlock Holmes*. There's no reason to be afraid I'll fail.

C-10: Failing was one way of defeating your parents and winning your independence and your integrity as a person. I wonder if you need that any more.

R-11: No, I don't. I'm looking ahead now to being a parent myself. And now I know I have the intelligence to be successful, and there is no reason for me to fail. I'll be independent enough with a wife and family of my own! (Picks up a book.)

Suppose you just gave me this book and said, "Read it!" What would I do?

C-11: Good idea. Tell me what you would do.

R-12: Well, you taught me how to skim. So I'd use that. First I'd skim. I'd look at the table of contents, then the first few pages. I'd feel free to go on a little more rapidly until I came to what looked important, then I might slow up a bit. If it looked very important, I'd decide to go back and look at that part again, after I finished skimming. Okay?

C-12: Very much okay. Once you skim, you know what you are getting into. Then, when you go back to read it more carefully, you have a purpose in going after it because, by now, it's somewhat familiar territory, since you've been over it once, though lightly.

R-13: So, I knew what to do, but didn't know that I knew.

C-13: That seems to be characteristic of you, doesn't it?

R-14: Yes, in so many ways.
(Silence.)

C-14: What are you thinking?

R-15: I was trying to figure out how you do what you do. I was thinking how I get a feeling of strength from you, but it's more that you help me get strength out of myself, out of something inside of me. I was sure lucky to find you!
But that's enough compliments for one day. I don't want to spoil you! Let's spend the rest of the time doing exercises. I brought my book.
(The remainder of the hour was devoted to rapid reading and testing comprehension. Both speed and comprehension show improvement.)

Discussion of the Thirty-first Interview with Ralph

In this interview there is a clear example of how a basic attitude expresses itself identically in two very different life situations: meeting a marriage challenge and meeting a reading challenge. The same pattern shows itself again and again. Ralph's demand for a guarantee against the threat of mistakes and failure has its roots in an unconscious wish to fail as a way of defeating the intimidating authority and establishing his own sense of self. He lacks the feeling of safety necessary for taking a reasonable risk, because all reasonable risks become blurred by the unreasonable wish for self-defeat—to establish integrity—which then creates panic, anxiety, and ultimate failure.

The reader must by now have seen why the therapeutic process takes time, and what a long and laborious chore it can be to incorporate new ways to replace old ones. Ralph formulates this process well when he says, "Isn't it funny how you can see a thing and then keep forgetting it, and then it comes up again in another way." (R-10.)

C-10 is an interesting statement from the point of view of timing. The counselor has waited until the thirty-first interview to say to Ralph a thought which she has held since the first or second interview. Now he is just on the threshold of saying it himself, and she helps him over that threshold. He is able to see it clearly and can quickly make it his own.

Thirty-second Interview with Ralph

R- 1: (Glowing and cheerful.) Well, I paid up what I owed you today. Here's the receipt. And I brought you some ice cream.

C- 1: Oh, thank you. It's just what I was wanting.

R- 2: Really?

C- 2: No fooling. It feels like spring, and you can hear kids roller skating. That puts me in the mood for an ice cream cone.

R- 3: (Laughs.) Me, too. Say, how would you like me to let you off early tonight? I'm so tired. I've been laying top-soil, and all day yesterday and today I was out riding motorcycles with Dad.

Dad and I are getting closer. When he's in old clothes I like him the best. When he is all dressed up he's different. I don't know . . . when we were working side by side on the lawn, it was awfully nice. (Smiles.) The whole family is showing more love these days. I like a family to be jovial and happy in the things they say and the way they act.

Mom came out to watch us today. She started yelling at Dad to get the dirt off the driveway. But they were teasing each other. It was all nice—joking around.

You know, with what problems I had about the family, I'm grateful it was small as it was. My friend Bob, he and his family are very high-strung and temperamental. It's terrible to go over there. My family was always nicer than that. It's terrible at their house. I could not live that way. They are always threatening to kill one another. Those people fight and argue all the time.

If Mom asks me to take her to the store, I'm always willing to do it. But *he* won't. With me he's grand. His mother wants me to explain to him that he should be nicer to his mother. I told her I couldn't interfere. I just told her, "Why don't you be calm, instead of flaring up and making matters worse." But I don't think she can do that.

I'm anxious to get back to college and to my routine. This time, everything's going to be different.

About my courses . . . I think the kind of business I'll go into, I wouldn't be able to get subjects to help me specifically in my work. Of course, you're a learned man when you have your degree in your hand. . . . I'd like to study about people. I could get that, couldn't I?

C- 3: Yes, you could get some work in child development, adolescent psychology, clinical psychology. . . .

R- 4: That sounds good to me. I'm going to see about it. They had me down as not eligible for a degree, because I had planned to transfer to a larger university. But it will all be straightened out.

Would you like me to read you a story today?

C- 4: If you like. What am I to hear?

R- 5: Well, now, there's a little article here on "Creative Reading." That title interests me.

C- 5: Good. Me, too. But first tell me what ideas you have on the subject, before you start reading the article, and what you hope to learn from it.

R- 6: (Teasingly.) Are you trying to "motivate" me?

C- 6: You are already motivated. What I'm driving at is developing a kind of attack upon the material.

R- 7: Well, I should think reading creatively means thinking about what you read, and adding something to it. And I don't know what I hope to learn from it, because I don't know yet what ideas the author has on the subject. Let's just say I'm approaching it with an open mind and curiosity.

C- 7: Fine! I'm all for curiosity and the satisfying of same.

R- 8: Say, aren't we in a good mood today? Do you suppose it's the weather?

C- 8: You've set the mood today. You came here feeling so nice and jolly.

R- 9: Yes, I feel wonderful. Well, here goes. Listen carefully.
(Ralph reads aloud with gusto and good expression. He stops to discuss ideas from time to time.)
Now, suppose I read another article, and you time me. By the way, when you study, do you believe in underlining sentences?

C- 9: Yes. I always try to buy my own books, so I can write in the margins, underline, indicate important points, add ideas—mark it all up. A book is to serve you, so you should not be intimidated by the book. You must not hesitate to make the most of it by making it your own.

R-10: I'm glad to hear you say that. I used to feel funny about getting a pencil mark in a book. I was always taught not to. In fact, in school we were fined for it. But lately I've been marking up my books, and I like to do it.
Okay, first I'll skim this article in sixty seconds, then I'll read it again and you time me. Or, I can time myself if you like; then you won't have to bother. You could read something yourself.

C-10: No, I enjoy doing that for you. Thanks, anyhow.
(Ralph skimmed the next article, then read it at the rate of 350 words per minute.)

R-11: And I felt as though I was taking my time. I know I reached for an ash-tray once, and I felt very relaxed. I bet I could have gone much faster. It all seemed like old stuff, very familiar. That's because I skimmed it first. Now to the questions:
(Ralph answers the questions quickly and accurately.)
My thinking is becoming more and more clear. I saw immediately why this had to be the answer, and not the other ones. This one I saw at once was not inclusive enough. I didn't stop to mull it over. I just *saw* the right one.

C-11: That's wonderful.

R-12: Yeah, it felt good. I had a feeling that I was in charge—almost like riding a horse. . . . Do you like horses?

C-12: Yes, but I can't say I know horses. I've had no experience with them.

R-13: (Very earnest.) I guess the reason I like horses is that they like me. I never have any trouble with horses. (He tells counselor some stories about horses until the end of the session.)

Discussion of the Thirty-second, Thirty-third, and Thirty-fourth Interviews

Ralph arrives in a cheerful mood each hour and leaves with a good feeling of growth and achievement, which is excellent. He is feeling friendlier to his parents, and seems to be more proud and approving of them. He is becoming less dependent on the counselor; he doesn't mind if he misses a few sessions.

The thirty-fourth interview contains some interesting symbolic material. "If you let the reins loosen, he'll go forward all the more," (R-2) describes Ralph's therapeutic development.

Thirty-third Interview with Ralph

R- 1: How many more sessions do you think we'll have?

C- 1: Why do you ask?

R- 2: I've been offered a job, and I'd like to start on the 19th. It'll run through the next month. I'm very well satisfied with the progress I've made. I don't think it matters if I miss a few hours. Isn't that true?

C- 2: Yes, you've done well. Suppose we work through the 14th, which gives us another month to finish up.

R- 3: That's fine. That'll be just right. . . . Did you get a report from Miss ———?

C- 3: No, I'm sorry. I'll show it to you as soon as I get it.

R- 4: Okay. You know, I should study children, because I love studying children. I was watching my little cousin. She is just beginning to walk, and it's so funny. A little walking doll, so awfully cute. I guess I'm prejudiced. I teach her little things to say, and she catches on right away.

(Ralph gave counselor a vivid and really excellent, detailed description of the little girl. He gave evidence of fine ability to observe and to recall his observations.)

Gosh, all the little things a baby has to learn! For example, she tries to stand up under a chair, and she keeps pushing with her head. You have to pull her out, else she'd hurt herself.

When she's standing alone, she's rocky, but if you take her hand, she feels secure, and she runs right along.

A lot of things happened this weekend. Jane's mother is moving to a smaller place, so she said we could have a bedroom set, a rug, a couch and a lovely breakfront. And Mom is giving me the desk and chair in my room. Well, it's wonderful. We'll save so much. We're very grateful.

Gee, everything is turning out so nicely. Like that job coming up now. I'll work for two months at fifty dollars a week, and it'll more than pay for our honeymoon.

So, if you're not afraid, things turn out right.

Usually, I asked those people for a job. This time they came to me and asked me if I could give them some time. So, that felt very good.

Say, did you see the movie, "Sitting Pretty?"

C- 4: No, I hear it's good.

R- 5: It was awfully good. Would you like to hear about it?

C- 5: Yes, thank you.

R- 6: Well, I'll summarize it for you. We'll use the movie as an exercise in summarizing.

(Ralph gives the counselor an interesting summary of the movie.)

Say, what do you think of marriage counseling?

C- 6: You mean for two young people planning to get married?

R- 7: (Laughs.) You know that's what I mean.

C- 7: Well, what do you think of it?

R- 8: It sounds like a good idea to me. I think people should get all the help they can, to know as much as possible, so they get a good start in their new life.

C- 8: Do you have anyone in mind you'd like to consult?

R- 9: No, I was wondering if you could suggest someone.

C- 9: I'll be glad to write out a few names for you, and then you can make a choice.

R-10: Thank you. Another thing: I brought my college catalogue with me today. I'd like to go over the courses with you today, if it's all right with you.

C-10: Good idea. Let's do that.

(Remainder of hour is spent in discussion of courses.)

Thirty-fourth Interview with Ralph

Ralph arrived a half hour late.

R- 1: I'm sorry I'm late. I was so interested in the work I was doing.

I was helping a friend build a house for his dog. Here's how we worked it: (Ralph gives counselor a detailed description, with drawings, of the project.)

He's such a genius, this guy! It's too bad about him, though (laughing). I tell him how a thing should be done, and he says, "Oh, that's no good." And then he'll do it *my* way and say it was *his* idea. But I don't mind. I can't say to him, "Oh, no, I thought of it first."

This morning I had two-and-a-half hours of beautiful horseback riding. They let me ride a horse they never let anyone else ride. It was like a circus horse. He knew five gaits. Did you ever see a horse gallop in place?

C- 1: No, I don't know anything about horses. You'll have to explain it to me.

(Ralph explains in detail.)

R- 2: I guess you do have to be an experienced rider to handle a horse like that. Every little move I made was a signal to him to do something different. (Gave examples.) I jumped him, too. It was so nice and smooth, it was wonderful. What a jumper! Once I tried to jump a horse that didn't want to, and he nearly threw me. . . . I love horses. I love animals, especially horses, as you know. . . . Another thing about this horse: you don't spur him, you just control him with the reins. If you let the reins loosen, he'll go forward all the more.

My friend got on my horse, and the horse got confused and started running away. Horses do take a beating from people who don't know how to ride. City cowboys come out and show off and really give the horses a terrible beating.

Well, to get back to me. . . . Everything is perfect. Life in general feels very good and very interesting. People are all nice lately.

Last week I didn't see Jane because she had to write a thesis. Jane wrote and told me there would be a formal affair at school. Usually I don't want to go to formals because of my tuxedo. It was given me by a friend whose brother had died. And it fits just awful. I feel like a waiter in it. So, Dad said he'd give me one for the wedding, but since there is this formal, he said he'd give it to me now.

I'm excited about getting married. I think we are going to have a good life together. Life is more interesting and more enjoyable than it used to be. After all, we only live once. Gee whiz, life is so short, even if you live to the maximum.

Gee, I'm excited about going up with my new tuxedo. I'll tell you how I felt before . . . I mean, I felt that I ought to hide in a corner, that everyone was looking at me; that's how my personality felt—you know? But now I'll step right up and want a spotlight on me. My new tux will fit so good and look so good, and my personality feels so good.

R- 3: Everything is so nice at home. Mom and Pop have been in a nice mood. Dad came to the city today with Mom to go shopping.

I've been doing a lot more newspaper reading. I didn't realize it was so interesting. I didn't find that out until I started doing it.

I'm eager to see Jane this weekend. It's awful to skip a weekend after seeing her every week. It's nice being in love and missing somebody as badly as that.

Say, I didn't show you this.

(Ralph shows counselor a letter from a store, asking him to come to work for them from the beginning of May through the end of June.)

R- 4: It's a little over eight weeks. That means over four hundred dollars. It'll more than pay for our honeymoon. I'm so happy the way everything is working out. This is a larger store than the other one, but run by the same people. It'll give me a little more experience, because it is a new and bigger place. It was very nice of him to ask me. It makes me feel that he needs me and wants me. The manager at the store where I usually work said, "Where does he get the nerve to take *my* help away!"

C- 4: You must be good, for them to be fighting over you.

R- 5: (Chuckles.) Isn't that funny? It sure makes me *feel* good. Oh, yes, everything is going along so nice. Naturally, every once in a while things will get rough, but I'll know I'm not going to be in that rut all the time, like I was. It feels good to know that I was in a rut but got out of it.

Mom and my kid sister and I have been kidding around a lot lately. We do a lot more laughing than we used to.

C- 5: You'll be interested in knowing that Miss ———— sent me the report on your test.

R- 6: Oh, good! Can you show it to me?

C- 6: Yes, we'll go over it together.

(The rest of the hour was spent in discussion of his Bellevue-Wechsler report.)

Thirty-fifth Interview with Ralph

C- 1: How was your party?

R- 1: Wonderful. I got proposed to. This girl said to me that as soon as I get rid of Jane, she'll be waiting for me.

(Both laugh.)

We were in New York Saturday, and Jane got a lot of clothes. (Tells counselor all about the clothes Jane selected.)

The dance was a little slow. Not many people were there at first, so we went out for something to eat. Everybody looked at us in our formal clothes.

Later, it got quite crowded. Say, I almost forgot—Jane and I won the waltz contest. We got a lot of applause. Gee, it was nice.

(Chuckles.)

I was thinking just now of Jane's brother. He always beats me at tennis, but yesterday I told him I'd beat him, and he was surprised to hear me say that. I played very seriously, and I won the first set, 6-4. So I got all excited and spoiled it, and he won the next two sets, 6-4, 6-4. I really did play exceptionally well yesterday, though. I learned I *could* do it.

I feel I have gotten an awful lot out of what we've done here. How many more sessions will we have?

C- 2: About four or five, I believe.

R- 2: Gosh, it makes me think how all I heard up there this weekend was how many more days to the wedding! Jane doesn't think of anything else. (Laughs.)

I'm thinking an awful lot about getting married. I'm sort of living marriedly in my mind. She was very lovable this weekend, very warm and passionate. She had a very beautiful and comfortable evening gown. It's rare you see such a beautiful gown that is also comfortable. (Describes Jane's gown.) And she didn't wear much underneath.

Well, I imagine you know pretty well how I feel today, and how I keep thinking about the wedding. (Grins.)

C- 3: A very pleasant preoccupation.

R- 3: Yes, and there are no troubles, none whatsoever. Gee, I felt good in that tuxedo. I told Jane I felt like a King and that she looked like a Queen. She's a good kid. Gosh, she's changed an awful lot lately, since that trouble I had with her. She really has. She *asks* now, instead of *telling* me. The trouble we had is all cleared up.

It didn't hurt Jane to hear this other girl say how wonderful I was. I seem to be very handy in fixing things. This girl's pocketbook had a broken frame, and I fixed it for her. And I typed Jane's thesis, and she said, "My gosh, you're good-looking today!" Another girl came in and said, "He *is* good-looking." It was all in fun. And she saw I had fixed Jane's bookcase, and she said, "He's handy, too!" The other girls began teasing Jane, and Jane said, "He isn't going to get tired of me if *I* can help it!" So that shows she's really trying.

So you can see I had a wonderful weekend.

C- 4: Yes, you certainly did!

R- 4: This morning I fixed the car all up. I changed the grease. It should be ready for the summer now. Just think, I won't need that poor excuse any more, of running out of gas! But I never had to do that anyhow. And now I'll want to get where I am going.

All the girls liked me this weekend. More than usual. They are always kidding around with me. I think they all like me pretty much. But this weekend I didn't pay much attention to them, and they all came to me. They are all girls I've known since Jane went to school there. So it's all friendly. Not like someone new trying to cut in.

(Ralph sings a little tune as he cleans out his pipe into the wastebasket.)

You don't suppose there's a match in this desk, do you?

(Counselor looked for matches, but could find none.)

Well, that's okay. Maybe I ought to do some reading now, anyhow. I'll read to you today.

(Ralph selected a book and read aloud. His phrasing was much improved.)

C- 5: Well, our time is about up now, so shall we stop here?

R- 5: Okay. You know, I usually think of something important to say on the way out. Shall we start to walk out? And I'll think of something? (Laughs.)

All I want to talk about is how much fun everything was this weekend. Jane was more warm and affectionate this weekend than ever before. Was it something different in me? Or was it that the rain on the roof of the car put her in the mood? Anyhow, it was wonderful. We sang all the way home.

Discussion of the Thirty-fifth Interview

All one can say about this interview is that it was the song of a boy in love. The last sentence is beautiful: "We sang all the way home."

Thirty-sixth Interview with Ralph

R- 1: That's a very pretty suit—is it new?

C- 1: Yes, do you like it?

R- 2: Yes, I like it very much.

I was thinking, out in the hall, I don't even remember what problems I presented when I first came here. It's a nice feeling, to not even remember what I came here for. In general I do remember, but so far as specific things go, it's all solved. It seems far away and long ago.

Now, let me think of what I can tell you today. What would you like to talk about today?

C- 2: Anything that occurs to you, Ralph.

R- 3: (Looks out the window, smokes thoughtfully.) Did I ask you to write to ———— (his college) about my tests?

C- 3: Yes, I'm glad you brought that up. You can help me plan the letter, if you like. What do you think we should write to them?

R- 4: (Laughs.) Inform them to turn the college over to me, that I have a lot of changing to do. I want to build the college up, not in size, but in strength.

Can we put a little emphasis on the fact that they should have done more for me before this?

C- 4: Suppose you dictate a letter, and I'll write it down.

R- 5: Shall I start at the beginning?

C- 5: Yes.

R- 6: Well. . . . Mr. ——— came to us early this year, for guidance. One of the difficulties was the fact that he had trouble with reading. We took all precautions to find out definitely if there was an eye difficulty. We were very fortunate to discover that Mr. ——— had aniseikonia, which had a great deal to do with his problem of reading. It has since been corrected, and we find it, along with other factors, has improved his reading speed greatly. New paragraph.

During the course of our work with him, a Bellevue-Wechsler Test was administered, and Mr. ——— fell into the Superior group. He was in the eighty-sixth percentile. He showed particular strength in the area of perceiving relationships. New paragraph.

He has worked through the problem of vocation, and has indicated a strong interest in the field of business administration. His plan is to take such courses during the remainder of his college course as will best prepare him for the work. New paragraph.

As Mr. ———'s reading difficulties diminished, his ability to study increased, so that at the present time he feels he has a good practical attack upon study challenges.

Well, that's enough, isn't it?

C- 6: That's a fine letter, beautifully written, clear and to the point.

R- 7: Thank you. About study habits. . . . Just the fact that I am able to read faster is the thing. When I first came here, I used to work all night on something and not remember about it in the morning. But now, since I take things thought by thought and not word by word, I am capable of noting thoughts instead of words. So now I can jot down thoughts, and then I remember them. Also, the ability of concentration is much greater. So, actually, there isn't too much difficulty about study habits. It was all in the reading ability—that had everything to do with it. And the way I felt inside had everything to do with my reading and my ability to concentrate. Gosh! How did they expect a book on study habits to clear up my difficulty! They should have done more. How many colleges do you suppose know what to do about problems like I had?

C- 7: I don't really know. More and more colleges are setting up guidance programs. It's a growing trend.

R- 8: I feel sorry for all the kids who don't fall into the right hands. I was just lucky, coming here.
(Picks up a mimeographed sheet that counselor had left on the desk for him.)
What's this. . . . "How to Review for Examinations." [4]
(Reads it aloud.)
This is good stuff. May I keep it?

C- 8: Yes, of course. And now let me ask you, if you had to study this book on "Glass and Bricks" and give a report on it tomorrow morning, how would you go about it?

R- 9: (Settles down thoughtfully to the task.) Well, first of all, I'd ask myself, "What do I already know about glass and bricks?" I'd run through all the little things I know about it. Maybe the book will include something on making bricks out of glass. I'd look for hints on the cover. There are glass bricks in the building on the cover. I guess that interests me because I like that kind of new building.
Then I'd skim the first page, and, if I notice something important, I might go a little into detail and stop to take a few notes. I'd skim through the whole book, and look at all the titles in heavy type, and at the pictures. Just by this picture here, I learn that glass was discovered many, many years ago. After I skim it, I'd go back and take notes on interesting and important facts, and make a note of the pages I find things on, so I can look it up again if I want to. Where I have stars marked in the margin, I re-read.
Finally, I would make an outline of what I want to say. I'd try to make my report as interesting as possible, and full of facts. If it's an oral report, I would talk right from the outline. If it has to be a written report, it wouldn't be too difficult once a good outline is done.
Say, now you've got me interested in this book. It looks good. (Ralph arose to turn on the lights in the room, since it was beginning to be dusk.)
This reminds me of how Jane dislikes the way my mother keeps the house so dark. Jane leaves all the lights on all over the house. And the shades up when it's light. Mom keeps the

[4] A study sheet by Professor Ruth Strang.

blinds down tight. I think she's hiding something. (Laughs.) I feel that a home should be a *home*, not a show-room. Even my own room—it's not my room, it's Mom's room. Well, it's too late now to change Mom. Just to give you an example: The other day I had a suitcase in my room, so Mom said it didn't belong there and it had to be taken right up to the attic. *My* apartment is going to be *home*. I won't plump up a chair cushion every time I get up off a chair.

The baby likes her Uncle Ralph very much. I'm really her cousin—second cousin, but I like the idea of being "*Uncle* Ralph." (Smiles.) She likes him the best. They were all calling her, but she came to *me*. She's just learning to walk. She got her first pair of hard-soled shoes, and she goes clopping around. It's really wonderful to watch her.

Well . . . enough fun for today. I'd better do a couple more exercises before our time is up. We're almost through the book.

Discussion of Interviews Thirty-six through Thirty-nine

Ralph's forgetting the original problems which brought him to the counselor for help shows excellent progress. Also, his statement that it is "too late to change Mom," shows greater freedom, maturity, tolerance and understanding. His own formulation of his gains (Thirty-ninth Interview, R-4), reveals a good awareness of the kind of growth that has taken place. "I've learned how to face problems and work them out instead of groping. . . ." "I don't let things slide. I face them and deliberately solve them." It is interesting to see how he tries to help Jane's brother profit by what he himself has learned.

Despite all this improvement, however, the counselor tries to arrange for more work in the fall. Ralph's troubles have been deep-rooted ones, and the counselor believes that more time and more therapy are required to consolidate his gains and make his new footing secure. However, Ralph does not feel he needs more help, and all the counselor can do is invite him to return, and then wait.

Thirty-seventh Interview with Ralph

R- 1: Well, everything is fine. Do you remember the paper you gave me the other day, on how to study for an examination?

C- 1: Yes.

R- 2: Well, it started a train of thought about my attitude towards examinations. I used to feel it was, "Make good or bust." So, since I was always thinking of "bust," it wasn't so good. Now when I go back to college, I'll really do much better because I'll have a better attitude. I've changed.

It's funny. . . . Sometimes you think that exams are unfair because of some teachers who pick up little details, and they could flunk you for the whole year if you flunked that last test. I had a psychology teacher who used to make out the trickiest true-false questions. And sometimes if there are just three essay questions, they might not hit on the same points that you happen to know.

C- 2: I used to study for an exam by pretending that I was giving the exam. I'd make out the exam questions and make sure I could answer them.

R- 3: That's a good idea. It would be a sort of outline of important ideas.

C- 3: That's right. I did not always select the same ideas for discussion that the instructor did, but I often hit several of them. It provided a focus for study; it meant being selective and deciding what was most important.

R- 4: I'm going to remember that. It sounds awfully good to me. You know, Jane got an exam this week, and they were allowed two hours for it, but they could take the questions home, or to the library, and use any material they wanted in trying to answer the questions.

C- 4: Did she like it?

R- 5: Yes, but it wasn't a snap, either, because with all that leeway, you felt you had no excuse for not doing a real good job. She learned a lot. . . . Do you remember I told you I tutored her on an exam?

C- 5: No, I don't seem to remember that.

R- 6: Well, I tutored her, and she got an "A" on it. She was so happy. It was fun helping her. That's where she'll be a big help to me next year. It's like one day we stretched out on a blanket near some lilacs that were in bloom, and we worked together translating my French lesson. It was fun. I got such a kick out of that. I learned a lot and enjoyed it, too.

Say, next Monday I might not be able to come here. Jane may

have to go down to ———— to see about a job. We'd drive down there Sunday and stay over. I want to go down and see about an apartment, too. One of my fraternity brothers gave me a lead, and I want to follow it up. Is it okay?

C- 6: Is what okay?

R- 7: If I don't get here Monday night?

C- 7: Oh, yes, surely. I have to be here Monday anyhow, and, if you don't arrive, I can just leave earlier than usual.

R- 8: You are always so nice. Don't you ever lose your patience, or scold?

C- 8: Do you deserve to be scolded?

R- 9: (Chuckles.) No. I think I used to feel that somehow I had it coming if people weren't nice to me. But lately I feel I'm a pretty good guy; I like myself. And people generally seem to be nicer.

I'm helping a friend of mine build a trailer. He's an awfully nice fellow. We're building this trailer in his garage. I never learned how, but I just started in, and I had no trouble at all. Look, I'll show you how it's done.

(There followed an excellent, detailed description, with careful drawings to supplement his explanation.)

C- 9: You've made it so clear, I think I could do it myself.

R-10: Sure you could! It's fun. And when we have it done, he'll be able to sell it for a great many times more than what it cost to build. Of course, he doesn't want to sell it. He plans to use it for his honeymoon.

He enjoys my company. It does get boring working all alone, and you really do need two sets of hands to work on a big thing like that. . . . Say, is our hour up already? Guess I used it up on building talk. Well, I'll read to you Wednesday.

Thirty-eighth Interview with Ralph

R- 1: Let's work on vocabulary today.

C- 1: Okay.

R- 2: Do you remember that method you taught me?

C- 2: The kinesthetic method?

R- 3: Yes. I like that. Let's spend this hour practicing that some more and learning some new words.

C- 3: Well, let's not do it out of context. Lists of words seem so meaningless. Let's read something, and you stop to look up words you don't know, and we'll make out cards for them.

R- 4:   Okay.

(Ralph selects a book from counselor's desk, and the remainder of the hour is devoted to work on vocabulary.)

Thirty-ninth Interview with Ralph

R- 1:   Here's the receipt for the balance of my bill. I just paid it.

C- 1:   Thank you, Ralph. How are you today?

R- 2:   Just fine, thank you. We went to ————, and we have a good chance of getting an apartment that we want. Three were available, but the fourth is the one we wanted. We'll know tomorrow. I don't know. . . . I'm afraid to refuse some of the apartments. They're so hard to get.

(Describes in glowing detail the apartment they hope will be available to them.)

C- 2:   Why, that's wonderful! It sounds like a good deal of space and comfort.

R- 3:   Yes. Just living in a place like that will be nice. And that private entrance I like. The other folks you don't see or hear. And it's beautifully furnished, as I told you, and has the new refrigerator and new stove. It's in the residential section of town, and walking distance from the college. Gee, it's great. . . . What are you smiling about?

C- 3:   It's pleasant to see you looking so happy.

R- 4:   I'm very, very happy. Let me tell you more. (Tells counselor more about the apartment and about a big leather chair he and Jane plan to buy.)

Everything is going along nicely.

I was trying to figure out in just what ways I've changed. I feel different, but I wanted to pin it down. One important thing is this: I've learned how to face problems and work them out instead of groping. I don't let things slide. I face them and deliberately solve them.

C- 4:   That's terrific.

R- 5:   Yes.

Well, our honeymoon is all planned and everything.

(Discusses in detail the plans for their honeymoon.)

C- 5: You know, today is our last session. Shall we make any plans for the fall?

R- 6: Well, I think I'm *cured*. I don't feel now that I'll need any more help. I'll know from now on if I'm slipping, and what to do.

C- 6: It's all up to you.

R- 7: I was thinking it might be a good idea to check things with you once in a while, if things get rough. But I'd have to cut a Saturday class to get here. You are not here ever on Sundays, are you?

C- 7: Suppose we put it this way: I'll be here for you if you need me. Just write or phone and we'll make an appointment convenient for both of us.

R- 8: Gee, that's perfect.

C- 8: Want to take a reading test today?

R- 9: No, I feel I don't need it. I'm satisfied with my reading now. It's not a problem any more. I don't need a test to tell me how I'm doing.

C- 9: Is there anything I can do for you?

R-10: Haven't you done enough?

C-10: *You* did it. I helped a little, but the major effort was yours.

R-11: It was all through you. You can't fool me about how much you've done for me.

C-11: Shall we say it was good team-work?

R-12: Yes, because it was. And I enjoyed it because I profited so much.

Jane and her mother want Jane's brother to go to a military college, and he doesn't want to go. I said to him, "If you don't have the feeling that you really *want* to go, don't go! If you are going just to please Jane and your mother, don't go!"

Jane whispered to me, "Shut up!" I said to her, "*You* shut up. I'm talking now to your brother."

"Family pressure is not right," I said to him. "It happened to me, so I know," I told him. "You should do just what *you* want to do."

I can see it so clearly, what they are doing to him. They are pressing and pressing. I said to Jane, "I'll say what I want to say. When you are talking, *you've* got the floor; when *I'm* talking, *I've* got the floor. I'll say what I want, and you won't stop me."

Her brother's only seventeen, and he can't think for himself. He was at the same academy I was at. He was in it for seven years, and he calls it, "The Prison." So how can he go to a military college?

Military training is supposed to teach you to be a man, but I don't think it does at all. It just teaches you to be a follower.

I was almost thrown out of the Academy once. Did I tell you?

C-12: No.

R-13: Well, I was called to the Commandant because the boy next to me at dinner dropped a spoon and pushed it under the table with his foot, intending to pick it up later, but forgot it. The Commandant said to me, "Who threw the spoon under the table?"

I said, "Sir, it was an accident." He said, "I want to know the boy's name." I said, "If you're going to soak him, I refuse to tell."

So, he put me on court martial. He picked up a paper weight and slammed it down and said, "Get out of here, you son-of-a-bitch!"

The superintendent called me in and said, "Just what is going on?" I said, "Sir, something very funny is going on." I told him the story. He had told me to come and explain.

And a few days after that, he called me in and told me it was okay. So, after the Commandant had threatened to kick me out of school, the superintendent told me it was okay.

Some military people are no good. They just crush you. They don't teach you to stand up. They hate you if you oppose them. They want to throw you out.

Just think—all because a boy sitting next to me accidentally dropped a spoon, and I wouldn't tell on him.

If it hadn't been for some strong family influence, I probably would not have got away with it.

(Thoughtful.)

I'm very anxious to get back to school in the fall. I had a good time talking to all the fellas. I have my ushers taken care of. Everything is all set.

C-13: And I think we have to stop here.

R-14: So . . . does that close the book on us?

C-14: It seems so.

R-15: Well, you know how I feel. I can't thank you enough.

C-15: (Extending hand for hand-shake.) Good-bye, Ralph. Best of luck to you. Let me hear from you from time to time.

R-16: (With warm hand-shake.) I will. . . . Good-bye. . . . And thanks.

A Follow-up Report on Ralph

The counselor did not hear from Ralph until she contacted him several years later, at which time she obtained the following information: [5]

"Dear ———:

"It was wonderful to hear from you. I am glad to be able to tell you that things are just fine and that I am very, very happy.

"So far as college goes, I stopped at the end of my second year. It was too much for me. But I got a good job, which I am very pleased with and like a lot.

"I got married, as planned, and the marriage has been a real success. We have our own home and we are expecting a baby in a few months.

"I'd like to tell you that that year with you changed my whole outlook on life. You made a man of me. If I am happy now, which I am, I owe it to you. I wish you would take a trip out to visit me, and see me in my present setting, so you would know how well things have turned out.

"I'll look forward to seeing you some day soon.

"Sincerely yours,

"Ralph ———."

[5] Identifying facts are disguised.

[5]

NEW THREADS FOR OLD

UNCONSCIOUS EMOTIONAL DIFFICULTIES were referred to in the first chapter as "underlying threads" weaving, among other symptoms, patterns of reading disability. Case material in subsequent chapters offered the reader an opportunity to watch the emergence of "underlying threads" and to follow the gradual replacing of new attitudes for old. If the reader tries to formulate just how the changes came about, he will recognize that his formulation is destined to be incomplete. The forces and influences in an individual's life are so many and complex, so hidden from view, that one can gather together only a few of the obvious components of growth and wonder about the rest. Keeping in mind that an over-simplified description would not be a true representation of the therapeutic process, the reader may extract from the case material some of the most important themes running through the drama of the struggle for maturity.

When Ralph came to the Reading Center, his presenting symptoms as he expressed them were: "Slowness, inability to comprehend what I read; slight difficulty in mind wandering; many times a lack of interest in what I am doing; I don't get from my reading the essential things of what I am reading."

Soon more of the "surface threads" became apparent: "I need help with retention; I cannot concentrate; I have the bad habit of reading word-by-word; reading makes me restless." As the interviews progressed, Ralph's unconscious fears emerged. The reader will have no difficulty finding the "underlying threads" in the case material.

For example, the thread, "I am afraid to take responsibility for a choice," runs all through the case of Ralph. It is revealed in the first interview when he discusses his vocational plans: "I've always thought I'd be an engineer . . . It was influenced by the family, of course, Dad's being an engineer." It is quite clear that he simply found himself preparing for this career without having taken responsibility for the choice. In fact, he had not made a choice. He had not selected engineering out of self-understanding, inner conviction or desire.

It was inevitable that Ralph fail the courses preparing him for engineering. Failure was his only way of communicating that he did not choose to be an engineer. This failure saved him from the terrifying prospect of competing with his father in the father's own field. To continue in this vocational direction would have led him into ever-increasing anxiety, for the closer he came to open competition with his highly idealized father, the more terrified he was by his unconscious wish to defeat his father, by his fear of being punished for this wish, and by his fear of being crushingly defeated by his rival.

It will be obvious to the reader that Ralph's fear of making choices is interwoven with many other underlying threads. For example, it is intimately connected with his perfectionism, his feeling that he can be acceptable to his parents only if he is perfect. Therefore, he cannot make any choices in life without a guarantee of perfect rightness and absolute success. This was expressed clearly in his reading and study problems. He read with painful slowness because he could not take any chances of making mistakes; he could not take lecture notes without trying to write down every word, since he dared not trust his own judgment in selecting important facts. (A young man with a similar problem spoke of it this way: "I can read one word at a time all right, but putting the words together to form concepts is always such a gamble!")

The seventh and ninth interviews show with particular vividness the role of perfectionism in the lives of Ralph and his parents. In the seventh interview Ralph says: "I keep feeling I want to *tell* my father . . . to make him recognize that I know *something* . . . to *prove* something . . . I guess I never felt he considered me worthy. It must have started a long time ago. It has something to do with his wanting everything perfect. It's like . . . being afraid to work on model planes if he was in the room. I guess I'm doing the same thing with Jane, trying to prove to her that I'm a *man*! It's like my grades at college, wanting to be *sure* to pass all my courses. You know, it might just be something within *me*. Maybe *they* don't need it from me." He continues later in the interview: "It seems to me I just never stopped feeling afraid. Always afraid to try to do things, because I knew I couldn't do them the way Dad wanted me to do them . . . *He* could be perfect if he wanted to, but he should not have expected me to be perfect. All I ever felt was failure, failure, failure."

In the ninth interview Ralph describes in detail his mother's demand for absolute neatness and cleanliness. Finally he relates her problem to his own: "I think I've got the same thing, too, that my mother has, come to think of it. For example, after I polish my car, people had better open the door by the handle, and not get fingermarks on the door! . . . Do you think I worry about things too much? . . . Yeah, I think I do."

This absolute orderliness is a symbolic representation of a perfect wall against the expression of hostile feelings. Ralph was in terror of his own unconscious rage, which he could not deal with constructively so long as he was not aware of its existence. He wanted, without knowing it, to escape his mother's vigilant control by not being the "clean" scholastic success she needed him to be. His feelings were no different in kind from anyone else's, but they were unusually intense and overwhelming because he was under so much pressure— from parents who were themselves, through psychological destiny, under considerable pressure—to be ever sweet, loving, obedient and perfect, with no leeway to express his frustrations, fears, protests and angers. This was the "wall" he complained about so bitterly, the wall against the free flow of feelings, since these feelings were considered dangerous.

Ralph's major problem, the reader is by now aware, was that he had for years hidden from himself his own real feelings. He was afraid of them. The "underlying thread" described as "I do not know what to feel" is a good formulation of his confusion that resulted from the long repression of his emotional responses to life. The major contribution of therapy was to help him uncover and understand these feelings. The counselor helped him by encouraging him to explore his true attitudes without guilt. Setting up a permissive atmosphere meant conveying to Ralph the idea that the counseling room was not a court of judgment; that he was not pronouncing sentence on his parents, peers or teachers; that whatever he said here could bring harm to no one, including himself. He began to understand that hostility repressed out of conscious awareness could cause more trouble than hostility clearly seen and consciously controlled. He understood that he could permit himself to sense his true feelings without having to express them hurtfully or unwisely. He shifted his focus from a wish to change his parents to a desire to understand them for the purpose of obtaining a new understanding of himself in relationship to them.

The therapist attempted at every opportunity to support Ralph's self-affirmation, not through reassurance but through clarification of his blind obedience to authority, his hidden resentments, his self-defeating trends, his feelings of hopelessness. As his fears lessened, he derived courage from within himself to take chances based on his own judgment and wishes. In the seventh interview he recognized that he could incorporate within himself the "new way of thinking," and that he could claim this "new way of looking at things" as a tool of his own, not something for which he must depend on the therapist.

All through the interviews, Ralph often formulated very well the "underlying threads" as he experienced them. In the thirteenth interview he said, "There are things in my mind that I have to bring out in order to face them." His understanding of his relationships frequently emerged clearly, as in the fourteenth interview: "I guess I've always wanted my mother's love because I knew I wasn't getting it." In the fifteenth interview he stated succinctly one of the interesting phenomena of therapy: "That's the funny thing about this. This is the kind of thing that has to come from within you."

Turning to the case of Donald, the reader will find that Donald, like Ralph, gradually became aware of feelings which formerly had been pushed out of awareness. For example, the "underlying thread" described as "Inner Resistance" is illustrated by Donald's withdrawal from parents who were over-directing, over-criticizing, over-channeling his energies. Donald needed the "freedom of his failures." As he himself so beautifully expressed it in the seventh interview: "They've got me so used to being told what to do that then I sink down if they stop telling. But she didn't stop for a long enough time . . . I mean, if she stopped nagging for a long enough time, that would give me time to learn how to do it without being nagged."

Withdrawal from parental nagging involved withdrawal from investing his energy in schoolwork, for he had more vital needs: He was struggling to preserve his integrity, his intactness, his feeling of being a whole person and a self-directing person. Taking care of these needs interfered with his academic success, which appeared impractical but which in truth was the most urgent kind of practicality. Just as he predicted, when the pressures were lifted, he did "make a mess of things" for a while, but in the long run he was able to integrate his energies around his own goals and to fulfill his promises to himself.

What was the therapeutic process that facilitated change in Ralph and Donald? The method has been called "psychotherapy," which has many definitions. "Psychotherapy can be defined as the treatment of mental or physical disorder by using mental influences." (75a) "Psychotherapy, if sound, ought . . . to generate a philosophy of life which, by permeating the home and society generally, would function as a preventive as well as a corrective." (48a) "Psychotherapy is in essence a process of helping a person mature." [1]

The kind of psychotherapy used by the writer has been demonstrated by the case material itself. It may be described as a treatment process based on psychoanalytic principles and training. It is an eclectic method, deriving from Freud, Reik, Horney, Rogers and others. It is modified to meet the needs of individuals; it may be changed from hour to hour or even within one hour, responding to the demands of the psychodynamic picture of the moment. The method of therapy used in the Reading Center was adapted to the framework and limitations of an academic clinic situation. For example, the exploring of unconscious material did not include work with dreams, fantasies or experiences of very early childhood. (58a) Nor were the clients seen more frequently than once or twice weekly.

An unusual modification of psychotherapeutic technique was the mixture of reading work with the exploring of personal feelings. Ordinarily, to include academic study in a process of therapy would be considered harmful to the therapy; it would tend to distract the client from following the line of his self-discovery. Whenever possible, the writer avoids the introduction of academic tutoring or testing once therapy has begun. However, including it is often unavoidable in a reading center. When this is so, the therapist can find ways to weave it into the situation in a manner that keeps the atmosphere permissive and therapeutic. Sometimes the skillful employment of reading techniques may implement the therapeutic process; for example, it

[1] Dorothy Baruch, *One Little Boy.* New York: Julian Press, 1952.

was extremely helpful to the emotional development of a twelve-year-old boy in the reading center when his counselor recognized his hunger to be babied. He had been told at a very early age that he must strive to be "a big boy now," though he was scarcely out of infancy. His counselor brought a supply of colorful picture books for him to look at, picture books designed for pre-school children. For weeks the boy enjoyed these "baby books" until he finally had his fill, then he gradually worked his way up to his twelve-year-old reading level, which now was no longer out of step with his emotional age. The counselor's introduction of the picture books was a non-verbal reflecting of the boy's unconscious needs. Similarly, the use of finger-painting for adults as well as youngsters with reading problems has produced some interesting results, though ordinarily one does not think of using finger-painting with adults, who can verbalize their problems. It has been found to be especially helpful as a transition between reading techniques and psychotherapy.

What are some of the basic procedures in psychotherapy? What does the psychotherapist do? In brief, he does the following:

1. He sees the client individually, in a quiet room, without interruption. This may seem too obvious and far too elementary to be mentioned, but it often requires courage and tact to ask the parents of an adolescent to please wait in the waiting-room for their own turn to be interviewed alone.

2. The therapist is a good listener. He not only permits the client to develop his own line of interest without intrusion, but he has learned enough psychodynamics, through training and experience, to recognize clues to underlying problems, and he exercises the necessary self-control to keep quiet and hold interpretations in his mind until the proper time to speak. He maintains a kindly, interested attitude while listening.

3. The therapist, being uninvolved in the client's conflicts, is able to keep a bird's-eye view for the client. He functions as the client's historian, watching for and remembering trends. The client may not be able to see the forest for the trees; the therapist, given time, keeps the whole forest in perspective.

4. The therapist educates the client. He shares with the client the benefits of his training and experience. He helps the client to see his own inner needs and feelings within the framework of the social picture. The client feels he alone has certain problems; he feels "dif-

ferent" and isolated. The therapist sketches in the missing scene, helping the client to see himself not only in relationship to his family and friends but in relationship to the culture.

5. The therapist does not try to keep the interview "cheerful." He does not impose his own needs or his own moods. He does not put upon the client the pressure of expecting the client to respond to "pep talks." This point may seem too elementary to require citing, but it is an important point which often is overlooked by the therapist who has not adequately clarified his own needs, and who feels personally threatened and like a failure unless he keeps the client "happy."

6. The therapist waits patiently and lets the client work at his own rhythm. He is not in a hurry to "find out." This is of particular importance in a reading center, where the client has not come for counseling in the first place. The client may prefer to select someone else in whom to confide. The therapist does not force on the client anything he does not want.

7. The therapist does not reflect feelings while he is still in the dark as to what the client's feelings are. A combination of knowledge acquired by experience, and what Freud called "unconscious tact," should help the therapist time his interpretations. Sometimes the therapist forever withholds an interpretation, yet works around it. For example, an adolescent boy who claims, "I could get better marks if I tried, but I just don't try," may be covering his fear of discovering that he cannot get high grades even if he does try. The therapist does not tell him this, but recognizes the need to strengthen the boy's self-confidence so that he may become free to formulate realistic goals. Then, one day, the boy announces that he is "studying hard, and will be satisfied if he gets B's instead of A's." Instead of "calling his bluff," the therapist had steered him toward exploring his feelings about his parents and their expectations for him, about his disappointment when they excluded him from discussions of family plans and budgets, about his conflict regarding growing up and becoming responsible and independent, or clinging to the unrewarding comfort of his mother's over-protection.

8. The therapist is not embarrassed or frightened by the client's expression of emotion toward him. It is especially in the area of "relationship" that the therapist's own self-understanding is of vital importance. A reading specialist was bewildered and deeply hurt when,

"out of a clear blue sky," the boy with whom she had been working said to her, "I hate you!" In relating the incident she said, with tears in her eyes, "But I've been so nice to him!" She had argued with the boy that it was not logical for him to hate her when she had nothing but the kindest feelings toward him. With some knowledge of psychodynamics and of her own needs in the situation, both she and the boy would have had a profitable rather than confusing experience.

What happens to the client in the process of psychotherapy? We cannot know what repercussions occur in the subterranean depths of personality, but we can grasp some of the effects of the teamwork between therapist and client. In greatly simplified form, we may enumerate them as follows:

1. The client comes with problems. He also brings his fears, conscious and unconscious.

2. With the help and support of the therapist, he uncovers and deals with his fears.

3. The relationship with the therapist strengthens his self-confidence and gives him courage to "take time out" from external and internal pressures while he tries to find out who he really is and what he really wants. Since the therapist is more tolerant and more forgiving of the client's hostility, awkwardness and imperfections than the client is himself, the client gradually begins to feel he is in a safe place, where he can stop blaming himself long enough to start understanding himself. It has been said that real "free association" does not occur until near the end of treatment; probably this is because the client is too self-critical to permit an uncensored, imperfect, poorly constructed stream of thoughts to emerge until he finally has the self-affirmation necessary for spontaneity. By this time he is ready to leave the therapist.

4. The client obtains from the therapist a way of looking at his problems that becomes his tools for meeting his life challenges. First he tests his new attitudes in his family relationship; later he tests them in his relationship with the therapist. For example: A client learned to look for evidences of her competitiveness in more areas than in the original competition with her mother. She recognized that when she felt annoyed with other students for "talking too much in class," she was competing with these students in much the same spirit as she had competed wtih her mother; that is, she could not really compete at all, since what she wanted was to be the *only* bright student, as

she had wanted to be her father's only girl. She began to see that she both admired and disliked her teachers, and that she wanted to displace them as she had wanted to displace her mother. It was important to encourage the client to talk freely about her feelings of competitiveness with the therapist. Unless this aspect of the treatment relationship is talked about openly, the client is burdened with secret misgivings that interfere with a complete understanding of herself and with the developing of a sense of safety. She may think, "Ah, yes, the therapist is nice to me now, but *if she knew* I sometimes wish I could take her job away from her, or prove I'm smarter than she is, and that I knew all this anyhow . . . If she knew all this, she would not think so highly of me."

These attitudes, as well as many hidden wishes often related to biological needs and not always consonant with social mores, create guilt and anxiety. When they are exposed in the process of therapy, guilt feelings are relieved. The client builds greater tolerance for himself and greater hope. A more understanding attitude toward himself leads him to a more spontaneous participation in his life situation. He becomes more social. His productive forces are freed for a more efficient approach to more realistic goals. By the time he leaves therapy, he is able to take responsibility for himself with strengthened self-confidence. This will be reflected in his life as a student, for his educational goals will represent attainable values in the real world rather than his former perfectionistic, grandiose, unattainable fantasy goals. When he finds himself as a person, he finds himself as a student, and he approaches his work with, as one boy said, "the feeling of running on all cylinders."

5. The client for a time is dependent on the therapist. Eventually he feels strong enough to become independent of the therapist, as he acquires the self-understanding and the self-confidence to face life on his own. Sometimes, early in the relationship, he may think he is all better and that he needs no more help. This spurious independence is often a defense against his fear of being hurt if he permits himself to feel dependent. Because he feels unworthy and undeserving, he ends many relationships almost before they begin, not only with the therapist but with others, too. He runs away before others get a chance to send him away, as he believes no one could possibly want to have him around. This defensive maneuver is frequently mistaken for healthy independence; there seems to have been "a quick cure."

However, if therapy progresses until true self-confidence is achieved, the client leaves finally with enough real independence to permit himself to enjoy realistic, collaborative interdependency.

In reviewing what happens to clients, we have to conclude that we do not know all the effects of our psychotherapeutic work; much of it is remote from our view, and unconscious forces operate like elves in fairy tales, busily and invisibly working in the night.

[6]

CONCLUSIONS AND
IMPLICATIONS

PEOPLE WHO COME to a reading center are asking for help. They believe that tutoring in reading is the kind of help they need. To give them, therefore, *only* tutoring in reading is to add nothing to their own diagnosis. It is the responsibility of the reading center to consider the total person and not just the reading performance. It is the responsibility of the reading staff to be aware of the linkages between reading difficulties and personality problems.

The recognition of reading difficulty as a symptom of a larger problem does not imply that reading centers must cease to function except as diagnostic and referral centers. One of the great values of maintaining reading centers is that people come to them. "Parents who would fight to the last before taking their child to a psychiatrist will have no objection to seeing his reading problem straightened out by a psychoanalytically trained remedial teacher working in the schools." [1] Therefore, instead of sending people away from reading centers to psychotherapists—a task which in itself requires skillful preparation for referral—it is suggested that psychotherapists be brought to the staffs of the reading centers. There are certain cases that must be referred elsewhere because of the severity of their emotional problems; for example, pre-psychotics and cases of severe neurosis. However, most of the cases that come into an adolescent

[1] Otto Spranger, "Psychoanalytic Pedagogy." *Psychoanalysis,* Fall, 1952, p. 63.

and adult reading center are adolescents with problems appropriate to psychotherapeutic treatment by a staff trained in psychotherapy as well as in reading and study techniques.

It is not the purpose of this book to teach psychotherapeutic techniques to reading specialists, nor to encourage the practice of psychotherapy without proper training. Rather, this book attempts only to sensitize reading specialists and teachers to the kinds of problems that lie beneath the surface of reading and study difficulties. It is hoped that these reading specialists and teachers will be stimulated to do one or all of the following:

1. Understand the need to make referrals to community agencies for psychotherapy when no psychotherapy is available in the reading center or school itself.

2. Undertake a program of training in psychotherapy, so that ultimately reading clinics and schools will have adequate numbers of trained personnel equipped to treat the psychological problems of those who come for help.

3. Where neither referral resources nor training are at present available, obtain sufficient awareness of the psychological needs of students with study problems to provide within the tutoring situation a helpful rather than harmful influence. (39a)

Like Moliere's "Bourgeois Gentilhomme," who one day discovered he had always been "talking prose," a great many teachers successful in remedial work might discover that they have been employing psychotherapeutic attitudes without knowing it. Further training to help them "know what they know" and add to their knowledge would increase the range of their helpfulness. The self-knowledge acquired in an adequate training program would also add to their own joy in life and satisfaction in their work. This would be of great importance in education; just as a happy mother is apt to be a good mother, so a happy teacher is apt to be a really helpful teacher. To prescribe "maturity," "serenity," or "interest" as requirements for good teaching, without helping teachers to remove their inner impediments to these healthy and desirable states of mind, is to burden them with assignments for which they have no adequate preparation.[2]

[2] The reader is referred to the forthcoming book: *Psychology in the High School*, A Report on a Conference of Teachers at Teachers College, Columbia University, July, 1952; compiled and edited by Arthur T. Jersild and Kenneth Helfant (to be published Summer 1953).

For reading specialists not trained in psychotherapy, it might be helpful to enumerate some of the criteria for referral to psychotherapists. One would consider for referral cases like the following:

1. Those who do not profit by the usual tutoring in reading skills, and whose intelligence would indicate that they are functioning considerably below capacity.

2. Those who read well, as objectively measured, but who cannot function well in response to school challenges. They procrastinate, they cannot finish reading books or writing papers, they forget assignments or come late to examinations.

3. Those who read and study effectively but who have the self-concept that they are poor readers. They need to investigate why nothing they do seems good enough.

4. Those who score high on vocabulary and low on paragraph comprehension. They cannot sustain attention to paragraphs. They complain of "mind wandering." They have trouble relating ideas.

5. Those who, on reading tests, achieve a very high degree of accuracy and a very low degree of speed. They lack the self-confidence to take chances, to trust their own responses.

6. Those who complain of headaches and breathlessness when reading, despite reports from doctors that there is nothing wrong physically.

7. Those who burst into tears during the interview, or in other ways convey feelings of acute anxiety.

8. Those whose reading development is hampered by poor vision or hearing, but who are diagnosed medically as having visual or hearing difficulties of psychosomatic origins.

9. Those who, after reliable medical examination, continue to report incapacitating fatigue, particularly when confronted with reading or other study assignments.

10. The rare cases of severe emotional illness, such as the person who can read nothing more difficult than a primer the first week, yet can read an adult's magazine the second week, and at the third meeting returns to the primer. This behavior reveals dissociation in the character structure and calls for psychiatric diagnosis and recommendations.

Another type of case for immediate referral is the adult who reads well but offers a bizarre, inappropriate reason for wanting to obtain tutoring; such as the middle-aged executive who said he wanted reading help "in order to know something my wife doesn't know." Further investigation revealed that he was severely depressed and in urgent need of psychoanalytic care.

There is also the occasional, infrequent case of extreme irritability, which sometimes indicates the presence of organic damage, and sometimes signifies borderline psychosis. The best service to this kind of person is referral for psychiatric diagnosis and recommendations.

The question often arises, "Since these people come for reading, how can you introduce something other than reading?" Preparing the client for counseling, or psychotherapy, or psychiatry, or psychoanalysis is an art in itself. It requires understanding of how the client feels about his reading problem. Has he a feeling of hopelessness, that despite all his efforts and expert tutoring he still is making little or no progress? Then he may be ready for the suggestion that he explore other possible areas of trouble. To do this saves him from the conclusion that he is "just too dumb to learn," that he is "a hopeless failure," that no one and nothing can teach him to study. Making a successful referral depends also on an awareness of how the client is feeling toward the reading specialist. Has the client had an opportunity, in time and in work, to know and respect the reading specialist and thus to take seriously a recommendation coming from this source? [3]

The interviews reported in this book may orient the reader to criteria for establishing that more than reading help is required in order to be of real service to the client. The case of Donald, for example, illustrates how an adolescent boy may come to a reading center for help in reading when his most urgent problem is to pass successfully through an adolescent crisis involving his attitudes toward himself and those meaningful to him. [4]

The case of Ralph is particularly interesting for the way in which his study problems expressed his personality problems as revealed by the psychotherapeutic process. It may seem disappointing that Ralph did not finish college. This raises the question of what the reading counselor's objectives should be. Surely one must not set ambitious goals for those whom one treats; rather, one tries to free

[3] The reader may explore the literature of social work to obtain information about the skills involved in preparing clients for referral.
[4] A follow-up letter from Donald appears on page 122.

the individual to establish his own goals, *really* his own, not the wishes of others which he self-deceptively presents as his own.

Both Ralph and the counselor were under the spell of a cultural attitude about the necessity of going through college. It was assumed by both that the treatment process would culminate in his successful completion of college work. This was unfortunate, for it meant that when Ralph finally gave up college, his turning to his own real interests seemed like second-best rather than first-choice. Had he been helped early in the treatment to face his disinterest in college, he not only would have experienced tremendous relief, but his energies would have been released for joyous investment in his own true goals. What he really wanted was to get a job, earn money, deal with people, construct interesting things with his hands, provide well for Jane, raise a family, and establish a home of his own. He rarely turned to books; he had no real interest in scholarship. He had turned away for so long from competing with his father in the area of knowledge, that now he had developed genuine interests in what originally had been compensatory interests. He glowed with enthusiasm whenever he told about building things, and he burned with ambition when he dreamed of the kind of father he would be to his sons. The one area where he felt he could compete successfully with his father was in the area of fatherhood; he felt that he had more understanding of people than his father had, and that he could therefore be a better husband and parent. He was impatient to realize his plans for family life.

The therapist considers Ralph's case a success because he himself feels that the treatment, as he expressed it, "made a man of me." [5] Also, he is not burdened by regrets over his withdrawal from college, which means he did achieve a measure of inner freedom. The Ralph case is perhaps the most dramatic example of the need for providing psychotherapy as an integral part of a reading center. Because of his belief in Christian Science, Ralph would not have accepted a referral to a psychoanalyst. Apart from Christian Science, many people are unable to accept this kind of referral because of the stigma it unfortunately still bears. A psychiatrist at the University of Michigan said in a lecture to a psychology class some years ago, "Once I put the word 'Psychiatrist' on my door, only a very small percentage of the students who need me will ever enter." [6]

[5] A follow-up message from Ralph is on page 263.
[6] This was Dr. Theophile Raphael, Professor of Clinical Psychiatry.

A reading center has the opportunity to meet the psychological needs of a great many people who otherwise would never show up anywhere for help. It has the opportunity to do important preventive work, catching personality problems in early years, alleviating them before they become crippling.

The reader may be interested in learning what happened to John, Mike, Sue and Betty. The following brief and necessarily over-simplified summaries indicate how important it was in each case to provide more than tutoring.

John worked one semester with a counselor in the Reading Center who offered him non-directive counseling as well as reading and study techniques, creative writing and public speaking. According to a report from his counselor, John achieved considerable growth in all these areas. Also, he became increasingly interested in the task of understanding himself, and at the end of the semester he formulated clearly his need for deeper therapy and asked to be referred to a psychoanalyst.

About Mike: The boy's day-dreaming and disinterest in school persisted until an underlying problem came to the surface. He had been preoccupied, without conscious awareness of his preoccupation, with worry about his small stature and his belated sexual maturity, both of which had made him feel unequal to the other boys who had grown taller and developed faster. The concern about his small size had nagged at him for years. He said, "I was big in kindergarten, but in the first grade they caught up with me, and I have been the smallest ever since."

The counselor asked Mike if he would like to see the staff psychiatrist,[7] who could examine him and tell him whether he needed endocrine therapy. His response was animated; in fact, he wondered if the psychiatrist could manage to see him the very next week. There was a marked change in the boy's posture and manner after his two interviews with the psychiatrist. "Well, Mike, how was it?" the counselor asked. "He says *I'm Okay*," was Mike's spirited response.

The psychiatrist reported to the counselor that he had been able to reassure the boy about the good possibility of his future growth, and that he had clarified Mike's confusion about his recent sexual maturing. They had had a good "man-to-man talk." The report stated: "This boy has learned from a friend that one can get injec-

[7] L. Clovis Hirning, M.D.

tions to make you grow. His friend knows someone who grew three inches in a few months! The patient says he has hesitated talking to his father about this for fear of worrying him—'giving him something else to think about.' "

A letter the following year from the teacher who originally had referred Mike read as follows: [8]

"Mike's general attitude has improved considerably all through the school. He changed his program, for one thing. He also went into intramural swimming this year, and not only has he shown great interest but he has done very well. He has also become interested in various other school sports and has attended all the basketball games and swimming and track meets.

"An active interest has been taken in a boys' club, and at present he is treasurer of the club.

"He has very definitely changed his attitude toward school, and is determined to finish high school and go on into forestry. He even has his college picked out."

About Sue: Objective reading tests revealed no reading problem. Sue tested in her proper age and school group. However, she was not functioning successfully in school, and the persons who worked with her in the Reading Center were agreed that her difficulties were rooted in emotional conflicts. She was given the specific tutoring which she herself asked for, and, in addition, had experiences in group activity, play therapy, and non-directive counseling, over a period of many months.

One year following the initial interview, the counselor called Sue in for a follow-up interview. She no longer looked like a little girl. She had grown taller, and she was dressed like a typical teen-ager, in wool skirt and sweater and the cherished loafers. Her hair hung softly to her shoulders, curled at the ends. The counselor remarked that Sue seemed to have obtained many of the things she had wanted a year ago, and Sue replied, "Yes, I can speak for myself better than before."

Despite this obvious growth in self-confidence, the counselor was in agreement with the worker who recommended that Sue be given further counseling to ease her through the usual problems of adolescence, which, in her case, were aggravated by a family of adults who

[8] Identifying data has been omitted or disguised.

fluctuated between treating her like a baby and expecting her to live up to high academic standards.

The case of Betty similarly showed how important it is to be prepared to provide more than reading techniques. Betty worked one semester with the counselor, talking through some of the conflicts interfering with her scholastic efforts. In answer to a letter from the counselor several years later, Betty wrote: [9]

"Since I last saw you, I successfully completed my college studies. I found that as my adjustment improved, my contentment with school increased. I carried quite a heavy program, and I did some tutoring on the side.

"Upon graduation from college, I acquired a job teaching third grade. The job is delightful in spite of the hard work. In addition, I do club-work one night a week.

"My social life has its ups and downs, but I don't imagine it's been too different from that of most girls.

"You ask in your letter why I didn't continue with you the following September. Frankly, I can't clearly remember any particular reason that I could now put my finger on. I know I did begin to feel better and seemed, to a certain extent, to be able to manage myself more fully.

"It might be interesting to you to know that as I think back I believe that I felt a certain amount of resentment toward the nondirective treatment I was getting. I do remember once saying to you, 'So I'm doing all the talking but you never say anything.' [10]

"I can only say now, after much more experience with people, I more fully appreciate what that talking did for me and how it did help. I find that now upon facing difficult situations, while some are harder to handle and some easier, they get taken care of with a good deal less worrying before they occur or after they're gone."

John, Mike, Sue, Donald, Betty and Ralph: Six persons who came to the Reading Center to improve their reading. If tutoring alone had been the treatment, how long would they have carried with them their secret problems, their unconscious fears, their anxieties, their self-

---

[9] Identifying data has been omitted or disguised.

[10] This is of particular interest, since the counselor had felt chagrined, when reading over the interviews, at having done *so much talking!*

defeating patterns? What other kinds of symptoms would have come to the fore, signalling the need for help? How many months or years would have been spent in a struggle against the self, with all the anguish and waste motions accompanying the struggle?

Though the presence of a reading problem suggests the presence of emotional conflicts, the absence of a reading problem does not indicate the absence of emotional conflicts. This book, dealing with "emotional difficulties in reading," does not wish to leave the reader with the idea that good reading per se is an indication that one has no emotional problems. Just as the alert teacher does not assume that the quiet child is a happy child, she does not assume that the good reader is necessarily functioning well in other areas.

The good student may often be the forgotten man. So long as he maintains his scholastic standing, no notice is taken of the fact that he is emotionally separated from the social life of which he needs to be an active member, or that he is suffering from secret fears of one kind or another. He may hold up very well until he has completed his academic career, but then, outside the school framework and under new and increasing pressures, he may suffer an emotional collapse. This may be the student who shows so much promise, yet never achieves fulfillment of the promise. "He was predicted in the yearbook to become the biggest financial success of his class, but now he cannot keep a job." . . . "She was pretty as well as intelligent, and social prominence was predicted for her, but now her marriage fails and she is depressed."

The plight of the good student is that no academic failure brings him to anyone for help. "We don't have to interview *you*," said a dean to an honor student. "We know *you* have no problems." This young man burst into tears after leaving the dean's office, and he did not know why he was weeping. Years later he said, "If that dean had only known what a strain it was to keep up a front! Good marks don't mean anything when you're as unhappy as I was."

Thus, it is necessary to consider the total person not only in a reading center, but in every school situation. Further implications of this book for education generally are as follows:

I. It looks upon reading as one aspect of the individual's total behavior; what he is and how he feels about himself are revealed in a reading situation as in any life situation which may confront him.

II. It challenges educators to re-define what they mean by "the whole child." Do they mean the unconscious as well as the conscious needs of the child?

III. It suggests that the concept of psychotherapy not be limited to its clinical applications, but that it be brought into education, since it *is* education.[11] Learning to know oneself in a way that helps one to live more fully also helps one to learn more willingly, readily and pleasantly.

IV. It challenges the teachers colleges to furnish to schools and universities, from nursery school through graduate school, trained personnel equipped to meet the unconscious as well as the conscious needs of students.

[11] Freud defined the essential function of psychotherapy as re-education. (Obtained from Theodor Reik, to whom Freud made this statement.)

BIBLIOGRAPHY

1. Alexander, Franz, M.D. *Psychosomatic Medicine*. New York: W. W. Norton & Co., Inc., 1950. 300 p.
2. Axline, Virginia. "Non-Directive Therapy for Poor Readers." *Journal of Consulting Psychology*, Vol. XI, 1947. pp. 61-69.
3. Baruch, Dorothy. *New Ways in Discipline*. New York: McGraw-Hill Book Company, Inc., 1949. 280 p.
4. Baruch, Dorothy. *One Little Boy*. New York: Julian Press, 1952. 242 p.
5. Bills, Robert E. *An Investigation of the Effects of Individual and Group Play Therapy on the Reading Level of Retarded Readers*. New York: Teachers College, Columbia University, 1948. 344 p.
6. Blanchard, Phyllis. "Reading Disabilities in Relation to Maladjustment." *Mental Hygiene*, 12:772-88, October, 1928.
7. Blanchard, Phyllis. "Attitudes and Emotional Disabilities." *Mental Hygiene*, 13:550-63, July, 1929.
8. Blanchard, Phyllis. "Reading Disabilities in Relation to Difficulties of Personality and Emotional Development." *Mental Hygiene*, 20:384-413, 1936.
9. Blanchard, Phyllis. "Psychoanalytic Contributions to the Problem of Reading Disabilities." *The Psychoanalytic Study of the Child*. New York: International Universities Press, Vol. II, 1946. pp. 163-187.
10. Blanchard, Phyllis. "Psychogenic Factors in Some Cases of Reading Disability." *The American Journal of Orthopsychiatry*, 5:361-374, 1935.
11. Challman, Robert. "Personality Maladjustments and Remedial Reading." *Journal of Exceptional Children*, Vol. 6, 1939. pp. 7-12.
12. Cooper, Miriam Dennie. "The Case of Madeline." *Journal of the National Association of Deans of Women*, Vol. IX, No. 35, June, 1947.
13. Davis, Louise Farwell. "Case Histories of Children Presenting Visual Difficulties of a Functional Nature." *Peabody Journal of Education*, 17:128-37, November 1939.
14. Dickenson, Irma C. "Emotional Factors as Contributing Causes of Reading Disability." *Virginia Journal of Education*. 31:254-256.
15. Eberl, Marguerite Thomas. "Johnnie Learns How." *Texas Outlook*, 29:13-14, December, 1945.

16. Edelston, H. "Educational Failure with High Intelligence Quotient: A Clinical Study." *The Journal of Genetic Psychology*, 1950. pp. 77, 85-116.
17. Ehrlich, Eugene. "Reading Problems of High School Pupils," *Journal of the National Association of Deans of Women*, Vol. XIII, No. 1, October, 1949. pp. 19-20.
18. Font, Marion McKenzie. "Orientation in Clinical Approach Through Remedial Reading Instruction." *American Journal of Orthopsychiatry*, 12:324-34, April 1942.
19. Fernald, Grace M. *Remedial Techniques in Basal School Subjects*. New York: McGraw-Hill Book Company, Inc., 1943. 349 p.
20. Freud, Sigmund. *The Question of Lay Analysis, An Introduction to Psychoanalysis*. New York: W. W. Norton & Co., 1950. pp. 123, 124.
21. Fromm, Erich. *Escape from Freedom*. New York: Farrar and Rinehart, Inc., 1941. 305 p.
22. Gann, Edith. *Reading Difficulty and Personality Organization*. New York: King's Crown Press, Columbia University, 1945. 140 p.
23. Gates, Arthur. *The Improvement of Reading*. New York: Macmillan and Co., 1947. pp. 200-405, 545-548.
24. Gates, Arthur. "The Role of Personality Maladjustment in Reading Disability." *The Journal of Genetic Psychology*. 59:77-83, 1941.
25. Gray, William S. "Case Studies of Reading Deficiencies in Junior High Schools." *Journal of Educational Research*, 10:132-40, 1924.
26. Gray, William S. "The Diagnostic Study of an Individual Case in Reading." *Elementary School Journal*, 21:577-94, April, 1921.
27. Gray, William S. "Growth in Understanding of Reading and Its Development Among Youth." *Keeping Reading Programs Abreast of the Times*. Supplementary Educational Monographs, No. 72, October 1950. Compiled and edited by William S. Gray, Chicago: University of Chicago Press. pp. 8-13.
28. Gunzburg, Herbert C. "An Intensive Reading Program in a Special School." *The New Era in Home and School*, 28:165-72, July-August, 1947.
29. Hansburg, Henry. "The Case of 'Arthur.' " *Understanding the Child*, 18:24-27, 1949.
30. Harris, Albert J. "Case Studies of Reading Disabilities." *How to Increase Reading Ability*. New York: Longmans, Green and Company. Chapter XVI.
31. Horney, Karen. *Our Inner Conflicts*. New York: W. W. Norton and Company, Inc., 1945. 250 p.
32. Hrastnik, Marjory. "Making Detailed Clinical Studies of Unusually Handicapped Readers." *Supplementary Educational Monograph*, No. 72, 1950. pp. 143-47.
33. Hutchinson, Linn. *A Study of Differences in Personality Organization Between Good and Poor Readers at the Tenth Grade Level*. University of Oregon, 1947. 82 p.

34. Jackson, Charles. *The Lost Weekend*. New York: Farrar & Rinehart, Inc., 1944. 244 p.
35. Jackson, Joseph. "A Survey of Psychological, Social and Environmental Differences Between Advanced and Retarded Readers." *Pedagogical Seminary*, 65:113-131, September 1944.
36. Jersild, Arthur T. *In Search of Self*. New York: Bureau of Publications, Teachers College, Columbia University, 1952. 145 p.
37. Klein, Emanuel. "Psychoanalytic Aspects of School Problems." *The Psychoanalytic Study of the Child*. Vols. III and IV. New York: International Universities Press, 1949. pp. 369-390.
38. Kunst, Mary and Sylvester, Emmy. "Psychodynamic Aspects of the Reading Problem." *American Journal of Orthopsychiatry*, 13:69-76, 1943.
39. Leavell, Ullin W. "Professional Guidance for the Whole Child." *Virginia Journal of Education*, 42:14-16, 45, September 1948.
39a. Lewis, Norman. *How to Get More Out of Your Reading*. New York: Doubleday and Company, Inc., 1951, p. 425.
40. Lichtenstein, Arthur. "A Case of Adult Reading Difficulty." *Journal of Juvenile Research*, 22:103-109, April 1938.
41. Margulies, Helen. "Rorschach Responses of Successful and Unsuccessful Students." *Archives of Psychology*, No. 271, July 1942. 52 p.
42. McAllister, James M. *Remedial and Corrective Instruction in Reading*. New York: D. Appleton-Century Co., 1936. pp. 127-140.
43. McCullough, Constance, Strang, Ruth, and Traxler, Arthur. *Problems in the Improvement of Reading*. New York: McGraw-Hill Book Co., Inc., 1946. 406 p.
44. Menninger, Karl A. *Man Against Himself*. New York: Harcourt, Brace and Company, 1938. 485 p.
45. Missildine, W. H. "The Emotional Background of Thirty Children with Reading Disabilities with Emphasis on Its Coercive Elements." *Nervous Child*, 5:263-72, 1946.
46. Monroe, Marion. *Children Who Cannot Read*. University of Chicago Press, 1932. 205 p.
47. Monroe, Marion. "Diagnosis and Treatment of Reading Disabilities." *Educational Diagnosis*. Thirty-fourth Yearbook of the National Society for the Study of Education. Bloomington, Illinois: Public School Publishing Company, 1935. pp. 201-228.
48. Morgan, Charles. *Sparkenbroke*. New York: The Macmillan Company, 1936. 551 p.
48a. Mowrer, O. Hobart. *Learning Theory and Personality Dynamics*. New York: Ronald Press Company, pp. 11-12.
49. Redmount, Robert S. "Description and Evaluation of a Corrective Program for Reading Disability." *Journal of Educational Psychology*, 39:347-58, 1948.
50. Reik, Theodor. *Listening with the Third Ear*. New York: Farrar, Straus, 1949. 514 p.

51. Reik, Theodor. *The Secret Self*. New York: Farrar, Straus and Young, 1952. 329 p.
52. Ribble, Margaretha A. *The Rights of Infants*. New York: Columbia University Press, 1943. 118 p.
53. Robinson, Helen M. "Clinical Studies in Reading." *Supplementary Educational Monograph*, No. 68, University of Chicago Press, June 1949. pp. 63-66, 70-72, 72-75, 81.
54. Robinson, Helen M. *Why Pupils Fail in Reading*. Chicago: University of Chicago Press, 1946. 257 p.
55. Robinson, Helen M. and Savery, Jean F. "A High-School Freshman Learns to Read and Write." *The Education Digest*, 8:42-44, December 1942.
56. Rugg, Harold. *Foundations for American Education*. New York: World Book Company, 1947. 826 p.
57. Russell, David H. "Research on Reading Difficulties and Personality Adjustment." *Improving Educational Research*, Official Report, Washington: American Educational Research Association, 1948. pp. 10-13.
58. Sherman, Mandel. "Emotional Disturbances and Reading Disability." In William S. Gray (ed.) *Recent Trends in Reading*, Supplementary Educational Monographs No. 49. The University of Chicago Press, 1939. pp. 126-134.
58a. Silverberg, William V., M.D. *Childhood Experience and Personal Destiny*. New York: Springer Publishing Co., Inc., 1952.
59. Simpson, Elizabeth A. "Reading Rate and Its Relationship to Good Reading." *Education*, 70:565-569, May 1950.
60. Soles, Edward M. "Emotional Factors in Reading Disability." *Hygia*, 19:940-943, 1941.
61. Spranger, Otto. "Psychoanalytic Pedagogy." *Psychoanalysis*, Fall, 1952, pp. 59-70.
62. Stauffer, Russell. "Clinical Approach to Personality and the Disabled Reader." *Education*, LXVII, March, 1947. pp. 427-35.
63. Stewart, Robert S. "Personality Maladjustment and Reading Achievement." *American Journal of Orthopsychiatry*, Vol. 20, 1950. pp. 410-417.
64. Strang, Ruth. *Examiner's Reading Diagnostic Record for High School and College Students*. New York: Bureau of Publications, Teachers College, Columbia University, 1938.
65. Strang, Ruth. "Personality Development and Reading Problems." *Claremont College Reading Conference: Tenth Yearbook*. Claremont, California: Claremont College Library, 1945. pp. 43-50.
66. Strang, Ruth. "Reading and Personality Formation." *The Journal of Personality*, Vol. 1, No. 2, April, 1951. pp. 131-140.
67. Strang, Ruth. *Study Type of Reading Exercises*. New York: Bureau of Publications, Teachers College, Columbia University, 1935. 112 p.
68. Tulchin, Simon. "Emotional Factors in Reading Disabilities in School Children." *Journal of Educational Psychology*, 26:443-47, 1935.

69. Vorhaus, Pauline. "Case Study of an Adolescent Boy with Reading Disability." *Journal of Projective Techniques,* Vol. 16, March 1952. pp. 20-41.
70. Vorhaus, Pauline. "Non-reading as an Expression of Resistance." *Rorschach Research Exchange,* 10:60-69, June 1946.
71. Vorhaus, Pauline. "Rorschach Configurations Associated with Reading Disability." *Journal of Projective Techniques,* Vol. 16, March 1952. pp. 3-19.
72. Watts, Phyllis W. "An Application of Clinical Diagnostic Techniques in the Classroom Situation for the Improvement of Reading at the College Level." *Journal of Educational Research,* March 1949. pp. 513-524.
73. Wiksell, Wesley. "The Relationship between Reading Difficulties and Psychological Adjustment." *Journal of Educational Research,* 41:557-558, 1948.
74. Witty, Paul. *Reading in Modern Education.* Boston: D. C. Heath, 1949. pp. 225-49.
75. Witty, Paul and Kopel, David. *Reading and the Educative Process.* New York: Ginn and Co., 1939. pp. 239-90.
75a. Yates, D. H. *Encyclopedia of Psychology,* edited by P. L. Harriman, New York: Citadel Press, 1946, p. 723.
76. Young, Robert A. "Case Studies in Reading Disability." *American Journal of Orthopsychiatry,* 8:230-53, 1938.